D0990022

BF 721 .C617 1988

Constructivism in the
computer age

Fairleigh Dickinson University Library
Teaneck, New Jersey

Constructivism
in the
Computer Age

The Jean Piaget Symposium Series
Available from LEA

SIGEL, I. E., BRODZINSKY, D. M., & GOLINKOFF, R. M. (Eds.) • New Directions in Piagetian Theory and Practice

OVERTON, W. F. (Ed.) • Relationships Between Social and Cognitive Development

LIBEN, L. S. (Ed.) • Piaget and the Foundations of Knowledge

SCHOLNICK, E. K. (Ed.) • New Trends in Conceptual Representation: Challenges to Piaget's Theory?

NEIMARK, E. D., De LISI, R., & NEWMAN, J. L. (Eds.) • Moderators of Competence

BEARISON, D. J., & ZIMILES, H. (Eds.) • Thought and Emotion: Developmental Perspectives

LIBEN, L. S. (Ed.) • Development and Learning: Conflict or Congruence?

FORMAN, G., & PUFALL, P. B. (Eds.) • Constructivism in the Computer Age

Constructivism
in the
Computer Age

Edited by

George Forman
University of Massachusetts

Peter B. Pufall
Smith College

LEA LAWRENCE ERLBAUM ASSOCIATES, PUBLISHERS
1988   Hillsdale, New Jersey   Hove and London

BF
721
.C617
1988

Fairleigh Dickinson
University Library

Teaneck, New Jersey

Copyright © 1988 by Lawrence Erlbaum Associates, Inc.
  All rights reserved. No part of this book may be reproduced in
  any form, by photostat, microform, retrieval system, or any other
  means, without the prior written permission of the publisher.

Lawrence Erlbaum Associates, Inc., Publishers
365 Broadway
Hillsdale, New Jersey 07642

Library of Congress Cataloging-in-Publication Data

Constructivism in the computer age/edited by George Forman, Peter B. Pufall.
        p.   cm.
    Bibliography: p.
    Includes index.
    ISBN 0-8058-0101-4
    1. Child psychology. 2. Computer assisted instruction—Psychological aspects. 3. Children
and computers.   I. Forman, George E., 1942–   II. Pufall, Peter B.
BF721.C617   1988
155.4′13—dc19   87–25389
                                                                                    CIP

Printed in the United States of America
10 9 8 7 6 5 4 3 2 1

This volume is dedicated to the memory of Joachim F. Wohlwill, whose contributions to the Jean Piaget Society and to the field of developmental psychology extend far beyond his chapter in this book. Although he will live on in his published work and in our memories, we shall miss him deeply.

Contents

Preface

In the Fall of 1983 the board of the Jean Piaget Society decided on the topic for the Fifteenth Annual Symposium to be held in June of 1985: Constructivism in the Computer Age. We stipulated, however, that this convention would be more than a computer fair to display the latest educational software. It was reasoned that computers will have a great effect on our research and our systems of education, and therefore needed to be evaluated in the light of developmental theory. Bill Damon (Clark University) helped draft a statement of purpose and the board recommended that it be sent to invited speakers. The following is a reprint of that statement of purpose for the 1985 symposium:

> Intellectual development has always been interwoven with cultural progress. Breakthroughs in the science of knowledge representation and information processing, made possible by inspired individual advances, eventually transform the learning climate for all members of the culture. This dynamic interplay was apparent to Piaget in his studies of genetic epistemology. It was Piaget's cherished belief that cognitive achievements in society and in the individual go hand in hand, and should be studied in the light of one another.
>
> At the present time we are witnessing a series of rapid cultural achievements resulting in an unusually sudden advance in our society's ability to process information. The source of this advance is the breakthrough in computer technology that has made powerful new computational skills and modes of representation available to wide sectors of the population. The miniaturization of memory storage devices, combined with inexpensive production techniques, has given the average person access to electronic tools for manipulating information and for representing events both physical and psychological. Just as paper and pencil make it possible to reason in ways that exceed the limits of our native short term memory, so too the microcomputer may allow us to extend our cognitive reach into further unexplored territories.

The computer revolution has occurred so quickly that we have not had time to examine some very basic issues related to the nature of computer-based intellectual activity. These issues are critical for an enlightened evaluation of the computer's proper use in education and knowledge construction. The following are issues that we believe need to be addressed at this time.

1. What is the nature of computer-based extensions of human intelligence? Is it mainly memory space that is being added when we use computers? Or does the computer enhance our symbolic facilities, allowing us to "see" our own thoughts in new modes of graphic representation? Could this cause us to understand self and world in different ways? In what sense does the computer externalize the functions of the human mind, and to what ultimate cognitive benefit?

2. What is the relation between natural language and artificial language? If we create a cultural network of intelligent machines that speak artificial languages like ADA or LISP, what will conversing with these machines do to our natural communication and problem-solving habits? What is the best level of abstraction for the building blocks of a computer language? Does making a language user-friendly place inherent constraints on the power of the computer language to improve our general problem-solving skills? Might we ourselves discover new communication skills from conversing with computers that inform us when and how we are not explicit?

3. What forms can the person–computer interface assume, and how can various forms be adapted to serve the educational needs of children at different developmental levels? Is the rush to teach children programming at the keyboard as misguided as our earlier rush to teach preschoolers reading? What are children learning when they learn to program in LOGO? At which developmental stages should digital systems, such as print, be introduced, given that kinetic icons are now possible as a viable alternative to print? Can computer applications be designed to foster the cross-modal integration of knowledge that young children need? Can computer techniques, such as hypertext, the simultaneous use of multiple modes of representation, increase the student's depth of understanding and range of application of subject matter?

This statement of purpose was a general guide for our speakers and the panel discussion that occurred among our speakers one Friday evening in June 1985. The book that you now see has taken some of these questions to task and added others. It should be an interesting study in the evolution of this project to compare the preface of this book with the epilogue, which is a summary of the actual 1985 symposium.

Several people deserve special mention. Barbara Presseisen (Research for Better Schools, Inc.), a diligent board member, worked many hours in helping to fund this conference and to formulate its mission. She was instrumental in obtaining a grant from the Research for Better Schools, Inc., to whom we are most grateful. I would also like to give special mention to Don Nix of IBM who gave a special workshop on interactive video disks and his authoring system called "Handy." This was an extremely successful workshop. We were also pleased that Alan Kay, then at Apple Computer, gave a plenary address on his pioneering work at the Xerox Palo Alto Research Center and his current ideas on computer enhancement of intuitive knowledge. While he was not able to write a chapter for the book, he certainly has influenced its content. Those of you who attended the symposium will also remember the fine contributions of James Levine (University of Illinois) and Roy Pea (New York University) who gave plenary addresses. Finally, our Series Editor, Lynn Liben did much to keep us on track and task as the book grew to full size and shape.

George Forman
Peter B. Pufall

Piaget in the Computer Age

Chapter 1

The Conservation of Piaget: The Computer as Grist to the Constructivist Mill

Seymour Papert
Massachusetts Institute of Technology

INTRODUCTION

Piaget taught us to say that the child has conservation when something is recognized as unchanged in the midst of flux. When water is poured from one glass to another, the height, the depth, the apparent color all change. Yet the child staunchly maintains, "It's the same."

When Piaget is poured into a new decade, much will change. Whether one has conservation of Piaget will depend on what one perceives as most important in the thinking of the great master. My own view is that the essential aspects of his work have not fallen by the wayside. On the contrary, they are stronger and more relevant than ever.

One of the most striking changes in this past decade is that computational objects have become a new and very prominent part of the lives of children. They are understood by children in ways very different from how traditional objects are understood and therefore warrant special study. Piaget might have liked to study these new objects, but the most we can do is conjecture what he would have thought. If our own research produces results that seem to challenge Piaget's thinking, then we might conclude that his ideas are wrong or obsolete. And in certain cases, what he actually said turns out not to be exactly true—but something better is true, something even more Piagetian.

Some of what Piaget believed will have to be changed. But whether one sees this as disproving Piagetian theory or as elevating it to its next stage of development depends on what one counts as most important in Piaget. Not everyone would agree with my perceptions. The Piaget I discuss here and find so relevant to the study of children and computers is not the same Piaget one usually encounters in standard American psychology courses. In my Piaget, stages and even most senses of "active learning" are quite secondary. I focus instead on his constructivism and structuralism.

The "conservation of Piaget" metaphor has a second meaning as well. In the new and vigorous field of research on children and computers, people are writing as if Piaget never existed. For reasons that might be obvious to a sociologist, educators and psychologists entering this field look for theoretical inspiration from areas of cognitive science that have not connected with Piagetian ideas. The examples I discuss here might convince them that Piaget offers them much that is valuable.

Thus, this chapter has two messages. For those interested mainly in Piaget, it draws attention to children and computers as an interesting domain for study. For those primarily interested in children and computers, it serves as a reminder that Piaget is a rich mine of ideas.

PIAGET'S CONSTRUCTIVISM AND STRUCTURALISM

The title of Piaget's seminal book on number is a good example of the way in which translation of Piaget to America has subtly yet systematically undermined his emphasis on constructivism. Compare: *The Child's Conception of Number* and *La genese du nombre chez l'enfant.*

To my ear, the English title suggests a static picture: there is a thing called number, and children have a particular conception of it. The French title suggests the dynamic, process-oriented way I read Piaget. Number is not something with an independent objective existence that children happen to have a particular conception of. Instead, the study of number is the study of something·in evolution, something in the process of construction. Children don't conceive number, they make it. And they don't make it all at once or out of nothing. There is a long process of building intellectual structures that change and interact and combine.

These remarks give only the faintest flavor of Piaget's constructivism, but they certainly show the contrast with studies of computers and children. The intellectual frame for nearly all these studies is an objectively given computer interacting with a child. There is little hint of any thought that the child's conception of the computer might be important and different from that of the researcher—and no trace of any idea of the child actually constructing the computer.

A striking exception to these deficiencies is Sherry Turkle's (1984) *The Second Self.* Turkle carefully distinguishes between "the instrumental computer" and "the subjective computer." The former is what exists out there objectively. The latter is what people construct in their minds. Her work on the issue of whether children believe that computers are alive is an excellent example.

Alive and Not Alive—
Construction of the Psychological

Piaget studied children's opinions on what is alive and not alive. Stated in the simplest terms, he concluded that young children think that whatever moves is alive—and they only gradually come to separate living from moving.

This is quite understandable in the case of traditional objects. People and pets are the prototypical living things, and they are the prime movers. Stones and clouds also move—and are seen as lifelike even by adults in poetic moods. Children always view stones and clouds as alive until they begin to use categories of thinking that distinguish between the spontaneous moving of an animal and the imposed moving of a thrown rock or blown cloud. But when it comes to electronic games that talk and beat you at tic-tac-toe but don't move, it is obvious at once, even to the youngest child, that what is most lifelike about them is related to their mindlike characteristics rather than to their motions.

The issue is not whether children think these games are alive or not. It is the discourse they use in talking—and presumably in thinking—about whether these things are alive. They do not talk about whether or how these computational objects move. Instead, they ask if such games think and feel, do they create or simply do what they are programmed to do, and can they be angry. Turkle (1984) makes the pun: motion gives way to emotion as the criterion for what is alive.

One can take three attitudes in relating these observations to Piaget's discussion of childhood animism. One can say he was just plain wrong. One can say that he was right about animals and sticks and stones and rivers, but we now see that he had only a partial picture. Computers lie outside the scope of his discussion. Or one can say, as I wish to, that these new observations expand rather than undermine the sense in which he was right. They bring out more clearly the constructivist and structuralist aspects of his work.

When Piaget listens to a child talk about whether a cloud or a stone or a river is alive, what interests Piaget is certainly not the cloud or the stone or the river, and hardly even the child. Instead, the child's opinions about what is alive and not alive serve as a sort of peephole into a completely different realm. Like the shadows in Plato's cave, the child's judgment provides hints of a different kind of actor in the development of the child's intelligence. The true story is the construction in the child's mind of the physical—in the sense of physics—and the animistic.

Piaget sometimes calls these entities *groupements,* sometimes *structures,* but the play we are observing through the peephole of judgments about alive and not alive is a story told roughly as follows. The child is born into an undifferentiated world in which self and other, animate and inanimate, are all one. The major line of construction is the structuring of this world into two large parts: the animate and the inanimate.

This is not a classification—not a mere attaching of labels—but something far more complex. For Piaget, such constructions are inextricably tied to the way in which the child makes sense of the world. At first, the child will say the stone *is* alive because you can throw it. Later the child will say it is *not* alive because you throw it. The process of changing from one opinion to the other is a process of making sense of the difference between spontaneous and impressed motion.

What we are looking at is the construction of understanding of the laws of motion. In short, we are looking at the construction of the physical in the sense of physics. When the child thinks that the stone is not alive because you have to throw it, but the river is alive, this opinion shows that the child's construction of the causality of motion has not reached the stage where the river can be seen as moving under the influence of external, impressed forces—in this case, gravity—so the river remains in the realm of the animate.

In summary, what Piaget looks at is the construction of large structures of thought—in this case, the construction of animate and inanimate around the criterion of motion. With this description in mind, let us rejoin the observations about the aliveness of computers.

Whether the computer is seen as alive or not alive has nothing to do with how it moves or what laws of physical causality are applied to it. So in this sense the computer is outside the scope of Piaget's particular analysis of structures. But when Turkle looks more closely, she notices that with increasing age, children's judgments about computers being alive or not alive parallel Piaget's observations about sticks and stones and clouds. Much as Piaget documented the development of physical sophistication, what Turkle observes is the development of psychological sophistication.

If we are to revise Piaget in Piaget's spirit, we do this by introducing another actor into the territory of structures. Besides the construction of the physical, we also take account of the construction of the psychological. And once more the judgment of alive and not alive is a window into something larger, into the child's construction of what it is to be a psychological being.

There is very striking similarity between this construction of the psychological and Piaget's observations on animism. Turkle reports that 5-year-old children say the tic-tac-toe game is alive because it cheats. These children do not yet make the distinction between spontaneous behavior that comes from itself and impressed behavior that comes from its program.

Computer-sophisticated 10-year-olds are quite unlikely to give cheating as a reason for the computer being alive. Their understanding of the "causality" of behavior is sufficient for them to make a clear distinction between doing it spontaneously and being put up to do it. In response to the question of computers being alive, a 10-year-old at the Hennigan School in Boston said, "Yes. They're more alive than trees, anyway—and everyone says that trees are alive." The way in which computers are more alive than trees is clearly psychological.

The issue of alive and not alive was certainly one of Piaget's interests and has become part of the social construction of Piaget. However, it is not on the main line of his development and certainly is not the clearest case through which to see the issues of structure. The example of number that I touched on earlier is a much better candidate.

The Mother Structures of Number

What is most striking about Piaget and Szeminska's (1952) study of children's notion of number is how little of the book focuses on what happens in the classroom or on the popular version of number. There is not much there about how children add 3 and 4 to get 7, or how they get to know the multiplication tables. Instead, Piaget is looking at the larger actors whose shadows we see in the way the child learns to add. These entities are large structures that can be identified, named, and studied in their own right. At different periods in Piaget's life, they were referred to differently. The clearest and simplest is probably the term he used after his encounter with Bourbaki, namely, *mother structures*—fundamental structures out of which number and other mathematical thinking is created.

Piaget sees these intellectual structures as precursors of number. They are elements in a process that leads to the emergence, or, rather, the *construction*, of number, even though they are in themselves something else. The central point is that for him, when children think about questions that appear to be related to the numerical, they are not using numbers in an incompetent and inappropriate way but instead are using something else appropriately and competently. I see his demonstration of internal coherence in children's thinking as simple and strong support for this view.

The various structures that Piaget has identified (order, topology, and algebraic structures) are, let us say, the mother structures that underlie the school structures. Piaget might be right or wrong in his identification of particular mother structures or in the completeness of the set he proposed to us. But I think it is very essential to his view of things that what you ought to study is the mother structures. Almost all the discussion of how to use computers in education bears more or less directly on school structures: how to improve this or that particular school structure in mathematics, or writing, or communication, or whatever. Very little of such discussions try to expand our understanding of the old mother structures or to see whether there are any new mother structures.

This view of number as having large and looming structures is in very sharp contrast to the dominant model of thought for information-processing theories of psychology—particularly in the form taken by the Carnegie-Mellon School. There, the ideal would show numerical behavior emerging from the possession of many atomistic and highly specific production rules.

These contrasting points of view identify a major issue—perhaps *the* major issue—in the study of learning that is not being confronted by contemporary cognitive theorists. This is just one way in which Piaget sits rather uneasily in the atmosphere of the decade after his death. Structuralism rings strangely for ears accustomed to the cognitive paradigm that came with the computer.

The Computer Challenge to Piaget: Phenomena and Theory

There are two methodologically very distinct ways in which the computer presence can affect Piagetian enterprise: explicative theory, and phenomena to be explained. Observations about what is judged to be alive or not alive show us phenomena which, on the face of it, do not fit Piaget's explanatory theory. As I have shown, there are ways of looking at the theory from another angle, ways that see these phenomena as strengthening rather than undermining his thinking. But regardless of which view you take, we are talking here about the computer presence throwing up phenomena to be explained. The question is: can Piaget's theory explain them?

We see something very different when we look at the discordance between Piaget's kind of theorizing and, say, Newell and Simon's (1972). The difference now focuses not on what phenomena are to be explained, but on the kind of explanation being given. In this case, the question is: which kind of explanation best fits the spirit and paradigm of these times?

The conflict between Piaget and Newell and Simon is not between modern computer models and old-fashioned structuralist models. One cannot identify Newell and Simon with the computer, and there are ways of thinking in computational terms that are closer to structuralism. For example, the *Society of Mind* (Minsky, 1986) approach to psychological theorizing allows one to postulate active entities with different degrees of complexity and of different sizes, so to speak, in the models being built. It encourages one to analyze the way of the mind in terms of active entities of all sizes. In contrast, the Piagetian view is that such active entities are large, encompassing structures.

Numbers of people (for example, David Klahr, 1984, Gary Drescher, Marvin Minsky, 1975, and myself) have developed computation models as alternative theoretical frameworks to Piaget's, and I see this kind of rethinking of Piagetian theory as a valuable pursuit to which I continue to devote some energy. My focus in this paper, however, is not on the kind of theory, but on the phenomena to be explained.

The Computer and New Mother Structures

When I was looking for ways of using the computer to enrich the development of mathematical thinking, I asked whether there might be other mother structures that Piaget had not recognized merely because they didn't appear clearly in the contexts that were familiar to him. The concept of the turtle arose from such strivings and speculations.

I was touched and impressed by being introduced at the 1985 Piaget Society Symposium not as the father of LOGO but as the father of the turtle, because the turtle is vastly more important than LOGO. From the wisdom of hindsight, the turtle captures a mother structure that has been fully as important to the historical development of mathematics as the mother structures identified in Piaget. This mother structure of the turtle is differential geometry—which is central to the construction of mathematical physics from Newton's time up to today.

One sees this structure most clearly when thinking about the motion of a particle. This motion can be represented by a differential vector that has a position, magnitude, and direction. So the turtle can be thought of as a mother structure to the motion of the particle. The turtle is logically simpler: its state has position and direction, but no magnitude. So this "turtle structure" has a family resemblance to many of the things that Piaget dealt with, but does not, in fact, fall cleanly under any of his structures.

Why is the turtle such an important mother structure? First of all, using the kind of terms that are very dear to Piaget, I got excited about it and began to think it was a mother structure when it first began to emerge from the crossing of two lines. Piaget told us over and over again to look for the intersection between the historical development of science—what has been important epistemologically in the development of any science of knowledge—and the psychogenesis of children.

The turtle captures that intersection because it is a mathematical concept that can be anthropomorphized. Euclid's point has position—but no other properties. When you are taught this definition in school, it usually evokes a laugh or a giggle of embarrassment, because you don't quite understand. What can that mean? A point has position but no magnitude or no color? This is the only example you have ever had of a formal object with very reduced properties, so it does not mean very much. When something has two properties, it makes more sense. A turtle has only two: position and heading and in its mathematical definition, that is what a turtle is. It is akin not to biological things, but to Euclid's concept of a point.

Yet the turtle is also different from the point, especially in two ways that belong to the two intersecting lines of development I mentioned earlier. From the perspective of science, the point is not really the natural way to do geometry. From Galileo on, especially in the hands of Newton and all later development of mathematical physics, we came to understand that the natural element for geometry is the differential vector, an entity tangent to the curve, having both position and heading. So the turtle really does capture an epistemologically key element in the evolution of mathematical science—mathematical physics especially, but mathematical economics no less.

Looked at from the other side, by giving Euclid's point a heading as well, the turtle gains in anthropomorphizability. You can't really identify with a point because it is very difficult to imagine having a position and nothing else. But having a position *and* looking somewhere, facing a direction you can walk toward, the turtle becomes much easier to identify with. So the turtle has a psychological dimension as well as a mathematical one. The fact that these two dimensions intersect in the turtle makes me think that it is a good thing. It touches on something important and powerful.

One can talk about anthropomorphizability in other Piagetian-like ways. This affinity between yourself and this mathematical entity allows you to assimilate the mathematical situation to schemas of personal knowledge. Without such a pipeline into personal knowledge, these mathematics would otherwise be abstract. But with this bridge between mathematics and your own bodily action schemas, sensorimotor experiences, and self-image, the mathematics becomes as tangible, real, and concrete as mud pies. I think that introducing this turtle gives a new facet and new perception to a fundamental theme of Piaget.

Why is the presence of computers so important to this mother structure? Well, the turtle can be introduced without computers, but I doubt that one can introduce it to children without computers. The two together—the turtle and the computer—make something that becomes very accessible to young children. They can take it up and make what they will of it. And you don't have to tell them to anthropomorphize it. You don't even have to call it a turtle, which suggests a kind of anthropomorphizability. Children anthropomorphize this thing quite spontaneously.

So we are looking at a new kind of structure and assimilation-accommodation process. Maybe if we had Piaget's taste for giving structures their "real mathematical names," we'd call this a *differential vector structure*. It would go side by side with structures of order, topology, and algebra. Piaget had not recognized this new one because he was in a different mathematical tradition. So he could not see the differential vector structure as sufficiently distinct—or in a form that appeared in the activities and thought processes of children. The computer's active nature enables us to introduce objects like the turtle that are more dynamic and anthropomorphizable than the kinds that existed before.

In summary, this account of the turtle shows how Piaget's constructivist and structuralist framework can be used as an heuristic for research. And certainly the idea that there might be a field of research called *La genese de l'ordinateur chez l'enfant* must—in everyone's view of things—be seen as reinforcement of the Piagetian approach.

A CRITIQUE OF THE FORMAL
AND OF PIAGET'S STAGE THEORY

I have already stated at some length that what I find to be strong and essential in Piaget is his constructivism and structuralism. What I find least powerful in Piaget is the stage theory. Here again, my focus is on phenomena to be explained—and the phenomena I present are differences in intellectual style that become evident when children are allowed to "construct the computer" in whatever ways are natural to them. But to make clear how these phenomena impact on Piaget's stage theory, I'll take a digression that has little to do with computers as such.

Gilligan and Kohlberg: Stages of Moral Development

This digression challenges the judgment that the formal and analytic is a superior and "ultimate" style of thinking. Its relevance here is that the formal stage may be the most troubled question in the exegesis of Piaget.

Larry Kohlberg's theory of moral stages (Kohlberg, 1969) is similar to Piaget's in some obvious ways. At the beginning, there is no differentiation of the self. Moral judgment is entirely egocentric. It gradually becomes externalized and takes into account other people. This externalization goes through various phases. The earliest is still very self-centered. That is, it is good for me to do something for you because you will do something good for me afterwards. Then beyond that, it is good to do something for you because that is in itself a justification. This progressive detachment of moral judgment from the self winds up at a stage where, detached even from other people, moral judgment is made in terms of general principles. It becomes a formal and abstract intellectual endeavor. And that is the last stage.

Carol Gilligan (1982) challenges Kohlberg in a number of ways. Her book, *In a Different Voice*, observes that this final, "abstract principles" stage of moral judgment is more often found among men than among women. She notes that many women who in every way are highly developed and sophisticated people— morally, personally, socially, intellectually—nonetheless always want to know the context in making moral judgments. Instead of being based on abstract principles, these women's moral judgments are made in terms of other people. Carol Gilligan says that perhaps these women do not "fall short" of the final stage of moral development described by Kohlberg. Perhaps they have taken a different direction altogether.

My purpose is not to enter into this debate. I mention it here as a model for asking a more general question about Piaget's stages of development. In essence, Gilligan challenges the idea that seems so straightforward, obvious, and natural to Kohlberg, that the ultimate development of human thought should be in the direction of abstract, detached, decontextualized thinking. This favoring of the formal and abstract is shared by Piaget.

A Different Voice for Thinking

For most people who have grown up in our Western tradition, it might be acceptable in the area of moral judgment to reject this analytic mode as being superior to the contextual; such a rejection in more logical and mathematical areas of thought is much harder to accept. The nature of the differences in intellectual style that are emerging from our research with children and computers, however, provides strong evidence for a different voice in this area as well.

For some children, it is not that they haven't reached a formal, analytic stage of reasoning. Their work certainly becomes more and more complex, sensitive, and sophisticated, yet it does not become more and more analytic. Computers are a domain where everyone expects the analytic to reign supreme, yet this situation makes it especially clear that for certain children, the development of intelligence and programming expertise can reach high levels without becoming highly analytic as well.

In observing children who are programming computers, a substantial number do hold to a path of development that seems in spirit to be like what Piaget and Kohlberg would say is the norm. By the time they are 10 and 11, that is to say, just about when Piagetians would expect to see them moving into the formal stage, these children do show a style of programming that fits the model of "the logical." Faced with a problem, they subdivide it, modularize it, deal with the parts one at a time, put them together and make a program that is clearly logically structured.

But other children demonstrate a different style—one in which a program emerges not through planning and subdivision of a problem but through something closer to the way in which a sculptor or painter makes a work of art—a process in which the plan of what is to be made emerges and is refined at the same time as the created object takes form. One might call it more of a negotiation between the creator and the material than an imposition of logical order.

This situation would not challenge the stage theory but for an observation that parallels Gilligan's. On any criteria other than an *a priori* commitment to the superiority of the analytic, children who follow a negotiational style are performing at an intellectual level that is fully as excellent and of high quality as the other children. Like the women Gilligan studied, these children as just as sophisticated, intelligent, well-educated, capable, and mature as the other children.

So, just as Gilligan describes another voice for moral discourse, perhaps we are seeing another voice for mathematical discourse—indeed, for the whole spectrum of intellectual endeavor.

Whether this theory will stand up is a matter for extensive research. But if it does stand up, what does this tell us about Piaget? Has the computer created an opportunity for a more Piagetian way of thinking in Piaget's favorite areas, logic and mathematics? Or does it mean that this voice has always been there, but the advent of computers made it clearer? My own opinion is the latter.

ACKNOWLEDGMENTS

We wish to give special thanks to Ms. Melissa Kaden at the University of Massachusetts/Amherst for her diligent work to transcribing the audio tape of Seymour Papert's address and to Ms. Winter Snow, editorial assistant to Seymour Papert, who greatly expedited both the revisions of this chapter and its timely completion.

REFERENCES

Gilligan, C. (1982). *In a different voice: Psychological theory and women's development.* Cambridge, MA: Harvard University Press.

Klahr, D. (1984) Transition processes in quantitative development. In R. Sternberg (Ed.), *Mechanisms of cognitive development* (pp. 101–140). San Francisco: Freeman.

Kohlberg, L. (1969). Stage and sequence: The cognitive-developmental approach to socialization. In D. Goslind (Ed.), *Handbook of socialization: Theory and research* (pp. 251–296). New York: Rand-McNally.

Minsky, M. (1975). *Semantic Information Processing.* Cambridge, MA.: MIT Press.

Minsky, M. (1986). *Society of mind.* New York: Simon and Schuster.

Newell, A., & Simon, H. A. (1972). *Human problem solving.* Englewood Cliffs, NJ: Prentice-Hall.

Piaget, J., & Szeminska, A. (1952). *The child's conception of number.* London: Routledge & Kegan Paul.

Turkle, S. (1984). *The second self: Computers and the human spirit.* New York: Simon and Schuster.

Chapter 2

Function in Piaget's System: Some Notes for Constructors of Microworlds

Peter B. Pufall
Smith College

The growing disenchantment with structuralism in general and the formal structuralism that marked the middle segment of Piaget's theoretical work has fostered a shift away from Piaget's genetic epistemology. Piaget aided and abetted his detractors by emphasizing structural over functional characteristics of mind. Statements as, "genesis emanates from a structure and culminates in a structure" (Piaget, 1967) left no doubt that Piaget conceived of mind as continuously developing, but did little to placate critics looking for precise theoretical statements about the processes by which one structural form is transformed into another. His final elaboration of equilibration was oriented toward a structural analysis of change differentiating types of equilibration in terms of the structures reorganized. (See Furth, 1981, for a clear presentation of equilibration.)

This leads easily to the conclusion that Piaget has little to offer any serious examination of "constructivism in the computer age." This is especially true if the computer age is conceived of as creating environments, "microworlds," that serve as incubators of "powerful ideas" (Papert, 1980). Both of these ideas are discussed fully later. However, it seems useful to lay out in general the meaning of *microworlds* in this chapter. A microworld, as the real world, embodies principles rather than didactically presenting them. The principles have been identified by other humans as important, and in many cases they embody a theory shared by experts about a physical or social phenomenon. In short, the heart of microworlds is that they are conceptual systems. In addition, they are fleshed out in contexts that, presumably, will make it easier for us to construct the principles through our transactions with that world.

The present chapter has two purposes. One is to look at constructivism in Piaget's theory by exploring his writings about functional aspects of mind. The second purpose is to consider the implications of these ideas for various meanings of constructivism. It is argued that only by keeping separate these meanings is it possible both to understand the kind of constructive impact "microworlds" might currently have on intellectual development and to appreciate the type of changes needed in microworlds if they are to have a greater developmental impact on thought.

PROPERTIES OF FUNCTIONALISM

Beilin (1983, 1984, 1985, 1986) argued persuasively that a "New Functionalism" is the most powerful alternative to structuralism. His historical analysis (Beilin, 1983, 1986) of functionalism may be argued to be too encompassing, even when restricted to its newest version, to serve as an alternative paradigm, metaphor, or a core of assumptions organizing programs of research (Overton, 1984). Whether or not new functionalism is a new paradigm will not be discussed, much less resolved in the present chapter. Three aspects of Beilin's (1986) are used to serve and analyze functional properties of mind in Piaget's theory.

Two are historical and the other methodological. Ironically, functional analysis has its historical roots both in comparative psychology and the study of consciousness. In comparative psychology, and in particular the various forms of learning theory that derived from a comparative perspective, function is taken literally. Adaptation requires doing or acting in a selecting environment. William James' functionalism starts with the assumption that consciousness is an adaptive function to be analyzed into its constituents, themselves adaptive functions. Contemporary functionalists may not accept James' view of consciousness, but they continue to employ his method of analyzing function into constituent functions (Beilin, 1986; Overton, 1984).

FUNCTION IN PIAGET'S THEORY

Piaget's link to comparative psychology is more obvious than his link to consciousness, Jamesian or otherwise. For Piaget, intelligence is an adaptive biological function. To know is to act, and, in the absence of action, the question of knowledge becomes mute within Piaget's system. As any biological function, knowing implies structure, and to come to know is to construct new structures. Within his system function is an inherent aspect of structure.

Insofar as function is inherent to structure, any analysis of mind necessarily implies the study of both. Function, or process, has been considered explicitly in his examination of *assimilative and accommodating functioning, semiotic functioning,* and *reasoning. Assimilation and accommodation* are concepts incorporated directly from biology. They were introduced in Piaget's first writings on intellectual development and remained an invariant fixture in his theory. *Semiotic functioning* was part of his early work on play and dreams, reemerging later in his examination of figurative and operative thought through the studies of perception, memory, and imagery. *Reasoning,* or thinking about explanations for physical events, marked the beginning—*Judgment and Reasoning* (1928) and *The Child's Conceptualization of Physical Causality* (1930)—and end—*Grasp of Consciousness* (1976) and *Success and Understanding* (1978)—of his empirical work on thought.

Three conclusions about Piaget's position on function should be stated at the outset to distinguish his meaning of function from meanings inherent in contemporary theory, especially theories associated with an Artificial Intelligence (AI) perspective. One, Piaget does not adopt the functionalist methodology of analyzing functions into subfunctions. Two, function and structure are related by "causal implication" and not "material causality." That is, structure is a formal property of intelligent functioning; structure does not have a physical reality and, therefore, is not to be compared to a machine state or a program, both of which materially influence the way the machine behaves and can be studied independent of the functioning of the machine. This is not to say that the relation between knowing and action has no material consequence. Drawing has both behavioral and figurative material results, as do all the schemata of thought. It does mean that the relation between function and structure is implied. Finally, function is never characterized as a mechanism or processor, formal or material, that manipulates or transforms particular kinds of sensory or symbolic information; hence intelligence is not reducible to symbol manipulation (Boden, 1980).

Assimilative and Accommodative Functioning

Even the briefest introductions to Piaget's theory underscores the fact that he views assimilation and accommodation as properties of all biological adaptive functions, which includes intellectual activity. Their general properties and purpose do not change, within domains of knowing, even as the structures they serve are qualitatively transformed over mental development. Neither do they differ between domains as structures of knowing adapt to various contents. In both cases, assimilation is conservative and, in that sense, egocentric. By contrast, accommodation is nonconservative and is directed toward the object to be known.

Constructivism is characterized as the continual restructuring of the relation between self and world (Kuhn, 1983), where *world* implies both palpable and ideational reality. It is useful to distinguish between self–world restructuring in the strict sense and self–object restructuring. The former refers to practical intelligent behavior including both sensory motor adaptations and conceptual systems or theories that can be shared with others. The self–object relation implies nonconscious structures of knowing that are implied in conscious thought. Within Piaget's theory these are the logical–mathematical structures. Every intellectual act, practical or conceptual, involves conflict between the epistemic acts of conserving (assimilative functioning) and changing (accommodative functioning), with the developmental potential for reconstructing the self–world and/or self–object relation (Furth, 1978).

In the extreme, these relationships appear to be disjointed. Adaptive perceptual-motor acts reconstruct the relation between physical reality and ourselves. For example, we change the shape of our grip as we grasp different-sized balls. In this case accommodation entails both the explicit sensory motor alterations of the hand and the firings of the nervous system set within the context of a stable (assimilative) scheme of grasping. These adjustments are temporary adaptations regulated by specific perceptual-motor feedback.

Conceptual acts reconstruct epistemic objects, which for Piaget include both nonconscious general structures of knowing, the logical-mathematical structures, as well as conscious knowledge about explicit theories, hypotheses, and hunches. The latter developmental adaptations are open ended. Even as they resolve previous conflicts in our thinking they introduce the possibility of asking new questions about our reality, or more correctly about our conceptualization about that reality. Whereas the self–world and self–object are offered as different psychological constructions, they are not necessarily separate in our ongoing intellectual functioning, but rather are two aspects of intelligence. We will return to their interrelation in the section on "Reasoning."

There is some Genevan research directed at the conditions of learning. Inhelder, Sinclair, and Bovet (1974) studied exogenous factors of development, which for them meant conditions that foster epistemic conflict. Conflicts were created by bringing ideas together that led to different predictions about the same event, for example, counting the elements in two lengths as well as comparing their relative positioning in space when making judgments about their relative length. They exaggerated the covariation of variables, for example, the relation of height and width in the conservation of liquid mass. And they emphasized reversibility of practical transformations, for example, pouring from one container to the next could be reversed.

They defined these conflicts not by examining the structure of the concept to be learned, but by looking at the conflicts revealed in previous research diagnosing the development of these concepts. That is, conflicts revealed by the child in his or her effort to structure the self–object relation. In short, they conspired to create conflicts by reflecting conflicts children had revealed themselves.

What message is there for developers of computer worlds in these considerations? From constructs as general as assimilation and accommodation it is impossible to derive precise directions for them to take, either in form or content. This is not to say that nothing can be gleaned. One message seems obvious to many but may be easily trivialized. There is a tendency to equate *constructive* with *interactive.* To assume that doing, especially if it is enthusiastic doing, is constructive in the sense of changing the self–world relation. Although this message may seem obvious, special care is needed, because creating interactive environments is educationally attractive and perhaps easy to accomplish in constructing computer environments. Moreover, children seem to be highly motivated to enter into an interactive mode with computers, though there is growing evidence of individual differences in children's motivation to interact with computers (Greenfield, 1984).

We are still not clear why children who interact with computer worlds are motivated to do so (Leeper, 1985). From a cognitive constructivist's perspective, that motivation must entail disequilibria of at least two kinds: One involves the self–world relationship and may involve temporary adaptations or fine-tuning our understanding, as is likely to occur in drill and practice. The other involves the self–object relationship, which has the potential for epistemic restructuring that is permanent. For example, once we understand class logic it remains part of our intellectual repertoire throughout development.

To go beyond this general perspective is to ask more specific questions relevant to how computer worlds can effectively create either type of disequilibria, but especially those leading to epistemic restructuring. One question is whether it matters what we think *in,* i.e., the medium or symbols representing knowledge, or *about,* the types of tasks or problems. The other is whether being conscious of our thinking is relevant. These two questions are dealt with in the next two sections, "Semiotic functioning" and "Reasoning." Though the former is relevant to the content and medium of thought and reasoning to consciousness, the two questions are so tightly intertwined that they cannot be considered in one section exclusively.

Semiotic Functioning

For Piaget, semiotic functions include language, art, play, perception, memory, and imagery. Language, art, and play formed part of Piaget's early work on semiotic activity. Their study seems a logical and necessary outcome of his work on the object-concept. The object-concept marks the beginning of the distinction between the self–object and the self–world relation. With objects as conceptual entities, children are in a frame of mind to represent things perceived: ideas and feelings. Language, art and play are specific to our need to represent.

Piaget stated that art and play are correlated with accommodation and assimilation, respectively. Artistic renditions are accommodations insofar as art is intended to be pictorially realistic, and play is assimilative insofar as situations are treated as if they are something else. Though admittedly overstated, the distinction draws out three important theoretical points. First, the full-meaning of semiotic functions cannot be captured by theoretical entities as general as assimilation and accommodation. Second, semiotic functions embody *both* operational knowing *and* the medium of expression. Third, although both assimilation and accommodation are present in any normal intelligent act and, in an effort to represent knowledge, either can and does gain prominence over the other (Furth, 1970). The fact that they are not always in balance may help us predict when developmental changes are about to occur and understand the relation between individual aspects or styles of intelligence and development. Concerning development, it seems reasonable to expect that there is a systematic relation between the degree of imbalance and the likelihood of change. An example may be the apparent shifts in the balance between assimilative graphic activity reflecting playful expression and its accommodative or constrained quality in pictorial representation, as expressed in the purported shift in the aesthetic quality of art between the preschool and grade-school years (Winner, 1982).

Differences between assimilation and accommodation may reflect cognitive styles in constructing or resolving conflict in the self–object and self–world relations. At the simplest level we may differ in whether we are assimilators or accommodators. These differences may lead us to choose one semiotic function as our preferred mode of representing the self–object relation. Accommodators may adopt a figural mode, emphasizing a more accurate representation of states, even series of states. Assimilators may look to formal modes of representation—language and mathematics—which more efficiently express transitions between states. In short, we need to be developing ways of characterizing the styles in which children interact with computer worlds and match cognitive styles to the style of representation in the microworlds.

Piaget's studies of perception (1969), imagery (Piaget & Inhelder, 1980), and memory (Piaget & Inhelder, 1973) were carried out during the 1960s and seemed to be extensions of his earlier studies of the logical-mathematical structure of thought. During this era the contrast between *figurative* and *operative* emerged. This contrast both embodies Piaget's constructivist position and sets the agenda for the research in each of the areas.

As a constructivist he assumed that the structure of thought, understanding, and problem seeking is derived from acting on and not from the reception of passive perceptions or the accumulation of images or memories. In fact, perceptions need to be "interpreted" in any act of reflective knowing, and images and memories are stored and retrieved as a function of operative activity. The latter is probably the most provocative aspect of the figurative–operative relation as it predicts that our memory for events is transformed with respect to changes in the logical-mathematical structure of thought. In sum, the figurative–operative distinction indicates the psychological priority of structure over representation in Piaget's theory; it does not represent a theoretical position of structure being ontologically prior to function.

The contrast between figurative and operative may have narrowed our view of these functions, and distracted us from seeing other values in the research Piaget offered as evidence for the contrast. An example of the narrowness is in his conceptualization of perception as a sampling process with individual samples construed as representations of reality. The methodology chosen to study perception was consistent with this view, forcing children to represent an event as a series of states. This had led to attacks from ecological realists such as the Gibsons (E. Gibson, 1969; J. Gibson, 1979).

It might be more appropriate to identify Piaget's view of perception contained in the figurative–operative distinction as "perceptual representation." It is in sharp contrast to his earlier characterization of perception as activity flowing out of sensory-motor activity (Piaget, 1954). That view is commensurate with those of his antagonists.

The value in looking at perceptual representation is that it shifts the focus to the role that forms of representation may play in cognitive development. Put another way, it changes our focus from Piaget's question: How does knowledge, operative structure, affect representation? to: How might a concept be represented within a particular medium? From a pragmatic-developmental perspective the new question is: What is the most effective medium within which the critical features of a concept can be communicated and constructed?

The graphics capabilities of computers might allow children to represent variant states of a spatial-temporal event, such as a tilting or falling object, in a systematic and self-paced manner. This would transform the experience from a self–world perceptual event, in which the information specifying falling is contained in the optic array, to a self–object conceptual experience, in which the information is contained in a series of static representations. This effectively separates the perceptual and representational so that the child can directly manipulate the representational.

Computer worlds could alter patterns of development we have taken as invariant by allowing us to interact with them in ways we cannot interact with our "real" world (Forman, 1985, and Papert, 1980). That interaction is not only altered in terms of the timing of the event, but in terms of the types of functions available for constructing new knowledge. VCR's have playback, reverse, and freeze-frame functions that modulate self–world interactions in ways qualitatively different from our direct experience with the world. This in turn creates the potential for thinking about the self–object relation within a new context for conceptualizing that relationship.

Through these technological functions children can think about self–object relations, for example, geometry (Papert, 1980), in new ways with the possibility of constructing a conceptual system sooner and interrelating it more easily and systematically with other knowledge. Forman (1985) provides a cautionary note as we consider these high-flying ideas. The value of these computer functions is not always perceived by preschool children, at least in the domains he has studied. Whether they learn to appreciate these functions at a particular period of development, that is, when metacognitive functions emerge during early and mid-grade school, when a certain level of conceptual understanding of a knowledge domain has been achieved so that the functions take on new intellectual value, or after extended media experience that allows children to understand the potential of these functions for understanding.

Reasoning

Piaget (1954) identifies two cognitive constructions marking the end of the sensory-motor period of thought: the "object concept," and the differentiation and coordination of "means and end." The developmental extensions of these qualities of mind were never integrated into a single conceptual system. The "object concept" marked the beginning of his quest for an answer to the question: How must the mind be structured to know that? It is a quest that led to his identification of necessary categories of reasoning such as the physical invariants and logical forms. His studies of "means–end" explore the question: How did the mind come to be structured in that way? This quest led him to identify strategies by which the mind evaluates the validity of theories about reality.

The previous discussion indicates that Piaget's analysis of intellectual development beyond the object concept emphasized structure over function. By contrast, his studies of development from means–end emphasize functional characteristics of mind. In particular, his examination of the genesis of consciousness and its functional value for intellectual development is central to functionalists with an intellectual lineage dating back to William James.

In this section on "Function in Piaget's Theory," three functional qualities of mind identified by Piaget are examined: practical reasoning, social constructing, and reflectivity. In contrast to the first two sections, specific implications of these functions for the development of computer worlds will not be explored immediately but will be reserved for the final section, "Constructing Knowledge and Computing."

Practical Reasoning.   Reasoning is inherently practical. In the context of unpredictable events, reasoning seeks definition of and solves problems created by what appears to be unpredictable events; or, in the context of predictability, it seeks explanations. This is not to say that what we think about is not theoretical. Isaac Newton did not dwell on the personal injury caused by the fallen apple but on a principled explanation that would subsume all fallen and yet-to-fall apples. At the same time, reasoning is not at all times or at all levels of development directed at theoretically sweeping explanations.

Developmentally the object of reason shifts from our actions that create an effect (Piaget, 1976) to our understanding of why those actions have to be patterned in that fashion (Piaget, 1978). Within the present context the object of reason shifts from the practical actions of self in the self–world relationship to the self–world relationship itself. Reasoning shifts from being conscious of what we are doing to understanding why in doing that we are successful.

In Piaget's early studies of reasoning (1928, 1930), he asked children to explain familiar phenomena, for example, "Why do clouds move?" and "Why do some things float?" In later studies (1976, 1978) he asked children to explain how they created a particular effect, or, as Piaget put it, to "grasp consciously" their own actions in creating the effect, and, finally, to construct their "understanding" of why a solution or procedure is successful. He examined children's thinking about familiar, directly observable effects, and in the later studies children could control and replicate the effects through their manipulation of variables.

Taken this way, reasoning must be both intuitive and planful. From a dynamic point of view, intuition and planning may be constituents of what Kuhn (1983) refered to as *searching for meaning,* or what Karmiloff-Smith and Inhelder (1975) refer to as "getting a theory." On the plane of action and in conscious thought, intuition is a semantic context specifying some of the variables, constructs, and interrelations among those elements, as well as implying a course of action. That is, it has both structural and functional qualities. For example, a child may explain floating in terms of an intuitive theory of force, that is, "the water pushes the boat up." Should the boat sink in his bathwater, a child with this theory might fill the bathtub to overflowing trying to make the boat float.

Intuitive thought may be conservative, looking for verification and not disconfirmation (Kuhn & Phelps, 1983; Piaget, 1928). It may tolerate contradiction insofar as some things are pushed up by water whereas other things are not. This aspect of thought creates a dilemma for cognitive theory. If thought accepts or does not even perceive its own contradictions, then how does thought even develop? What is the source of the conflict?

Social Constructions.   Why do children leave an *objectively confused* state of mind if they are *subjectively certain* in their thinking? In general, Piaget resolved the dilemma by proposing that human thought is self-equilibrating. Even if one accepts that premise, the question of what is the source of any conflict still remains. At a metatheoretical level, conflict necessarily arises because every cognitive act implies assimilation and accommodation. At the behavioral level it can be seen as the potential outcome of social exchange. In defense of social transaction Piaget states: "Never without the shock of contact with the thought of others and the effort of reflection which this shock entails would thought as such come to consciousness" (Piaget, 1966, p. 144).

Taken literally, this suggests that our search for meaning entails a search for shared meaning between knowing systems. Conflict and the ensuing consciousness of our own thought comes with others challenging us to think about the adequacy of our own thought. This is not to restrict the importance of social interchange to the birth of consciousness in general or on particular issues. In fact, its relevance may increase rather than decrease as the object of thought moves from the practical to the theoretical level. Cross-cultural research provides indirect evidence to support this hypothesis. Cultures are more likely to differ in terms of whether or not individuals achieve the higher stages of intellectual development, particularly formal reasoning.

In this context, one way of characterizing intellectual development is as a process of becoming more and more aware that the object of thought is not reality per se but our understanding of it. One dimension of cultural variation is the presence or availability of formal schooling, and one of the strategic implications of formal schooling may be to focus our attention on our cultural and personal conceptualization of reality and how these are often contradictory. The significance of our failure to move to a formal level of reasoning in a particular domain may not be a statement about individual capacity as much as it is a statement about the practical value society places on our thinking about thinking in general and about a specific domain in a formal manner.

The developmental value of social challenges may be related to who offers the challenge. Piaget speculated in his early work on moral development that social cognition develops in different ways depending on whether adults or peers presented the challenge. At younger ages adults may reinforce egocentricity (Furth, 1978). Parents may enter into children's conceptualizations too readily and, therefore, may be less likely to challenge them to explicitly think about the pretense they are constructing. By contrast, peers force each other to be explicit, to objectify their thought even if they are constructing a pretense.

The differential role of peer and adult, especially parent, may change during the pre-teen and teenage years (Youniss, 1980). Peers present challenges but do so in the context of mutual trust. Perspectives are willingly shared, and there is often an effort to mutually construct a common perspective. The self–object relationship is the focus, but object is "objectified" so that two selves can reflect on it simultaneously. The dynamic when interacting with an adult is compliance, not mutuality. The cognitive relation reconstructed is not self–object but, rather, self–world, as the youth's expectation is to accommodate behavior to the prescriptions of the adult.

It may be that these dynamics, especially during adolescence, have more impact on social cognition than on other areas of thought. At the same time, it would seem foolish to imagine different logics developing out of peer and adult encounters. The difference may be on how, or even whether, children engage in learning a subject matter, especially one in which they have to question or to construct a conceptualization of a phenomenon as a hypothesis or theory. Though these are uncharted areas, there is every reason to believe that the transformation of novice to expert is regulated by the form of intellectual relationship between novice and expert (Renninger & Wineger, 1985).

Social challenges that lead to reconstructions of mind may take various forms. They may include articulate alternative conceptualizations, challenges to specific aspects of one's thought, requests for clarification or examples, and inquiries about how one would generalize from the prototype. In all of these the social challenge rarely specifies a clear plan by which the mind can reconstruct itself. We are left to our own devices if we are interested in constructing a new self–object relationship.

Reflectivity. Social challenges provide the context and the motivation for intellectual development; the constructive processes that bring about development involve something more. What that something more is depends on one's conceptualization of mind. "Reflecting on" is central to many constructivist theories. One manifestation of reflectivity is our ability to understand what we know as well as what we need to know. Meacham (1983) noted that this duality might take various forms, it may vary over development, and it may even represent cognitive styles, as some of us are problem seekers or question seekers, tolerating ambiguity and searching out uncertainty, whereas others are answer seekers, always seeking closure and trying to eliminate uncertainty. In all these cases, reflectivity implies the awareness of two states and, by implication, knowledge of strategies appropriate for coordinating them or transforming one state into another.

This analysis of reflectivity is reminiscent of William James' conceptualization of consciousness as the leading edge of intellectual functioning. Piaget's (1978) work on understanding reflects a similar concern for consciousness—he refers to it as "cognizance." Cognizance is the goal-directed quality of mind, that sense of seeking after a more coherent conceptualization. Cognizance is to be contrasted with nonconscious intellectual development. The latter not only goes on nonconsciously, but the abstract structures constructed are nonconscious in their functioning. These structures are similar to syntactic structures; they function to organize conscious thought, but are not conscious in the act of knowing.

Piaget (1978) referred to the abstraction process leading to conceptual restructuring as *reflexive,* and the process leading to structural reorganization as *reflective.* Both restructurings could go on simultaneously in an intellectual act, or it is conceivable that we reflexively reconstruct our thinking without reflectively reconstructing the formal structure of thought. This might occur if we abandoned a metaphor because its entailments did not lead to accurate predictions. For example, "sweating glasses" is figuratively accurate but literally suggests that glass is a permeable membrane. Reflecting on the nature and function of containers should lead one to abandon this biological metaphor as the appropriate scientific model. Clearly containers that are porous are functionally useless, to say nothing of being messy. As well, we might recognize that people sweat when the atmosphere and their bodies are hot, not when the former is hot and the latter cold. Anyone making this observation would not necessarily construct another metaphor or structurally reorganize thought. This observation leads to questions about and the search for a new understanding that might result in our constructing principles of relative density, permeability of membranes, condensation, and so forth.

Piaget's examination of these two forms of reflectivity reveals changes in his thinking about what is abstracted and the interrelations of these abstractions. First, the structure of thought reflectively abstracted is not identified with logical-mathematical structures but with general properties of organization, for example, reciprocity, coordinations, compensations, and so on. Second, conscious states are not identified exclusively with logical necessity but include "significations" connected by "significant implication."

CONSTRUCTING KNOWLEDGE
AND COMPUTING

The foregoing examination of function provides a general framework within which the issue of "constructivism in the computer age" can be examined. To this point there have been some hints about the connectedness of the two. In the following sections these connections will be elaborated. Particular emphasis will be given to the constituents of reasoning, and "computer age" will be restricted to "microworlds." Microworlds is restricted further by using Papert's (1980) world of Turtle Graphics and the specific study of that world by G. Fein, E. Scholnick, P. Campbell, S. Schwartz, and R. Frank, chapter 7 in the present volume, as prototypes.

Constructing Knowledge and Microworlds. Microworlds need not be identified with computers, though perhaps their most elegant forms are run on computers. Microworlds are not simulations of reality, as in the case of flight simulators. In fact, simulations may only take advantage of established self–world relations rather than challenging children to think about how other humans conceptualize reality.

In general, if successful, microworlds are environments within which we can think more clearly and, presumably, develop intellectually more efficiently. Bruner's (1964) analysis of mind in terms of modes of representations (motoric, iconic, and symbolic) has been credited as one of the intellectual forces in the development of microworlds. Embedded with his analysis is the belief that given the appropriate environment, an effective and comprehensible mode for representing knowledge, children can learn anything, or at least their intellectual development will be greatly facilitated.

The picture-logic world created by Furth (1970) and the various environments created by Donaldson (1978) and her colleagues are examples of microworlds that are not computer dependent, either for their existence or their functional value, although Furth has recently constructed a computer micro-world called Symbolic Picture Logic. Both create environments that at least facilitate the possibility of children demonstrating what they know already. What is difficult to specify are the characteristics of an "environment" that make intellectual development more likely.

Donaldson created environments with plausible and storylike structures so that the relevant relations are easier to detect and the child less likely to be distracted by trying to figure out what the situation is about, rather than being able to concentrate on the question to be answered. Domain familiarity will not account for the developmental potential of Furth's (1970) picture-logic world. To be sure, Furth (1970) used familiar forms. These forms are figuratively related to the symbolized object (e.g., a mandala for the sun) and logical functions (e.g., → for "is an instance of"). However, the most significant psychological change when transcribing picture logic to a computer microworld may be more interpersonal than technological. Children are free to choose the level at which they wish to enter the program, the form of feedback they wish to have, and, perhaps their most important choice is to take risks by interacting with a "knowing system," (see chapter 3 by Furth in this volume).

These microworlds are limited in varying degrees by the potential for intellectual growth. Furth's picture-logic task does not include all of the forms of propositional logic, though there is no reason that it could not. Donaldson's worlds are micro-microworlds. They probe specific conceptual areas and do so in specific contexts. In neither case is it clear that the knowledge tapped is generalized to other contexts, that is, that the self–object relation has been transformed so that it is not bound to a single context.

These qualifications are true of all basic research. They are not offered as criticism but to set these cases of microworlds off from ones with more ambitious goals. Some microworlds presumably create environments in which it is easier for children to construct knowledge than their "ordinary" world. Their microworlds must be places in which the child not only learns effective procedures for working in that world, the self–world relation, but also constructs a new understanding of the principles that regulate that relationship, that is, reconstructs aspects of the self–object relation.

The Microworld of Turtle Graphics and LOGO.   Microworlds with such ambitious intent embody rather than conceptualize limited domains of knowledge. They do not prescribe what the child should know, they set the context within which the child can construct knowledge. Papert's Turtle Graphics embodies geometric principles; it does not present them, as geometry texts do when they systematically introduce axioms of geometry. The world of Turtle Graphics invites children to create an understanding of geometry from their practical constructive manipulations of the "turtle." Fein et al, (chapter 7) capture the point more forcefully when they say that with LOGO children can teach the turtle new tricks. Children can teach it to go beyond its primitive commands by sequencing them into modules.

Turtle Graphics and LOGO are the critical elements of the Papert micro-world. The former not only locates a form—the cursor—within the screen, it specifies its direction or orientation within that space. That means that graphics can be conceived of as vectors, not merely geometric elements like lines, angles, and so forth. Working with LOGO as their programming language, children can create patterns—paths—forms. By having children program the turtle to figurally construct a form, the actions of construction must be set out in specific procedures, procedures that can be consolidated into modules to be used again and again. In short, programming externalizes and operationalizes an intelligent act as symbol manipulating (Boden, 1979).

The conceptual environment of Turtle Graphics and LOGO is offered as an "incubator for powerful ideas" (Papert, 1980). Powerful ideas is a metaphor, and, as any useful metaphor, has intriguing entailments. Powerful ideas have a structural and functional side. On the structural side they are coherent, and as a consequence of using the ideas, by reflecting on them, that coherence becomes more evident. For example, the case of geometry this implies being able to demonstrate that the sum of the interior angles of a rectangle equals $360°$.

Functionally, ideas are powerful if they are not literal. They can be used figuratively, as in the case of metaphor or analogy, to give coherence to other domains of knowing. A simple example is Papert's use of a turtle as the meta-phor for the cursor; it is powerful insofar as it transforms a geometric entity—a line—into a path of action and presumably facilitates children thinking in terms of vectors.

Microworlds and Structurally Powerful Ideas.   The turtle, its behavior, and the world within which it behaves are neither simulations of turtle ecology or the biomechanics of a turtle. Children playing within the world of the turtle are not programming the turtle to negotiate the ecology of a real turtle. The procedures for moving the turtle do not require the child to consider the energy expended to move through the space, to start, to turn, to stop. The space is a topographical void that makes no energy demands on the turtle.

Whereas the ecology of the turtle is neither a simulation of a turtle's nor of our sensory-motor space, it was Papert's intention that our sensory-motor knowledge and our knowledge of turtles would make Turtle Graphics less ab-stract and the functions for moving it about more easily understood. The turtle was chosen so that children would assimilate it to their knowledge of movement. Turtles as visually guided organisms have both location and direction. Thinking about the cursor in this way changes it from a charming or attractive image to an epistemic idea, which allows one to think about space as paths and vectors. Papert's hypothesis is that geometric principles would be abstracted more efficiently from a vector space than the Cartesian space in which they are typically embedded.

In short, adaptation to the world of the turtle is not going to restructure the self–world relations of sensory-motor knowing; those relations are not part of the interactive experience when using Turtle Graphics. Papert created a microworld self-object interactive experience for constructing principles of geometry. The microworld of the turtle embodies a conceptual system; the graphic world of the turtle is constrained by elementary principles of geometry. The child must learn to move the turtle through space by learning the rules of the language, and of course how those rules affect the behavior of the turtle. The ultimate objective is to reflect on sets of rules that create geometrically interesting effects, for example, rules for constructing various rectangles, and abstract from them the embodied geometric principles.

The process of reflexive abstraction may be enhanced because the turtle's world is digital both in terms of the primitive commands and the movements on the CRT. The sizes of linear and angular units are specified as primitives in the system. An extended line is programmatically constructed by the number of times the forward command is repeated; an angle, in terms of the number of times the directional change command is executed. In the land of Turtle Graphics curved paths are created by changing the turtle's direction or heading before it moves forward. The smaller the change of direction and distance covered in each move, the more faithful the approximation of the digitized form to a smooth curve.

These constraints sharpen the distinction between constructing in Turtle Graphics and the sensory-motor acts of drawing, which are basically analogic. The fact that the self–world constructions in sensory-motor graphics is distinctly different from the self–world constructions in Turtle Graphics may give the latter an advantage as an interactive systems within which to learn conceptual systems like geometry. Children in Piaget's studies of imagery and perception had to construct a discrete representation of a continuous spatial event. When operating in the Turtle microworld children are working in discrete space. This constraint provides a context within which children can think about discrete space as *real* and not about discrete space as *an abstraction* from the analogue world of sensory-motor experience. If this transformation has developmental value, children should reflectively abstract principles of geometry more efficiently, that is, do it earlier in development, and effectively, that is, construct more general geometric principles.

Microworlds and Functionally Powerful Ideas. The fact that children communicate with the turtle by way of a programming language rather than move the turtle as they would a stuffed animal, means they have to *represent* their intent in terms of the means for achieving that intent. Moreover, the means to that end has to be given in an explicit manner. Making thought explicit seems functionally equivalent to conceptualizing thought in Piaget's system. In both cases thought is conscious and as a consequence is open to reflection; however, in contrast to social constructions these are not shared reflections.

Communication in this mode is declarative. The child cannot say to the turtle: "Tell me all about yourself." Of course, the child could ask an adult or another child to write a program that would achieve a particular intent. That might effectively deal with the self–world relation in the short run; however, depending on what the other did, it might not lead to a reconstruction of the self–object relation. That seems most likely when the child transforms questions about the ways of achieving a particular end into a testable hypothesis: "If this is true, then by programming the turtle this way . . . ." That is, the child is forced into a functional mode of experimenter.

The presumed cognitive benefit of communicating in this way is that children must adopt a procedural orientation to problem solving. Some, (as Fein et al., chapter 7, this volume) suggest the possibility that children abstract higher order relations like reciprocity, recursion, and embedding from the programs they develop to construct patterns, and there is evidence that children's programs contain sequences of commands that are instances of reciprocals, recursions, or embeddings.

Such predictions are reminiscent of Piaget's reflective abstraction, abstracting formal relations from the structure of action. It may be that with these relations preserved in programming language, rather than in the flow of action, the abstraction process will be facilitated, and may be so in two ways: First, it may be in module procedures—once the properties of recursion are understood in one program, they may be easily reconstructed in another program; and second, recursion, may be a concept within which to understand and differentiate types of spatial (repeated designs) and temporal (musical rhythms) patterns. Unfortunately, to date these are provocative promises with little evidence on which to judge their validity. There is no doubt that both promises are well worth pursuing.

Microworlds, Procedural Thinking, and Metaphor.   There are several special, "really powerful," functional ideas that may be induced by microworlds of the sort created in Turtle Graphics. Microworlds in which solutions have to be programmed would appear to have general problem-solving implications. Programs are testable; if they run they represent a solution to the problem. Because every symbol and every step or command in the program have to be defined in the system, they are explicit, something valued in all problem solutions.

For Papert, programming becomes a powerful idea when we adopt a procedural orientation to problem solving. Its general cognitive value is that this orientation is independent of any particular programming language, and, in fact, it does not even demand that a computer be involved. The computer seems to serve the same purpose as a social agent. Through continued interchange between two knowing systems, the meanings of terms are clarified and the procedures for ordering terms are constructed. In either case, when the novice recognizes the value of procedural thinking it becomes a powerful tool for analyzing all problems.

With all good things there is risk. Characterizing problem solving as procedural thinking runs the risk of thinking of thought as exclusively a rational sequential process. It suggests that thinking is a process with precise symbols and well-specified rule systems. It would be foolish to say this is not *part* of human thinking. It is *all* that is critical to the functioning of computers. Therefore, it is essential that we become efficient in procedural thinking if we are to effectively communicate with them.

Another aspect of human thought is particularly central to problem solving. It is nonrational insofar as it does not necessarily involve the logic of deductive reasoning. Problem solving often begins with understanding a problem as if it were something else—it is "playing with ideas" in the technical sense of play as a semiotic function and a vital property of thought.

Let me recast this and call it the metaphorical side of thought. I am sure that this side has several levels; two are emphasized here. At one level, metaphorical thinking operates without our knowledge, or at least we are not fully aware of its influence on our thinking. At another level, the metaphor is well defined and used systematically to help us think about something new or something not well understood. The computer and the camera as metaphors for the mind and eye respectively are examples. At both levels the metaphors' entailments regulate how we look at the details of the problem; they allow us to take it apart. We think about the mind as composed of hard- and software, that when configured in this way it is in memory mode, and so on. Metaphors have their limits insofar as they are not isomorphic structurally with their referents, and there are functional dissimilarities: Vision is not to be equated with the chemical processes occurring when film is exposed to light. Eventually we have to switch metaphors or abandon metaphorical thinking and think about the problem per se and not *as if.* There exists, of course, debate over whether or not that type of shift is possible. That is not the issue in closing this chapter; the issue is to explore the challenges metaphorical thinking brings to the development of microworlds based in computers.

The Turtle as Metaphor.   Fein, et al. note, in chapter 7, this volume, that the kindergarten children they tested were biased to use the forward command to the neglect of the one for backwards. They interpreted this to mean that one element of reciprocal commands was differentiated before the other, and that the process of learning efficient programming had the successive steps of learning one command, differentiating that command from its reciprocal, and then coordinating the two. Yet another interpretation is that Papert's decision to anthropomorphize the cursor has some consequences hidden in the entailments of the turtle metaphor.

Visually guided animals, the turtle being one of them, face the goal, thereby increasing the likelihood of success and decreasing the likelihood of disaster. If the cursor is assimilated to this understanding, children do not fail to differentiate or coordinate forward and backwards but, rather, organize their programs with respect to their knowledge of animate locomotion. Children would not produce the most efficient programs until they abandon the animate metaphor and looked at the problem as a programming problem per se.

This example indicates that aspects of a metaphor can, in the same problem-solving situation, be conscious and nonconscious. There seems to be no reason to believe that children fail to discriminate between the triangular cursor and a turtle. In that respect the child is intuitively sensitive to the contrast between figurative and literal. At the same time the child may not be aware that the metaphor's behavioral entailments constrain their choice of commands by giving meaning to them richer than that contained in the computer's meaning for those commands. For the child, "forward" stands for the type of action guided by "heading for" a target.

It seems unlikely that any child would remain ignorant of those entailments over an extended period of time. Gaining insight may mean different things to different children (Turkle, 1984), depending on the microworld with which the child is interacting. If permissible within that world, some children may develop new programs to make the metaphor more apt. They might try to program the cursor's movement so that the methodical and awkward gait of the turtle is simulated. Others might abandon the metaphor and explore programming within the context of the CRT. In short, I am suggesting as Turkle (1984) has that each of these would be interacting in technically the same microworld, but they would make quite different things of it, because the object in the self–object relation is categorically different.

In ordinary discourse, in our social constructions, we become aware of our metaphors. In microworlds this process is truncated. The metaphor is not the children's construction, though it is chosen to be enticing for them. It is specified in both the instructions and the visual display. The microworld is organized so that it operates within the confines of the metaphor but is not privy to it. It cannot interpret its own metaphor to itself or to the child. Moreover, the computer is in no better position when it comes to understanding the metaphors brought by the child to the microworld.

The fact that the computer does not function as a coconstructor of knowledge is a critical limitation. It may be a contemporary problem. Kay (1985), for one, predicts a breakthrough in computer technology revolutionizing information processing so that, for its part, the computer can function in the microworld by taking "hints," by paraphrasing, as well as by offering alternative interpretations of our suggestions and questions. If his predictions prove to be true, the differences between human and computer discourse will be diminished, and in fact the computer may be decidedly more patient than another human in muddling through our mixed and ill-formed metaphors. Until that time, it is not only important for us to choose our metaphors wisely but to recognize that this cautionary note is even more important in constructing computer-based microworlds that are blind to their own and others' metaphors.

CONCLUSION

Within this chapter I have explored "Constructivism in the Computer Age" by examining function in Piaget's theory and the implication of his meanings of function for microworlds, a special construction of the computer age. The core meaning of function for Piaget is adaptive interaction of self and world or self and object. Self–world interactions construct sensory-motor adaptations and pragmatic solutions. Self–object interactions construct explicit conceptualizations or theories about self–world relations.

From a functional perspective, Piaget sees the child's motivation to solve practical problems transformed by social transactions that force children to think about their own thinking. Ultimately, the reorganization of the self–object relation is brought about by our capacity to reflexively abstract new conceptualizations from the relation between proposed solutions and outcomes as well as from the mutual constructions of two or more knowing systems.

Microworlds are conceptual worlds, and as such can be argued as satisfying the need to challenge children to think. Essentially they are saying. "Think about the world in these terms." Indeed this may be true of microworlds such as Papert's world of Turtle Geometry. It embodies ideas rather than stating them explicitly. It challenges children to construct ideas by solving practical problems within the microworld. It challenges them to think precisely by making solutions dependent on constructing programs or procedures that will move the turtle through space. In short, they have to represent the steps in their solution in detail.

One criticism that can be brought against this microworld is the limited information on whether children construct a "deeper" understanding of geometry by having thought in this microworld. In the absence of convincing data one way or the other, it seems reasonable to continue to pursue the promises contained in the microworld.

Another criticism is more telling and at the same time more interesting to both cognitive developmentalists and computer scientists. How do we preserve the value of social constructing in microworlds? The conceptual domain of microworlds is not mutually constructed. The child is adapting to the conceptual system embodied in the world, paradoxically a system to which the computer is blind. It cannot reflect on its own structure, much less the structure created through the interaction between child and the software of the microworld. Finally, the computer is immune to the metaphor giving meaning to the world, as well as to any metaphor the child brings to that world. In short, microworlds are even more egocentric than humans. Broadening their perspectives may unravel significant issues involved in social construction of knowledge.

REFERENCES

Beilin, H. (1983). New Functionalism in Piaget's Program. In E. K. Scholnick (Ed.), *New trends in conceptual representation* (pp. 3–40). Hillsdale, NJ: Lawrence Erlbaum Associates.

Beilin, H. (1984). Functionalist and structuralist research programs in developmental psychology: Incommensurability or synthesis? In H. W. Reese (Ed.), *Advances in child development and behavior* (Vol. 18, pp. 245–257). New York: Academic Press.

Beilin, H. (1985). Dispensable and nondispensable aspects of Piaget's theory. In T. S. Evans (Ed.), *Genetic epistemology: Yesterday and today.* (pp. 107–126). New York: The Graduate School and University Center, City University of New York.

Beilin, H. (1986). Current trends in cognitive development research: Toward a new synthesis. *Cahriers do la fondation archieves Jean Piaget.*

Boden, M. A. (1979). The computational metaphor in psychology. In N. Bolton (Ed.), *Philosophical problems in psychology* (pp. 111–132). London: Methuen.

Boden, M. A. (1980). *Jean Piaget.* New York: Penguin Books.

Bruner, J. (1964) The course of cognitive growth. *American Psychologist, 19,* 1–15.

Donaldson, M. (1978). *Children's Minds.* New York: W. W. Norton & Company.

Forman, G. (1985). The value of kinetic print: Digital symbols with analogical properties. In E. Klein (Ed.), *New directions for child development: Vol. 28. Computers and children* (pp. 19–35). San Francisco, CA: Jossey-Bass.

Furth, H. G. (1970). *Piaget for teachers.* Englewood Cliffs, NJ: Prentice-Hall.

Furth, H. G. (1978). Children's societal understanding and the process of equilibration. In W. Damon (Ed.), *New Directions for child development. 1: Social cognition* (pp. 101–122). San Francisco, CA: Jossey-Bass.

Furth, H. (1981). *Piaget and knowledge: Theoretical foundations, 2d.* Chicago, IL: The University of Chicago Press.

Gibson, E. (1969). *Principles of perceptual learning and development.* New York: Appleton–Century–Crofts.

Gibson, J. (1979). *The ecological approach to visual perception.* Boston: Houghton Mifflin Company.

Greenfield, P. M. (1984). *Mind and media: The effects of television, video games, and computers.* Cambridge, MA: Harvard University Press.

Inhelder, B., Sinclair, H., & Bovet, M. (1974). *Learning and the development of cognition.* Cambridge, MA: Harvard University Press.

Karmiloff-Smith, A., & Inhelder, B. (1975). If you want to get ahead, get a theory. *Cognition, 3,* 195–212.

Kay, A. (1985). Software's second act. *Science 85, 6,* 122–126.

Kuhn, D. (1983). On the dual executive and its significance in the development of developmental psychology. In D. Kuhn and J. A. Meacham (Eds.), *Contribution to human development* (Vol. 1). New York: S. Karger.

Kuhn, D., & Phelps, E. (1983). The development of problem-solving strategies. In H. W. Reese (Ed.), *Advances in child development and behavior* (Vol. 17). New York: Academic Press.

Leeper, M. R. (1985). Microcomputers in education: Motivational and social issues. *American Psychologist, 40*, 1–18.

Meacham, J. A. (1983). Wisdom and the context of knowledge: Knowing one doesn't know. In D. Kuhn, and J. A. Meacham (Eds.), *Contribution to human development*, Vol. 1. New York: S. Karger.

Overton, W. F. (1984). Comments on Beilin's epistemology and Palermo's defense of Kuhn. In H. W. Reese (Ed.), *Advances in child development and behavior* (Vol. 18, pp. 273–286). New York: Academic Press.

Papert, S. (1980). *Mind-storms: Children, computers, and powerful ideas.* New York: Basic Books.

Piaget, J. (1928/1966). *Judgment and reasoning in the child.* London: Routledge & Kegan Paul, Ltd.

Piaget, J. (1930). *The child's conceptualization of physical causality.* Totowa, NJ: Littlefield, Adams.

Piaget, J. (1954). *The construction of reality in the child.* New York: Basic Books.

Piaget, J. (1967). *Six psychological studies.* New York: Vintage Books.

Piaget, J. (1969). *Mechanisms of perception.* New York: Basic Books.

Piaget, J. (1976). *The grasp of consciousness.* Cambridge, MA: Harvard University Press.

Piaget, J. (1978). *Success and understanding.* Cambridge, MA: Harvard University Press.

Piaget, J., & Inhelder, B. (1973). *Memory and intelligence.* New York: Basic Books.

Piaget, J., & Inhelder, B. (1980). *Mental imagery in the child: A developmental study of imaginal representation.* New York: Basic Books.

Renninger, K. A., & Winegar, L. T. (1985). Emergent organization in expert–novice relationships. *The Genetic epistemologist, 14*, 14–20.

Turkle, S. (1984). *The second self: Computers and the human spirit.* New York: Simon & Shuster.

Winner, E. (1982). *Invented worlds: The psychology of the arts.* Cambridge, MA: Harvard University Press.

Youniss, J. (1980). *Parents and peers in social development: A Sullivan–Piaget perspective.* Chicago: University of Chicago Press.

Chapter 3

Piaget's Logic of Assimilation and Logic for the Classroom

Hans G. Furth
Center for the Study of Youth Development
The Catholic University of America

The purpose of this chapter is twofold: On the theoretical side, a plea is made for a balanced understanding of the place of logic in Piaget's theory and, beyond that, in a school that aims to foster creative thinking. On the practical side, it describes an educational computer program for exercising logical thinking, namely, Symbol Picture Logic (SPL), suitable for children who have achieved their first logical operations—Piaget's "concrete operations," and the concluding section discusses the advantages of setting SPL in a computer microworld. Perhaps paradoxically to many, the advantages cited are related to the implicit social–interpersonal as much as to the explicity graphic and electronic context.

LOGIC IN PIAGET'S THEORY

Two critical comments frequently voiced about Piaget's work are on the one side (Gruber, 1982), that the theory is overly logical and abstract, that it deals with a logical subject that has no links to flesh-and-blood existence and no emotions or social context. Knowledge in Piaget's theory is said to be devoid of any specific content or at best is relevant merely to the understanding of physical laws, such as space, causality, or conservation of quantity. On the other side (Ennis, 1978), some consider Piaget's logical models of concrete and formal operations to be seriously deficient both from a logical and a psychological perspective. In short, too much logic for the one, not the right logic for the other.

From the Logic of Action to the Logic of Thinking

With this as background, I will explore the function of logic in the context of Piaget's theory. For that purpose you must divest logic of its textbook connotation, that is, the logic articulated by logicians, and become familiar with a more humble status of logic, namely the logic of biological and sensorimotor actions. Certainly Piaget made no new discoveries in adult logical thinking. Rather, he sought how that adult logic came to be. In this search he found a logic in the tentative sensing and movements of small infants, long before articulated consciousness or language. All biological actions require coordination, between organism and environment and within the organism. Coordination is but another word for a hierarchical and temporal ordering (of input and output, sense and motor, etc.) and all this implies regulation, structure, and organization. Here, according to Piaget, is to be found the source of logic, where logic is *within* the action, not at all disconnected, abstract, or content free, as real and as emotional and social as the action itself.

This is the kind of logic Piaget brought to the foreground of his investigations, the logic implicitly present in the external—and eventually internal—actions of children. He observed that with development, what changes is not the logic itself, but its quality, that is, the way it is used. To illustrate this change, compare the linguistic knowledge in a 3-year-old child, a 10-year-old child, an adult, and a linguist. They all know the same language and grammar, but they use it in qualitatively different ways. Similarly, for Piaget logic has a rock-bottom, absolute quality, different from any other lawful regularity, and he rejects the notion of different types of logic. He considers logic in itself as invariant across all developmental changes or individual and cultural differences. As Piaget puts it, if $x + y = z$, then $z - y = x$, and this is as true for the poor as for the rich, for the gifted as for the retarded, for people living today as for their ancestors thousands of years ago, and for the North as for the South.

However, qualitative *changes* across an invariant function are the essence of Piaget's stages. Generally, stage progression is a change in the manner of using logical structures. The logic of biological regulations at birth is followed by the logic of sensorimotor action, leading at around age two to the logic of the "permanent object." This ushers in a qualitatively new form of knowledge, potentially separated from action. As a consequence a new form of signifying appears: Objects of knowledge can be made psychologically present ("represented") as symbols. The three major forms of symbols are gestures and play, internal images and fantasy, and socially shared communication and language.

The symbolic world of gestures, images, and communication characterizes the human, personal world; most particularly it establishes the quality of personal-social relations through which we recognize others and ourselves as persons. Between ages two and five the psychology of children is dominated by the newly achieved symbolic ability and is described in remarkable similarity by both Freud and Piaget as relatively disordered and at the whim of personal desires. However, a *relative* disorder does not mean the total absence of logical order. On the contrary, the symbolic constructions of young children are precisely the first steps in using the logic of symbols. This logic, though adequate to form symbols and symbolic attachments, is as yet inadequate to put logical order into the symbols. Factual resistances that physically limit *sensorimotor* possibilities no longer constrain *symbolic* possibilities. So how does Piaget's theory envisage developmental progress and from where does the necessary constraint come?

Piaget's surprising answer is that logic is both the motor and the constraint that will put order and objectivity into symbolic constructions. And once having done so, the necessity of logic becomes the counterpart of the infinite openness and the creative potential for newness characteristic of symbolic thinking. Whereas logicians concentrated on the logical operations of educated adults, Piaget discovered earlier forms of logic in infants and young children. But he also described mature forms of logic, generally neglected by logicians, as early as ages five to seven. He called these logical achievements *concrete operations.* Even though they are only stepping stones to the more comprehensive formal operations of later years, there is nothing childish or immature about them. They are the real thing and provide the children for the first time with a genuine experience of the full power of logic. Compared to the daylight of reversible operations the mental world of children between ages two and five is a twilight zone and a somewhat chaotic conglomeration of knowledge and desire. Without the system of logical operations, children cannot reliably distinguish between knowledge and desire, fact and fantasy, among what is, may be, must be, or cannot be.

But now for the first time concrete operations empower the child to do precisely that. This logical experience is a revolution in children's psychology, comparable to the earlier logical transition that around age two turned sensorimotor infants into symbolizing children. Concrete operations are autonomous logical systems, notably the systems of classes or classification, of sequence or sequential order, and of numbers. They are called *concrete* in that these operations are applicable to concrete (actual or possible) situations. When children are able to move freely within the system in any direction ("reversible"), they can then make logically necessary inferences, "it *must* be so because it follows from the system."

Try to appreciate what it means to a six-year-old child to realize—in whatever implicit manner—"I am thinking," in the sense of "I can infer this notion and can justify it as being logically necessary." This is no longer the playfulness of childish ideas; it is children's first entry into the public, socialized arena of adults. It may take them 10 to 20 years to accomplish this step fully. Nevertheless it is an exhilarating experience that makes the child exclaim with the poet: "But now I am six, I'm as clever as clever . . ."

Logic and Social Relations

Logical development is badly conceived when it is enclosed within the child (or worse, within the brain of the child), almost as if it were some automatic happening to which the child has no choice but to submit. Against this mechanistic, thinglike perspective, Piaget describes development as something alive and done by the children. It cannot occur without their active emotional efforts. By the same token this is not accomplished in isolation, but in continuous relation and communication with other people. Piaget equates operatory logic with an intellectual exchange and goes so far as to insist that the basic desire to share with others—to be respected and to respect the viewpoint of others—is the one necessary condition without which development is unthinkable.

For Piaget development always implies a twofold movement: Forward looking, it is the construction of a new equilibrium, backward looking, it is a compensation for an experienced disequilibrium. The recognition of a mental gap or dissonance, that something is amiss, elicits the need for developmental change. A cognitive moment must be coupled with the motivation for making the required effort. This is a motivation internal to the life of logic, which caused the disturbance in the first place, even as it tends toward a new restructuring.

Note therefore in Piaget's theory the social and emotional conditions that invariably surround logical development. Why indeed would a child—or anyone, for that matter—give up a position once reached and acknowledge its inadequacy, unless the desire to share and be part of the community of peers is stronger than the displeasure of loss of face? In the final analysis all knowledge is an interpersonal exchange, a sharing of viewpoints, a justifiable consensus of a multitude of people mutually respecting each other. The logical operations children achieve first around age six are in a literal sense the product of cooperation and belong to individuals only insofar as they are desirous of sharing the common humanity and rationality embodied in other people.

Formal Operations

Piaget's name for the completed logical structures characteristic of healthy adults is *formal operations*. These are beginning to be constructed around ages 11 to 13, but keep in mind that all ages relative to stages are approximate and are not to be interpreted as normative and across all content areas. Whereas concrete operations apply to concrete situations, formal operations deal with formal propositions and verbal statements. Similarly, they focus on hypothetical possibilities rather than factual reality. Finally, formal operations take account of a total network of possibilities and from their systematic combinations infer valid conclusions.

Piaget did very little research on formal operations insofar as his main aim was to explain how they came to be and he took their presence pretty much for granted. There is considerable research (Neimark, 1975) which claims to show that only a minority of adults in the United States succeed on tests of formal operations and that this proportion is even smaller in non-Western cultures. Then again there are some (Commons, Richards, Armson, 1984) who suggest that adult thinking requires postformal stages. Both opinions are somewhat out of place, the first one in exaggerating the requirements of a standardized test geared toward science and mathematics, the other in misjudging the scope of Piaget's formal logical thinking. Operations are procedures of *potential* logical thinking. To what extent and in what content area they are used is very much a matter of individual differences, motivation, and, above all, societal opportunities. By no means should formal operations be equated with high intelligence scores.

Response to the Critique

What about the charge that Piaget's theory is overly logical and neglects entire areas of human knowledge? I do not know whether in these pages I have succeeded in demonstrating that the scope of Piaget's logic is as broad as human life. It should have become obvious that for Piaget logic is endowed with actions and feelings, with biological and interpersonal life, in a manner that sets it a world apart from the logic of things or textbooks with their dry formalisms.

This leads to the second charge that Piaget's logic is poorly articulated. Up to now we have talked about the child's logic, but the present criticism is about the way Piaget attempted to formalize his substantive findings. I have never paid much attention to his logical models and in my understanding of the theory have never felt the worse for it. They are not a major component of Piaget's theory. He was fully aware that logical model building is a relatively arbitrary affair and was quite prepared to change the models. During the last 20 years of his life he had less and less recourse to logical models; he published an entirely new version of the equilibration concept, based much more on psychology and experience than on extensional logic and mathematical probability.

These and similar criticisms are unfortunate in that they reinforce a formal, almost mechanistic interpretation of Piaget's work, when in fact the theory is quite the opposite. Logic is not at all inimical to imagination, freedom, social relating, or interpersonal feeling. Without human logic there would be none of these things. Piaget's theory is unique in showing how they are related. The decisive link is the logic of the separate object and of symbol formation as the base of the critical self–other differentiation. *Object* in this context does not mean a "thing," but "another," that is, another person vis-à-vis the person who is the self. Object formation, Piaget's "permanent object," is thus the birth of the self-in-relation-to-another, and this is precisely the characteristic of what it means to be a person. Object formation, beginning around age two, is therefore person formation, and the latter is as much an emotional as a logical transformation (Furth, 1987).

It seems therefore unfair to blame Piaget's theory for a misplaced emphasis on logical thinking in the teaching of children at the cost of neglecting approaches far more consistent with the purpose of education. To make this claim (Egan, 1983) seemed to show both a misunderstanding of what does go on in schools and of Piaget's developmental logic.

If there is one point on which there is almost universal agreement it is that schools do not provide enough challenge and opportunity for creative logical thinking. Educational computer software, too, is criticized for this reason (Schank, 1986). Yet if Piaget's theory were adequately understood it could provide a valuable guide toward this very purpose. For in his theory the function of logic is precisely to be the firm anchor of logical necessity against which constructive personal freedom and the opening up of new possibilities can come into play.

An elementary school that would have as its major aim to foster what I have elsewhere called "intellectual health" (Furth & Wachs, 1975) would be a place where the students are challenged to use their logical powers in a creative way across different domains. In such a "School for Thinking," logical thinking would be experienced as a developmental achievement that students are encouraged to exercise just as in physical education they exercise movement coordination and muscle strength for no ulterior motive beyond bodily health. To put this philosophy into educational practice requires some expertise in designing activities that are intellectually challenging. I believe this is the chief way in which Piaget's philosophy can have some very practical and decisive application. If— and this is a big *if*—you want to have a School for Thinking, Piaget's theory can help you recognize high-level thinking and plan an appropriate curriculum.

SYMBOL PICTURE LOGIC

Some years ago I published two small volumes (Furth, 1969/1986a; Furth & Wachs, 1975) in which I suggested a variety of suitable thinking activities for the elementary grades. Included was a description of a course of symbolic logic which was used successfully in a variety of educational and rehabilitative settings. This course is now available as computer software (Furth, 1986b). It is called *Symbol-Picture Logic;* SPL for short. Two unique features render it especially appropriate for young children. First, each complete SPL sentence includes, besides the symbolic-logic component, a pictorial instance. Second, SPL is essentially nonverbal. In fact, I first introduced it to deaf students (Furth,

1966) whose deficiency in the comprehension of societal language is recognized as their chief educational burden.

Why are these features important for the purpose of challenging the thinking of young children? Because at that age logical thinking is invariably ahead of verbal skills and is most suitably exercised and tested for its soundness in relation to concrete actions and examples. This reply may sound controversial when logic is primarily associated with the capacity of abstraction and verbal articulation. But this is precisely the reason why a novel theoretical perspective is fruitful. Make no mistake, Piaget's theory is novel and revolutionary. Recall how he conceptualizes knowledge as an interpersonal relation and describes logic as both necessary and free, as alive and developing, as interpersonal and transpersonal (objective), as free of all content but present in all action and knowledge. Leaving these theoretical points aside, I will conclude by demonstrating the power of logic as shown in children working on the SPL program.

Around age six many children begin to understand SPL sentences like:

$$S \rightarrow \text{☼}, \quad H \rightarrow \text{⌂♀}, \quad T \rightarrow \text{⌂♀}, \quad S \nrightarrow \text{⌂♀}, \quad \overline{S} \rightarrow \text{♀⌂}, \quad \overline{S} \nrightarrow \text{☼}.$$

On the left side is a symbolic statement consisting of a letter ("There is a sun," "There is a house," etc.) or a letter with a bar, the bar standing for negation ("There is no sun"). In the middle is an arrow ("goes with") or a crossed arrow ("does not go with"). The pictures on the right are concrete instances. Of course, none of these verbal explanations are part of the program. The children have to discover the rules of the game by playing it.

Understanding this symbolic language requires a clear grasp of the difference between the *logical* reality of affirmation ("there is"), negation ("there is not"), and judgment ("does or does not go with"), versus the *concrete* reality of (the picture of) a house, a tree, or a sun. This differentiation was mentioned as a potent consequence of concrete operations. Therefore most children by around age seven and above find these logical thinking games challenging, that is, they experience them as being at the limit of their present logical comprehension. SPL gives them the opportunity to practice in an explicit fashion what they are spontaneously doing all the time in an implicit manner, namely, meaningful understanding. To understand something it does not suffice merely to define a thing as a known fact, one must also know how the thing relates to its overall class, what the thing is not ($\overline{}$), and to which possible instances the definition can ($\rightarrow$) or cannot ($\nrightarrow$) be applied.

Further, the children around age seven and above enjoy the challenge of putting into practice their newly acquired insights into logical necessity. Given the problem $\overline{S} \nrightarrow ?$, the picture situation on the right *must* include a sun; in fact $\overline{S} \nrightarrow$ is (and *must* be) equivalent to S $\rightarrow$. This kind of double negation ("The absence of sun is not instantiated") is something these children can master in the SPL format, but surely not as verbal sentences in English: their knowledge is ahead of their language.

Some two to four years later many children have developed logical comprehension beyond these elementary operations. For these the second volume of the SPL program introduces two new logical connectives, the • as conjunction ("both . . . and") and the v as inclusive disjunction ("either . . . or . . . or both"). As an example, given the two SPLs, $\overline{H} • T\not\rightarrow$? and $\overline{H} v T \not\rightarrow$, which *one* picture would be a correct response to *both* statements? The answer is: "a sun, but not a house or a tree."

A further logical complexity (suitable even for high school and college students) is added by having the negation bar over the connectives: $\overline{•}$, $\overline{v}$. In this SPL format the youngsters can discover the equivalences of $H \overline{•} S = \overline{H} v \overline{S}$ and of $H \overline{v} S = \overline{H} • \overline{S}$ (known in formal logic as *deMorgan's Law*). Again it should be clear that these logical insights cannot be appropriately "taught" or expressed in verbal sentences. Nevertheless, this logic is psychologically real and operative as an integral part of the students' development. Moreover, to grasp the full meaning of $\overline{•}$ or $\overline{v}$ seems a good illustration of Piaget's statement that formal thinking is an operation upon an operation: The negation of a logical connective is clearly a hypothetical proposition, twice removed from the reality of concrete action.

In conclusion, SPL demonstrates the growing logical abilities of children of elementary school age. In these children, logic, as suggested by Piaget's theory, is an operational (action) power, linked to the achievement of concrete operations and the comprehension of logical necessity and logical reality (propositions). It is not directly dependent on verbal language and thus is suitable as a challenging, high-level thinking experience regardless of verbal achievements.

The Computer as Participant in Constructing Logic.   The computer format removes the child from the pressure of having to perform according to an outside model and evaluator—from a situation that by itself is developmentally restrictive and as such not conducive to high-level thinking. Piaget referred to this as an interpersonal relation based on unilateral respect and contrasted it with the more constructive relation based on reciprocal respect. To the extent that children consider interaction with the computer a situation of mutual equality, they experience a social precondition favorable to developmental growth and constructive learning. The logic recognized by the computer is the same as the logic operating in the children. The computer does not impose anything on the children they themselves would not construct on their own. Thus, the "honesty" of the computer is matched by the "honesty" of the offered material.

Logic is not an arbitrary subject matter, relative to a particular school curriculum; it has its share in all human acts. Similarly, the computer treats its operators with an evenhanded, responsible fairness and removes the children from attitudes and motives that could potentially interfere with constructive learning, such as pleasing a superior, showing off, fearing displeasure, suspecting another's fairness or bias, or wanting to control or annoy another. If children work on the program, they do so for the best possible motive that Piaget considers intrinsic to the logic of constructive assimilation. Anyone observing children responsive to the challenge of logical problems cannot but be impressed by the intrinsic motivation of autonomous thinking. It is not uncommon for young children to spend an hour or more on SPL tasks paying close attention to the logical possibilities and subtleties. In ordinary educational settings I have not yet come across children of 10 years or younger who would find this explicit logic program and its challenges either boring or irrelevant.

One notable feature of SPL, as in most real-life situations, is its potential openness: A given problem can be solved in many different ways. Here the computer shows another advantage; while encouraging serious cooperation it is supremely tolerant. In the "free-for-all" units a student (or the teacher) locks in an incomplete SPL, for example, $v^- \rightarrow$ ☼ . The number of possible solutions is then shown on the screen; in this case, eight (namely, $H \vee \overline{D}$, $S \vee \overline{D}$, $T \vee \overline{D}$, $S \vee \overline{T}$, $T \vee \overline{S}$, $D \vee \overline{H}$, $S \vee \overline{H}$, $T \vee \overline{H}$). There is no pressure or penalty for not doing all of the solutions. The children are left free to judge for themselves how much mental effort they are prepared to expend. Just as with all of us, students should not be expected to work constantly on their highest level. This principle of responsibly choosing their own challenge—made possible by the computer's neutral attitude—is a marvelous thing for building self-knowledge and self-respect. It is perhaps the main reason for the computer's popularity with children in elementary schools.

It follows from the link between logic and social relations that autonomous thinking (the desirable endpoint of Piaget's development of knowledge), even though it means "regulated from within," does not on account of this imply *unrelated to* or *unconcerned about* what other people think. On the contrary, even though outwardly the children may work alone, this is not and is not experienced as a solitary activity.

This social link can also be observed insofar as the entire program can be used advantageously in such a manner that two or three children work together on specific units. In fact some of the units demand that the format of questions given by one be answered by another. A high degree of helpful cooperation has invariably been reported, an indirect indication of Piaget's claim that the opportunity to show autonomous thinking allows the children to become intellectually socialized. It is a growth situation in which they discover and respect logical norms mutually binding on all. In this connection a recent report from The George Washington University Learning Center using SPL is significant. Children with social and emotional problems were found to have difficulties when paired with others, whereas the vast majority of other children, including those with so-called learning disabilities, preferred working in groups of two or three—to the mutual cognitive and social advantage of all concerned.

As said earlier, logical operation for Piaget is the flip side of a social and emotional attitude of mental cooperation. As such, logic is an essential ingredient of intellectual and social health. An educational curriculum aimed at high-level thinking should not neglect its active power in the mistaken view that logic is merely a mechanical skill of manipulating empty symbols. Moreover, computer worlds such as SPL should be recognized as capitalizing on the child's perception of computers as neutral, nonevaluative, and honest agents encouraging mutually responsible construction of operatory knowledge. Piaget's theory with its focus on the "logic of life" (in contrast to the "logic of things") can be a useful guide in overcoming this prejudice and evaluating the worth of a challenging thinking program.

REFERENCES

Commons, M. L., Richards, F. C., & Armson, C. (Eds.). (1984). *Beyond formal operations.* New York: Praeger.

Ennis, R. H. (1978). Conceptualization of children's logical competence: Piaget's propositional logic and an alternative proposal. In Siegel, L. S. & Brainerd, C. J. (Eds.), *Alternatives to Piaget* (pp. 201–260). New York: Academic Press.

Egan, K. (1983). *Education and psychology: Plato, Piaget, and Scientific psychology.* New York: Teachers College.

Furth, H. G. (1966). *Thinking without language: Psychological implications of deafness.* New York: Free Press.

Furth, H. G. (1986a). *Piaget for teachers* (2d ed.). Washington, DC: Computer Age Education. (originally published 1969).

Furth, H. G. (1986b). *Symbol-Picture Logic (SPL),* 2 vol. Washington, DC: Computer Age Education.

Furth, H. G. (1987). *Knowledge as Desire: An essay on Piaget and Freud.* New York: Columbia University Press.

Furth, H. G., & Wachs, H. (1975). *Thinking goes to school: Piaget's theory in practice.* New York: Oxford University Press.

Gruber, H. E. (1982). Piaget's mission. *Social Research, 49,* 239–264.

Neimark, E. D. (1975). Intellectual development during adolescence. In F. D. Horowitz (ed.), *Review of child development research, (vol. 4,* pp. 541–594). Chicago: University of Chicago Press.

Schank, R. C. (1986). Thinking about computers and thinking: A response to Papert and his critics. *New Ideas in Psychology, 4,* 231–240.

Computers and the Developmental Relation Between Intuitive and Formal Knowing

Chapter 4

Knowledge in Pieces

Andrea A. diSessa
University of California, Berkeley

Nobody thinks clearly, no matter what they pretend. Thinking's a dizzy business, a matter of catching as many of those foggy glimpses as you can and fitting them together the best you can. That's why people hang on so tight to their opinions; because, compared to the haphazard way in which they're arrived at, even the goofiest opinion seems wonderfully clear, sane, and self-evident. And if you let it get away from you, then you've got to dive back into that foggy muddle to wangle yourself out another to take its place.

—Dashiell Hammett

How one intends to use computers to aid learning depends in a dramatic way on what one thinks is important in learning. In this chapter I outline a central theme of my work with computers and learning which follows from certain empirically and theoretically driven predilections concerning the nature of knowledge and its development. The fundamental question is: How do we view the transition from commonsense reasoning about the physical world to scientific understanding? Leaving aside the nonconstructivist "accretion" model—new knowledge by transmission from textbook or teacher—there are still very different views of learning that motivate different approaches to the uses of computers.

My own view is that the transition to scientific understanding involves a major structural change toward systematicity, rather than simply a shift in content. After outlining this view by contrasting it with another that presumes a more evenhanded trade of content from prescientific to scientific apprehension, I will discuss uses of computers that follow more or less directly from the structural-change perspective.

INTRODUCTION

What is the character of the knowledge that people spontaneously acquire about the physical world? How do people think the world operates based on their experience with it? This is a subject on which Piaget and his colleagues have spent many productive years. It has come into focus again in recent years at ages beyond those Piaget usually studied, late high school and early college years. In this setting, there has been less emphasis on cognitive development and more on developing understanding in more formal situations: science and mathematics courses. Intuitively developed physics is revealed in interaction with the concepts and theories that physicists hope to teach.

In very brief summary of this line of work, it seems that intuitive physics is a rather well-developed and exceedingly robust system that can potentially interfere with "proper" textbook understanding. A large set of probes has been developed in which students give relatively uniform, but incorrect or at least nontextbook answers, long into the educational process that is meant to provide a proper understanding of the laws of nature.

To sharpen focus on this phenomenon, I would like to contrast two opposing views of intuitive physics. The first is an example of what I call "theory theories," and holds that it is productive to think of spontaneously acquired knowledge about the physical world as a theory of roughly the same quality, though differing in content from Newtonian or other theories of the mechanical world. Michael McCloskey of Johns Hopkins is probably the most visible of the theory theorists at the present time (McCloskey; 1983; July 1983). He described his research as follows: "We show that . . . people develop on the basis of their everyday experience remarkably well-articulated naive theories of motion. Further, we argue that the assumptions of the naive theories are quite consistent across individuals. In fact, the theories developed by different individuals are best described as different forms of the same basic theory" (McCloskey, 1983, July, p. 299).

McCloskey went so far as to tell us what the core theory is that essentially everyone has: It is a version of the impetus theory developed in the Middle Ages, standing historically between two great landmarks, Aristotle's physics and that developed by Newton. I will provide some details shortly.

On the other side, my own view is that this is a highly misleading representation of the actual state of affairs. Though it gives signs of being quite robust, intuitive physics is nothing much like a theory in the way one uses that word to describe theories in the history of science or professional practice. Instead, intuitive physics is a fragmented collection of ideas, loosely connected and reinforcing, having none of the commitment or systematicity that one attributes to theories.

There are many implications to the dispute, but they become particularly pointed when it comes to educational implications. The garden path and frequently advocated strategy on the theory theory side is to attempt to provoke a theory change: to expose and confront the intuitive theory with evidence and argumentation so that students can switch theories. My own view is that a much broader attack needs to be made. Indeed, "attack" is certainly the wrong word. Not only is a one-by-one attack of the knowledge fragments that constitute intuitive physics a hopeless task, but the only material we have to develop scientific understanding in our students' heads is precisely those same fragments. One must not throw the baby out with the bath water. And, although there is surely some trading of one content for another, the issue of form is equally, if not more important. *Building a new and deeper systematicity* is a superior heuristic to the "confrontation" approach many theory theorists have taken.

In the second major part of this paper I develop images of computer-based pedagogy appropriate to science education in view of the character of intuitive knowledge and its relation to textbook physics. These come in three flavors. The first involves engaging naive knowledge on the level that makes best connection to it: experience. Computers provide an excellent medium for designing activities that build and integrate pieces of knowledge. Integration, however, needs special attention, as we need do more than just let children play with simulations and scientific models of the world.

The second use of computers involves replacing static and abstract formalism of the past with ones that are better linked with intuitive knowledge. Symbols like equations and numbers require substantial internalized knowledge to operate and to connect meaningfully with the "real world." On computers we can craft systems that are at once more expressive of dynamic and interactive aspects of the world, and, because they operate more like real-world systems themselves, are easier and more engaging to learn.

Finally, at a level above both of these described roles, our students should learn more about the nature of the development and integration of knowledge itself so as to better monitor and control their own learning. Computers don't play any single special role here, but instead, as with other educational tools, the goal of developing awareness and skills "at the meta level" will influence in many ways what we should do with technology.

TWO INTERPRETATIONS

I will begin the comparison of the impetus theory theory and my "knowledge in pieces" on some of the former's strongest grounds. This is a context that provides some of the best evidence that there is such a thing as an intuitive impetus theory. In this way, I can give a reasonably compelling, though brief, presentation of the impetus theory and at the same time test my alternative view on more-than-fair grounds.

The Impetus Theory

Consider the following simple problem: What happens when you throw a ball straight up into the air and catch it? A "cleaned up" protocol of a high school or college student might run something like the following: "When you give the ball a toss, you give it a force that propels it into the air. But this force is working against gravity, and as it dies away, gravity begins to take over. The peak of the trajectory is the point at which gravity is just balancing the force you gave the ball, after which gravity overcomes that force and causes the body to fall downward at an increasing rate."

The "force" you give the ball that propels it into the air against gravity is impetus, an internal force that can be imparted to an object, and it is, according to McCloskey, the central actor in the impetus theory that characterizes naive ideas of motion. Impetus has other characteristics. It spontaneously dies away, or it may die away as a result of things like friction. There are some fine points. Notably, there are two kinds of impetus, linear, as in the above example, and circular, which we shall encounter below, but this little sketch highlights in capsule form the main ingredients of the impetus theory theory.

A physicist's analysis of the toss involves only one force, that of gravity acting constantly downward. Any upward force ends when the hand loses contact with the ball. There is no "balance" at the peak of the trajectory, nor any "overcoming" on the way down. There *is* a construct in physics that has some of the properties of impetus. It is momentum. In fact, momentum is transferred to the ball in the initial stages of the toss, and the momentum is, in a way, "responsible" for the ball moving upward. But momentum is not a force, it doesn't die away of its own accord, and it does not combine or conflict with other forces in the way the impetus explanation of the toss suggests. These caveats having been made, impetus does not make a bad preliminary metaphor for momentum, and I will frequently use it in this productive way.

There is no doubt that people sometimes give protocols that look like the above fiction, but the central question here is whether this is indicative of a widespread theory of motion or, instead, might arise in a quite different way.

Knowledge in Pieces

My alternative view (diSessa, 1983) is that intuitive physics consists of a rather large number of fragments rather than one or even any small number of integrated structures one might call "theories." Many of these fragments, which I call "p-prims" (short for *phenomenological primitives*), can be understood as simple abstractions from common experiences that are taken as relatively primitive in the sense that they generally need no explanation; they simply happen. For example, why is it that you get more result when you expend more effort, say, pushing a big rock? There is no ready explanation, nor really any need for one. One has so much experience with things that work like that, that the phenomenon is encoded simply as an expected event. There is need for further thinking only when things *fail* to work in that way.

Let me list some examples of p-prims. Table 4.1 gives a sampling that will prove very useful to us in returning to the tossed ball.

TABLE 4.1
A List of P-Prims Together with Key Attributes That, in Part, Define Them, and a Prototypical Circumstance from Which the P-Prim Might Be Abstracted and to Which It Applies

Name	Key Attribute	Prototypical Circumstance
Ohm's Law	Agency (also "resistance")	Pushing a box with variable effort on different surfaces
Force as a mover	Violence	A throw
Continuous force	Steady effort	A car engine propelling a car
Dying away	Fading amplitude	Sound of a struck bell
Dynamic balance	Conflict	Equal and opposite competing forces
Overcoming	"Success"	Greater force overcomes weaker

Ohm's Law is one of the most fundamental and pervasive p-prims. It is really an enlarged version of the "more effort begets more results" primitive mentioned before. It consists of an agent or *impetus* (*impetus* in a different sense than in the "impetus theory") that is exerting some effort to achieve a *result* through some *resistance*. In such circumstances the proscribed behavior is that increased effort begets increased result; increased resistance begets reduced result; and so on. Not only is this the commonsense interpretation of Ohm's Law, which describes the relations between voltage (the impetus), resistance (the resistance), and current (the result), but it also interprets a very broad range of physical, psychological (e.g., "trying") and even interpersonal situations such as "influencing." The key attribute, agency, is one that plays a central early role in intuitive physics, and it has a long and interesting development, though one I cannot describe here.

Force as a mover is a simple abstraction of a throw. It involves a directed impetus, a rapid pattern of effort, then release, and a result in the same direction as the impetus. The result, which is modulated by Ohm's Law with respect to the impetus and the resistance (weight, etc.), may be either a net result (distance) or a more local one (speed).

Continuous force shares a common abstraction with force as a mover in that a directed impetus achieves a geometrically parallel result according to Ohm's Law, except that I believe these two are separately encoded. Such redundancy is typical of intuitive physics and is one of the reasons for its apparent robustness. The two p-prims differ in the pattern of amplitude, which is described as "violence" for force as a mover and "constant effort" for continuous force. Such patterns are an important class of attributes for cuing and encoding of physical p-prims.

That sounds, motion, and so on, all *die away* of their own accord is another phenomenon involving a characteristic pattern of amplitude, in this case, gradual fading. This is also a good case of a p-prim being "relatively primitive" in that, even though it is generally taken to be a fact of life that needs no further examination, people will often find excuses for it, such as competing influences (gravity wears away the linear motion of a rolling ball somewhat like it makes us tired in walking).

Dynamic balance involves a direct conflict between opposing forces. Presuming they are equal, neither gets its way; but if one becomes stronger or the other weaker, the stronger will win out, "overcoming" the other, perhaps with a crescendo of "result." Thus the potential action called *overcoming* is closely connected to dynamic balance as an expected possibility. In general, balance and equilibrium is a rich, salient and very important class of primitive phenomena in intuitive physics. *Being in equilibrium* is frequently given as a primitive explanation for why things are as they are.

Let us take another look at the toss of the ball in terms of these p-prims. The first part of the toss, the action of your hand on the ball, is essentially never described at all because it is entirely unproblematic. The p-prim of force as a mover describes and explains precisely this situation. Descriptions given by subjects are often as interesting for what they don't say as for what they do. Indeed, many of the explanations given by subjects must be expected to be comments on what are seen as problematic or puzzling aspects of a phenomenon rather than reductions to a fundamental set of principles, which is what problem solving means in a more formal context. In this case the existence of force as a mover explains why people never make any analysis of the first fraction of the toss, though it is certainly warranted from a physical point of view.

In contrary manner, the rest of the toss is intuitively problematic. There is evidently a conflict involved in the situation; although gravity wants to cause the ball to go down, it continues upward until the peak of the trajectory. So already p-prims having to do with conflict are cued. Even more, the peak of the trajectory in its commonsense interpretation of "stopped," fairly oozes *balancing* and equilibrium. The down side of the trajectory looks like archetypical *overcoming*. But what is balancing the evident force of gravity? What is it that gravity is overcoming on the downward path? Consider also the upward trajectory which, interpreted as a nonviolent *continuous motion* (result), needs a continuous force cause. In other words, the problem context cues a number of schemes that all have one missing element, an element that some sort of upward force residing within the ball could occupy. That force, if it *died away* (another natural phenomenon) would solve the problems posed. It would be the conflicting partner of gravity that, while greater than gravity, would propel the object upward, while equal to gravity, would balance it at the peak, and as it decayed, would leave gravity to overcome it.[1]

What I am saying is that something like impetus is an invention particular to this or some relatively small class of problems rather than a fundamental theoretical construct of intuitive physics. To be sure, the idea shows a significant resonance with many elements of intuitive physics; it can essentially be derived in the context of a toss from the set of fragments enumerated above. Yet, as I will indicate below, it hardly has the priority that would mark it as the core of a systematic, theoretical view. Instead, I claim that understanding intuitive physics necessarily means understanding the kind of pieces into which I have just decomposed impetuslike explanations.

Showing a decomposition of impetuslike explanations into a set of plausible pieces that do not include the notion of impetus is one piece of evidence undermining the impetus theory theory. But we must look to a broad range of circumstances to really prove the case. We should find the following phenomena that distinguish the impetus theory from the p-prims theory:

1. Because the impetus theory is a pattern that emerges from more invariant pieces, we should see those pieces in other contexts, either alone or in other combinations with no hint of impetus.
2. Indeed, the list I have presented is hardly exhaustive, according to the p-prims view, and it should not be hard to find situations in which subjects give reliable responses that have nothing whatsoever to do with impetus or any of the p-prims in the short list I presented here.
3. We should expect a significant spread in answers subjects give to problems like the toss. Even if they all have the same set of p-prims at the base of their intuitive knowledge, we should not expect that they all uniformly derive an impetuslike explanation in this context. Many of these should involve the same or similar p-prims, but in other combinations and attached to other features of the problem.
4. We need to look in some detail at the dynamic of the generation of impetuslike explanations, even if they reliably occur. There should be an

---

[1]It is worth noting an additional consonance between impetus and naive p-prims. The force residing in the ball is a particular manifestation of the kind of animism that Piaget describes in some children's descriptions of physical events. A moving ball exhibits an independent motion and can even exhibit agency in making other things move in collisions. Yet it is not alive; it cannot initiate its own motion. Because it does not originate in the ball, children see the ball's agency in terms of something that is *transferred* to it. Naive p-prims having to do with substance and transfer approximate the state of affairs in description by reifying the quality of motion transferred (roughly, its direction and magnitude), as a restricted kind of life. In children, we might call this "animism." Physicists call it "momentum."

observable genesis; impetus should not emerge instantly and fully. There should be "waffling" and uncertainty and no great commitment to the impetus idea. The notion should be somewhat unstable even if it is generated, and should occasionally give way to other kinds of descriptions and explanations that may be consistent with the above or an extended list of p-prims, but not with impetus as a guiding notion.

Even though I have not personally studied the toss problem in detail, I do not think it is very hard to find evidence for 3 and 4 above. In the best of cases, one finds explanations smacking of impetus occurring in less than half the subjects, even by McCloskey's own reckoning. Because it is almost impossible to find subjects to admit a strong commitment to any particular interpretation in a problem context, let alone to that interpretation as a general fact that determines a fundamental law of nature, waffling, alternate explanations, and so forth, are really the order of the day in essentially any intuitive physics protocol.

Instead of pursuing those lines, I will provide some examples in categories 1 and 2 above, of other contexts where one sees impetus-fragment p-prims without impetus, and where one finds situations governed by p-prims having nothing to do with impetus or even the list of p-prims given above.

It turns out that it is terribly easy to find situations that do not generate impetus explanations. In fact, if one asks for a description or explanation of what happens when one simply drops a ball from rest, the second half of the toss, one almost never sees impetus responses. From the p-prims view, this is easy to explain. There is no conflict, there is no balancing, there is nothing, in fact, that needs another agency like impetus to explain it. Gravity simply gets what it wants, the ball falls down without the aid of any internal impetus.[2]

In this regard, it is useful to look at the history of science, at one who was really trying to build theories. Galileo took a look at impetus as an explanation of the toss at one stage in his dialogues. He saw clearly the need to find a way to extend that analysis beyond the initial context that suggested it in order to test and develop the notion into a genuine theory. After looking at the toss, he developed a clever, but hardly intuitively compelling, explanation of the fall of a dropped object using impetus. But the intuitive thinker does not develop sophisticated arguments to extend the scope of a notion, neither does he even feel the need to talk about tossing and dropping in uniform terms.

Galileo provides a good study of intuitive versus theoretical knowledge systems in other respects. He systematically highlighted intuitive arguments that

---

[2]McCloskey explains this particular restriction in domain of application of the impetus theory by asserting it: impetus does not apply to situations of carrying. Besides being subject to the question, "Why?" my conjecture is that if one studied many problems at the edge of the common range of use of impetus ideas, one would need many such unmotivated patches. Theory theories, in general, will not provide a small enough grain size to cope with people's commonsense physical ideas. The problems that follow in the text continue to make this point.

counter his ideas as part of his expositional technique and, one by one, defused them. One can not only build a compelling list of p-prims from this (to appear), but again one sees how hard it is to build any core of ideas into a theoretical coherence that extends beyond a very limited context. At every turn, intuition suggests other ways to think about the situation. Even more impressive is how many contexts and arguments it takes to clarify and make precise even the core ideas. Galileo runs through at least one-half dozen intuitive frames of analysis simply to explain and make plausible the single idea that an object dropped from rest accelerates uniformly, which idea he took to be one of his greatest accomplishments. For the historically interested, I highly recommend rereading the relevant Galileo in the light of these issues (Galileo, 1954, p. 165, and surrounding).

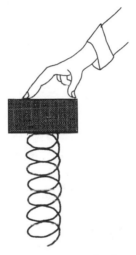

FIGURE 4.1.   How far must one compress a spring in order for it to toss an object into the air?

Figure 4.1 shows a problem that cues certain p-prim fragments, but no impetus. The question is: How far must one press a brick down onto a spring, compressing it, before the spring will be able to toss the brick into the air when one releases the compression? Students frequently see this as a straightforward situation of dynamic balance and overcoming. If you compress the spring until it is pressing upward harder than gravity is pressing downward, the spring will overcome gravity on releasing your hand, throwing the brick into the air. If one writes down the equation expressing this condition, it turns out one has only specified the equilibrium point where the spring is compressed enough to support the brick unaided. Instead, the problem *really* is a question of impetus from the physicist's point of view; can the spring provide a net positive impetus (momentum) to the brick by the time it has completely extended itself? It is not enough that the spring supplies a force greater than gravity at the beginning of the "toss."

(a)

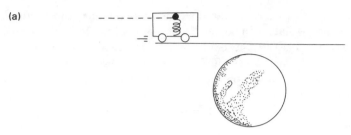

FIGURE 4.2.   A boxcar in space whizzing past a planet. What path does the mass on the spring take?

Figure 4.2 shows an equally striking situation that does not provoke impetus responses even though, in this case again, impetus responses would be more appropriate than the p-prims that are actually cued. A mass is attached to a spring, which, in turn, is attached to the base of a boxcar (and constrained so that it cannot flop over). The boxcar happens to be running at a constant and huge speed along a perfectly straight railroad track in space. As the boxcar passes a planet (and the mass feels the gravitational pull of the planet) what path does the mass travel along?

(b)

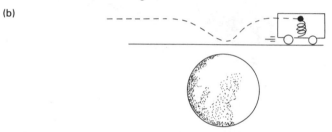

Figure 4.2b is an enormously attractive answer. Not only is the answer visually appealing, but everyone knows that springs compress an amount that is somehow proportional to the force on them. As the force gets symmetrically stronger and weaker while the boxcar flies by the planet, the spring's compression should follow suit.

(c)

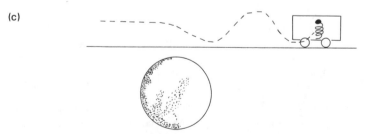

Figure 4.2c is the correct answer. The mass acquires a downward impetus (momentum) from the pull of the planet, which carries it downward even after the closest approach to the planet. Thereafter, the mass will oscillate on the end of the spring as the gravitational perturbation dies out.

Students show an amazing resistance to thinking about this problem dynamically, in terms of impetus, momentum, or any other dynamic concept. Instead, it seems so obviously a question that can be answered by what I call the "spring scale" p-prim—squishy things compress an amount proportional to the force on them—that often not even an hour or more of probing that highlights the dynamic nature of the problem can shake the conviction of even bright MIT students that "spring scale" is the right way to think about it.

Circular Motion

I would like to report briefly on another context in which p-prims can be compared to the theory theory, and to the impetus theory in particular. McCloskey claims that rotational problems are handled by a branch of the impetus theory that holds that there also exists a second kind of impetus, circular impetus, that works in basically the same way as linear impetus. The difference is only that circular motion is involved rather than straight-line motion. Circular impetus acts to continue circular motion after a circular push has stopped.

Rather than put this idea to a test at the extremes of its predictive power, Tamar Globerson (from the School of Education, Tel Aviv University) and I decided to test it with only very small variations of a single problem. Again, the point is not whether subjects ever give any indication of circular impetus explanations, but whether impetus is any sort of complete characterization of or even a reasonable approximation to people's knowledge state as far as circular motion is concerned. We used variations on Piaget's sling problem: What happens to a ball twirling around on the end of a string if one cuts the string? The important thing is that, from the point of view of Newtonian mechanics, and even from the point of view of the impetus theory, the problems are all identical: What happens when a circular motion is aborted by removing the circumstances causing it? A physicist or one who holds an impetus theory should see through the small variations and give a uniform response.

In addition to the ball-and-string form of the problem, we used the following variations, among others:

1. A ball is moving in a circular tube. What happens when it leaves the tube? Suppose one adds a short circular extension to the tube, then removes it just as the ball is about to enter it? Does anything change?
2. A ball is moving on a table under a circular tunnel. If the tunnel is removed, what happens?
3. Instead of asking subjects to predict the results, what happens if subjects are asked merely to react to the plausibility of various paths presented in a computer simulation of the cut-string problem?

4. Suppose one asks subjects to rethink their responses on the basis of suggestions that "some other people think . . ." or are merely prompted to remember particular phenomena related to circular motion?

In a preliminary study that involved early elementary school children (around first grade), late elementary school children (around fifth grade) and "physics naive" adults, we found striking variability in the answers and justifications that subjects gave. Subjects frequently gave multiple kinds of predictions and explanations, and these answers changed according to the circumstances of presentation. Literally no one gave and maintained a pure circular impetus explanation. A particularly strong example of the variability came with respect to the issue of centrifugal force. Whereas "a pull to the outside" (not necessarily known by the name *centrifugal force*) was perceived in the ball-and-string presentation, few thought the same thing happened inside a tube. The explanation for this seems to have something to do with the overt and focused "tug to the center" offered by the string as opposed to mere "guidance" offered by the tube. Few of our subjects were sophisticated enough to spontaneously see a force acting inside the tube.

Mild interventions aimed at prompting remembrance of centrifugal phenomena—"Do you remember what you feel when you drive rapidly around a corner in a car?"—frequently caused subjects to shift predictions. In particular, the prediction that the ball should move outward at a 45° angle to a tangent to the circle became quite salient after such an intervention. The explanation subjects gave for this prediction is that the ball feels two tendencies: one to keep moving forward (either straight or in a circle) and one due to the outward pull. Thus it will actually follow a compromise, the 45° path. Note how far such prediction is from a simple, exclusive adherence to a circular impetus that has no provision for centrifugal force or for any principles of combining multiple influences in circular situations. Although not a single subject in our study gave this answer spontaneously, more than a quarter of the subjects who were prompted to think about centrifugal force declared they preferred this prediction to all other predictions, either self-produced or offered by us, at the end of the session. In view of such data, it is evidently an extreme oversimplification, at least, to attribute theorylike status to circular impetus responses.

One of the most striking effects noticed in this experiment, and one which needs follow-up study, has to do with modality of presentation. First, it must be noted that the youngest and oldest subjects gave quite different predictions, explanations, and justifications. For example, a significant percentage of the younger subjects said the ball would stop after it left the tube or the string was cut "because it wouldn't know which way to go," whereas none of the older elementary school students or adults gave such a response. In contrast, when asked merely to rate the plausibility of various results depicted in a computer simulation, essentially all age differences disappeared. It is as if a visual and inarticulate ability to judge plausibility of various motions develops quite early whereas more articulate explanations and theoretical constructs continue to evolve substantially.

PUTTING THE PIECES TOGETHER

I have motivated a view of intuitive knowledge in physics that poses fundamental educational problems in terms quite different from disabusing students of a theory competitive to Newton's. Indeed, perhaps the most fundamental problem is the simple fact that students come to physics classes with no theory at all, but instead are used to dealing with the world on a catch-as-catch-can basis, where it is quite fair to change tactics whenever the problem is minutely varied. There is an entirely different style of thinking involved when one comes to the stage that, for example, all the circular motion problems that Globerson and I cooked up are perceived and acted on as trivial variations of the same problem. I firmly believe that students who can articulately espouse *any* systematic view of the physical world would be far better prepared for physics courses than those who can be coaxed into reciting the right words, yet behave as if every new problem were an occasion to invent another explanation. This section is aimed at commenting on the uses of computers in education that are consonant with "knowledge in pieces."

Microworlds

Let me begin by going back to an old idea. When we ask ourselves where people get the funny ideas that they have, we must, like Piaget, look to experience not just experience as judged from an abstract view of what people are doing, but experience as felt internally, as judged by the extent to which people discern structure in the experience, and to the extent that this structure is contributing to the development of new mental structures. The key here is continuity. We cannot expect to have students learn things radically distant from their current state of understanding. Nor will they learn things that have a radically different character, such as the extremely systematic view of the mechanical universe provided by Newton, except by progressing through stages of understanding that, by degrees, approximate the final state.

So we should begin with experiences that have roughly the same character as those that generate and support intuitive physics as we find it.[3] This is the idea of microworlds, constructing artificial realities that intersect enough with students' ideas that they can immediately begin to manipulate them, but whose "deep structure," if you like, leads inevitably beyond those initial perceptions and conceptions. I and others have talked and written much about this idea in other contexts (see, for example, diSessa, 1982, and Papert, 1980), so I won't belabor it here, except to note that computers are so flexible as a design material that we should soon see, if we have not already begun to see, a boom in materials-based, experiential learning. Computers are so versatile in crafting interactive environments that we are more limited by our theoretical notions of learning and our imaginations. We can go far beyond the constraints of conventional materials, which are limited to an interaction of "push, pull, poke, and position" in a high-friction universe.

There are two particular ideas extending the notion of microworlds that are appropriate to the discussion of fragmented knowledge. These are relatively new ideas for me, or better, ideas whose importance has only gradually impressed me as I have come to see more of the fragmentation of intuitive knowledge and the educational problems that it poses. Rather than being closed-form ideas, these are more heuristics to help guide the design of microworlds.

The first is what I will call *mega-microworlds*. Simply put, the idea is that a single perspective is almost never enough to build a well-integrated and widely applicable understanding of the sort that we would want to call "scientific." The most carefully crafted experience just won't do it by itself. Instead, one needs to build clusters of these so that students can become involved in many ways over an extended period of time. Even from my own practical experience in building microworlds, it seems we must have quite limited expectations for any particular one, but must turn to building a multiplicity of them with a common thread. A bit metaphorically, we must find proper contexts to express all of the right collection of perspectives, the right set of p-prims that can be integrated into a new scientific understanding. This idea is developed in diSessa (1986).

The second extension of the microworld idea I call *textured microworlds*. This is an optimistic position that we are almost in a position scientifically to note, perhaps not one by one, but at least by the general class, the p-prims that we expect students to be abstracting and recombining in their microworld expe-

---

[3]Here, by the way, we find another shortcoming of the theory theory. If theories are the stock and trade of naive understanding of the physical world, surely it is important to ask how these theories develop. What replaces in people the historical and social forces that create theories in public science? In contrast, at least some parts of the beginnings of the phenomenological physics that I have described are comparatively unproblematic. People make many relatively simple observations about the physical world, keep them, for the most part, relatively isolated from one another, and only gradually percolate some of these up to a level at which they can even be surprised that these phenomena do not hold in some circumstance or another.

riences. This amounts to saying we can nearly chart the essentials of experiential knowledge. Instead of just designing an activity or set of activities, hoping for the best, we should begin to have more precise expectations about what exactly students will learn from various contexts. Such microstructure should allow us to do more than see success or failure when we have designed and built a microworld and let a student go off for a while to play in it. We should begin to expect to be able to assess partial successes, to "debug," if you like: find the places where knowledge must be patched. In microworlds that come with such a rich, theoretical texture, we should be much more capable of making principled interventions. The beginnings of such a texture for a microworld for learning Newtonian mechanics are presented in diSessa (1982).

The concepts of mega- and textured-microworlds, of course, need not be limited to computer-based materials. In fact, Marlene Kliman (presently a graduate student at Harvard) and I have tried to chart in a much more refined way than has until now been attempted the intuitive knowledge that becomes involved when children interact with a relatively common and nonelectronic piece of pedagogical instrumentation, the balance scale. The result is a data base that we hope will add tremendously to a teacher's ability to watch a child and know what is going on, to know what knowledge is being used, where it comes from, and where it might go developmentally (Kliman, 1987). The data base is an excellent place to accumulate profitable interventions.[4]

Mediating Between Formalisms and Experience

Computers have a very special niche at the interface between, on the one side, formalisms—those grand unifiers of science where one can write down "F = ma" and summarize all of Newtonian Mechanics in a little box—and, on the other side, experience with its apparently infinite fragmentation. A major problem with formalisms in past pedagogy is that they have stood quite apart from intuitive knowledge. Indeed, they are often made to be the antithesis to intuitive ideas, rather than to be productively engaging of them. The computer can play a multitude of important roles squarely between these poles, making for productive transitions in both directions. Generally, programming and computer modeling can profitably interject formalisms into an otherwise experiential microworld. But I would like to give more specific examples that I think are indicative of the richness and importance of this way of viewing the role of computers in science education.

---

[4]Even in such a context, computers may play a significant role in helping teachers keep track of their students' knowledge state and in helping to suggest interventions out of the large data base of intuitive knowledge. Advances in artificial intelligence should eventually allow us to entirely automate this feedback loop.

The first example is a microworld I designed a number of years ago for optics. The core of the microworld is a "simulation" that allows one to place a number of optical elements of different kinds, lenses, mirrors, prisms, and so on, into a field, and then shoot rays singly or in clusters through the constructed optical system. This is an automation of a little formalism called *ray tracing* that was developed in order to help people think about optics. From the way the rays travel through the system, one can figure out all other optical properties of the system.

Unfortunately, I discovered that, for the most part, this microworld was a dud. Students would sit down and play with it for a while, and they would happily do exercises I assigned to them on it—it is a much better tool than paper and pencil—but an important ingredient was missing. The system simply does not have any of the experiential feel of optical phenomena in the real world. The most immediate consequence of this was that students were not motivated to play and try things out, but instead treated it like the formalism it really was, as a tool to be trotted out when absolutely forced to.

Now, I think I know how to fix this microworld. A student of mine, Ed Lay, added a single feature to the system which has entirely changed the feeling of the system. The feature is that in addition to placing optical objects down, one can place *things to see* and can ask the system to show you what is seen from any vantage point. All of a sudden abstract questions become experiential and immediate. We had the experience within our own research group. (I have not yet had the chance to actually try this modified microworld with students.) You just poke around a bit and all of a sudden, "Grief, why is the picture upside down now?" Or, "Why is it in or out of focus?" Design criteria, magnification, lack of distortion, become directly observable. And the formalism, ray tracing, is always available in the same context to supply precisely what it is best at, careful analysis. The formalism is seen as a powerful tool, not to be mistaken for the object of study itself. Building analytic or other formal tools right into experiential environments should become more and more a standard part of microworld design.

Intuitive understanding of traditional formalisms is hard won because the phenomenology of operating with them is so subtle, so far away from daily experience and naive p-prims. Could it be that with computers we can design more dynamic and interactive formalisms that transcent this problem? The idea is not to juxtapose experiential and formal points of view as above, but to fuse them. One seeks to build things that are understandable and engaging in their own right, so that students have a painless and productive engagement with them, but things that happen also to be good formalisms for representing and thinking about a broad range of phenomena. I call manipulable systems that can serve as general and precise formalisms but which retain for students a sense of familiarity and evident controllability *semi-formalisms*. Semi-formalisms will often take the form of construction kits to make things that can be viewed either as toys or as formal models.

Both of the following are examples of flow systems in which some "abstract" stuff flows from node to node according to rules that specify how it should flow. In fact, both of these might be constructions in an as-yet only partially implemented construction kit that allows many types of flow systems to be simply generated. Stuff moving around from place to place is understandable and interesting in its own right, yet happens also to be a powerful and extendible way of modeling many real-world situations that may or may not literally involve flow. I have for years advocated flow as the core to a rigorous but intuitively accessible way of thinking about many areas. (See, for example, diSessa, (1980). Computers can build on this initial accessibility by providing more precise means of control and analysis in what remains familiar and experiential.

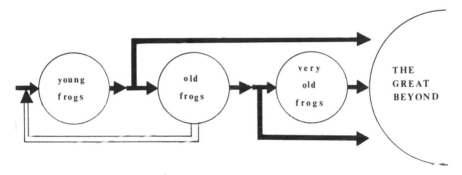

FIGURE 4.3.   A flow system used to model a simple ecological system.

Figure 4.3 shows a mock-up of a flow system used as a model of a simple ecological system. Each of the nodes represent the number of frogs at various age levels. Numbers or some thermometer-type analog display can show how many frogs occupy each node. On the left, one has young frogs. In the middle are older frogs, and on the right are very old frogs. Now, the connections show the routes that frogs can take as they age. Some young frogs grow into older frogs. But some, because of famine or disease, go to "the great beyond." Older frogs have the same options. The oldest frogs have no choice, but go directly to the great beyond. There is a single control line in the system as shown; the number of young frogs entering depends on the number of older frogs and is independent of the number of young and very old frogs.

Even with such a simple setup, one can see interesting phenomena. For example, if one artificially sets up a surge in births at one stage, a wave in populations will ripple through the system, and secondary waves will be generated as each baby boom reaches the fertile age.

Things get even more interesting if we introduce, for example, the number of flies in the ecological system. It should control the branching ratio of frogs that go on to older age levels compared to frogs that go to the great beyond. If we add a negative influence between the total population of frogs and the number of flies (more frogs eat more flies), then one can get extremely intricate patterns of behavior.

What makes this an interesting environment is that it has independent layers of understandability: First, as a system that moves "stuff" around according to a simple set of influences and controls, one can set up and play (perhaps literally as games) with systems with few parts, all of whose interactions are simple, but, in the large, exhibit complex and sometimes subtle behavior. Just as well, one can use this as a little formalism to experiment with various realistic and unrealistic models of actual physical systems, of which the ecology system is only one example.

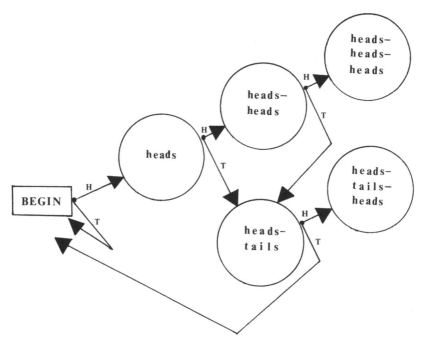

FIGURE 4.4.   A marker "flows" along a state transition graph, showing progress toward two goals.

Let me show another example of a very different modeling function built out of the same formalism. Figure 4.4 shows a system that solves a problem in probability theory relating to coin tosses. Consider a question such as: What can you say about the likelihood that you will toss a sequence of heads–heads–heads before heads–tails–heads? Figure 4.4 depicts what is called a "state transition graph" and works as follows: Suppose you first toss heads. Then you can move a marker, which shows the state of your progress toward the two goals, from "begin" to the "heads" node. If you subsequently toss heads or tails, you would move your marker along the appropriately marked path to "heads–heads" or "heads–tails" respectively, moving closer to one goal or the other. If you toss in sequence heads, tails, and then tails, then you must follow the path marked T from "heads–tails" back to "begin," because you are nowhere near either of your goals and must effectively start from scratch. On the other hand, a tails after heads–heads puts you in position to reach the heads–tails–heads goal with a subsequent heads toss, which is equivalent to having tossed heads–tails. (In this case, the initial heads is no longer relevant.)

Of course, one could make this little system with paper and pencil, and move markers around, but imagine how much easier it is with a computer system designed for such things. Imagine, as well, children have already encountered the flow system, perhaps with frogs, so that they know how to build their own systems, set them up, make them run automatically, and so forth. They can start a million coins at "begin," then watch them all move from node to node, one-half taking each path from each node on each toss. Or one could take a single coin and run it a million times through the system, taking the heads or tails path out of a node each time by chance. Incidentally, although it is no more likely that you will throw a heads–tails–heads than a heads–heads–heads in three coin tosses, you have a much better chance of reaching a heads–tails–heads goal before a heads–heads–heads. This should be apprehensible from the flow pattern represented in Figure 4.4, even without running it.

All in all, the flow kit should serve as an interactive formalism for modeling many sorts of systems. What makes it a semiformalism is that the "formalism" is itself something that is comprehensible and something with which one can immediately play because it is based on a simple metaphor, movement of things.

Intuitive Epistemology

I would like to mention a final area of leverage in using computers to attack the fragmentation one finds in intuitive knowledge systems. I have done some preliminary study of an area that I call "intuitive epistemology." This is another intuitive knowledge system that, however, concerns the phenomenology of personal intellectual functioning rather than phenomenology of the physical world. People have perceptions about what happens, about what causes what, about what is important and what is not concerning knowledge, its development, and its deployment. In some cases these ideas also seem to be almost theoretical, but the same caveats are warranted here as with intuitive physics.

In diSessa (1985) I develop two case studies of students with remarkably contrasting intuitive epistemologies. One of these looks in many instances to be similar to my own p-prims epistemology, particularly with respect to the relation of intuitive knowledge and textbook physics. The other might be caricatured as a theory that physics resides only in the equations and formalisms and that intuitive knowledge is only so much confusion. One would guess that the second student might be at a distinct disadvantage in learning physics with such a poor model of what it is he is trying to learn. Indeed, this appeared to be the case to the limits of this small study.

One would really like to walk up to the second student (and, in my experience as a physics instructor, there are many like him) and say, "Look, you have a fragmented, piecemeal jumble of an intuitive knowledge system, and that's fine; it contains a lot of the right pieces. You must find, cultivate, and refine these pieces. And, above all, you really need to concentrate on integrating that system. Science is, after all, at least as well characterized by its systematicity as by its content." Of course, that is bound to fail if you do it like that. That is the confrontational approach of the theory theory. Even if such students could understand literally what was said, even if they believed you, they still need to have some sense for what it feels like to use intuition properly or to be scientifically coherent; they need to have some sense for what one does to unify.

Again, because confrontation will not work does not mean the battle is lost. Again, computers can be extraordinarily helpful in providing students with experiences that meet their intuitive ideas and develop them toward more integrated and profitable points of view. Here, I will make a short list of techniques. Details appear in diSessa (1985).

Amplifying Qualitative Phenomena.   Much science education is dominated by analytic methods. Problems are posed in terms of known and unknown quantities. So problem solving is often perceived by students as finding the right equation, which represents knowledge to them, and grinding through a little arithmetic or algebra. Instead, their images of knowing and learning should be different if they deal constantly with phenomena at the qualitative level. This is microworlds at the meta-level. Experimentation and research on real-world systems could serve this role, except we have much greater difficulty designing such experiences to have the important ideas represented near the visible structure and in the direct principles of manipulation of the system. Semiformalisms and related computational devices have a role here too in providing nonanalytic but still technical help in solving problems.

Undermining Naive Realism.   If analytic methods provide poor models of knowledge, the absence of salient alternatives can lead to assumptions that knowing (after learning) is simple and direct, even if problem solving is not. What one would like to have are explicit schemes that represent the world in a powerful way, yet which have a visible human genesis and must be used carefully. Indeed, the notion of representation—of a schema that one builds, but which accurately reflects some reality without being mistaken for it—is central and visibly pervasive in computational systems. Every time one builds a simulation, one selects or invents a representation of reality, discovers it is not quite right, throws it out, and rebuilds or invents "patches" to overcome inadequacies. This can be a much better process from which to abstract ideas about knowing than always having been supplied with a thoroughly debugged and apparently simple law.

Changing the Quality and Time Scale of Exercises. One of the great experiences of my scientific career was to discover in high school that I could profitably think about a problem for weeks, that I could get valid insights, make progress, see things gradually fall into place, rather than just "find the solution" like a needle in a haystack. Yet I had this experience in none of my classes, but on an exam for a summer science program for which I was applying. Indeed, the vast majority of work done by students in school classes is of the 20-minutes-or-less-per-problem type. This is hardly fertile ground to promote awareness of learning processes that may be months or years long. Instead, I believe we must engage students in research and design in many ways more typical of professional practice than schoolish exercises. In the same way as computers have become indispensable tools for scientists and engineers, they are nearly essential here. Engaging in research and design is not easy, and without significant help in terms of good areas to research (microworlds), good tools with which to do analysis, and good material to design with, it may be nearly impossible for students. In my years of teaching research and design courses to high school students and undergraduates, not a single student has *not* used the computer, even though I never hinted that it was necessary, and I even occasionally encouraged students to work with materials other than the computer. This is due to more than the fact that computers are fun. For certain things, their utility is more than obvious to everyone.

Changing Subjects That Are Taught. Intuitive epistemology changes our pedagogical agenda. We are not only concerned with the "stuff" that students learn, but the process that they go through, and the meta-cognitive abstractions that they make from that experience. Some things to learn may be significantly more or less attractive from this point of view. Indeed, some of the best things to learn from this point of view may be unteachable without computers. Some readers may know the book I wrote with Hal Abelson on Turtle Geometry (Abelson & diSessa, 1981). Anyone who does cannot doubt that teaching that material would be difficult or impossible without the computational experiences built into the book. Learning computational geometry without touching a computer would be like learning physics never having touched, pushed, or pulled a physical object. I cannot begin to try to convince that learning Turtle Geometry is good for your intuitive epistemology here, so I refer the interested to the book and to things that have been written about it (e.g., diSessa, 1979). I am not sanguine about when the educational establishment can accept such radical changes at the core of its sacred curriculum, but computers can at least be an edge in.

A CLOSING NOTE

The fragmented system of intuitive knowledge that we find in our students poses significant educational problems. We need not throw up our hands, however, but should roll up our sleeves and get to work with the best tools we have. Computers are such tools.

With all my optimism about computers, I must emphasize that they are not magical instruments to engage and integrate intuitive knowledge. They will not help independent of what we do with them. We need not design microworlds or attempt to devise semiformalisms. We certainly need not change the subject matter we teach with them. Indeed, the first guesses for how we should integrate computers into education did none of the profitable things I listed here. One can easily teach the same old things with the same old 20-minute exercises. We could easily undermine qualitative methods, and emphasize numbers and other formal methods so that the computer is really just a number or symbol cruncher. The choice is ours whether computers will help solve or aggravate the problem of knowledge in pieces.

REFERENCES

Abelson, H., & diSessa, A. (1981). *Turtle Geometry: The computer as a medium for exploring mathematics*. Cambridge, MA: MIT Press.

diSessa, A. (1979). Learnable representations of knowledge. In J. Lochhead & J. Clement (Eds.), *Cognitive process instruction*. Philadelphia: Franklin Institute Press.

diSessa, A. (1980). Momentum flow as an alternative perspective in elementary mechanics. *American Journal of Physics, 48* (5), 365–369.

diSessa, A. (1982). Unlearning Aristotelian physics: A study of knowledge-based learning. *Cognitive Science, 6* (1), 37–75.

diSessa, A. (1983). Phenomenology and the evolution of intuition. In D. Gentner & A. Stevens (Eds.), *Mental models* (pp. 15–33). Hillsdale, NJ: Lawrence Erlbaum Associates.

diSessa, A. (1985). Learning about knowing. In E. Klein (Ed.), *Children and computers: New directions for child development (28)*, (pp. 97–124). San Francisco: Jossey-Bass.

diSessa, A. (1986). Artificial worlds and real experience. *Instructional science, 14* (3 and 4), 207–227.

Galileo Galilei (1954). *Dialogs concerning two new sciences* (H. Crew & A. deSilvio Trans.). New York: Dover.

Kliman, M. (1987). Children's learning about the balance scale. *Instructional Science, 15* (4), 307–340.

McCloskey, M. (1983, July). Intuitive physics. *Scientific American,* pp. 122–130.

McCloskey, M. (1983). Naive theories of motion. In D. Gentner & A. Stevens (Eds.), *Mental models* (pp. 299–324). Hillsdale, NJ: Lawrence Erlbaum Associates.

Papert, S. A. (1980). *Mindstorms: Children, computers and powerful ideas*. New York: Basic Books.

Chapter 5

Some Pieces of the Puzzle

Jack Lochhead
University of Massachusetts

Ten years ago Jean Piaget spoke to the Piaget Society on the topic of "Corre-spondences and Transformations." As one ought to expect from any great mind addressing a society named after himself, Piaget began by questioning the basic assumptions of his own theory. He indicated that although he had originally believed that mental processes could be understood solely in terms of transfor-mations, he no longer believed this to be the case.

Piaget stated that the use of correspondences is a necessary precursor to the ability to think in terms of transformations. One reason for this is that transfor-mations require mastery of some form of reversibility, whereas correspondences do not. Two objects can be exactly alike, indistinguishable, but they cannot be absolutely different, thus there is no inverse correspondence. But even though correspondences appear to be simpler than transformations, the issue of how they can be performed is far less easy to ascertain. To determine difference, one need only find a comparison that fails; to determine sameness, one needs to perform possibly an infinite number of comparisons.

Although it may well be impossible to determine true identity, it is fairly easy to create vague similarities based on sloppy criteria. This roughly, is what Vy-gotsky's (1962) preconceptual thinker does when he formulates heaps. It is also similar to what Rosnick (1982) referred to as the "generation of undifferentiated conglomerates."

I believe there are some interesting correspondences between these ideas expressed by Piaget, Vygotsky, and Rosnick, and those in diSessa's chapter (chapter 4) on knowledge in pieces. In all cases there is the suggestion that before knowledge can be organized in comprehensive global structures it first must be collected piecemeal. Coherence and self-consistency are not possible in the early stages of knowledge acquisition and in fact are meaningless prior to the imposition of reversible structures. A meaningful level of coherence can be perceived only if one is able to move back and forth (reversibly) between the various nodes within a knowledge domain, checking for consistency. Thus something akin to transformational reasoning must preceed the development of consciously coherent schemes. A learner in the early stages of knowledge construction can do no more than develop islands of competence devoid of a coordinated structure for connecting the islands.

The students diSessa describes are capable of formal operations, and they certainly can construct transformations. Thus the analogy I see between diSessa's perspective and Piaget's does not concern intellectual development but rather knowledge construction in moderately novel domains. The piecemeal system typical of physics students and possibly many other novices is a network of incoherent knowledge, negotiated via a process of drawing correspondences between events and a set of phenomenological primitives (p-prims). The relationship between p-prims and explained events need not be reversible and certainly lacks much of the precision of a transformation. The analogy also holds at a second level. The inconsistent knowledge produced by this process cannot be scrutinized because there are no transformations for moving between (relating) different nodes in the network. The system cannot self-correct because it has no means for seeking coherence.

Because it is my belief that we are still in the early stages of our investigations into high-level mental processing I think the knowledge-in-pieces perspective ought to apply to our current knowledge about the field and in particular to this chapter. One of the benefits this view has over more conventional theoretical perspectives is that it relieves me of all that tiresome baggage of consistency and coherence. My intention therefore is to offer a few disjointed comments on student knowledge in the hope that at least one of them may provoke the reader's curiosity and lead to a further examination of the issues that have been raised.

THE MESS WE ARE IN

Let me start by saying that I find diSessa's descriptions of student behavior to be consistent with my own experience both as a teacher of introductory physics and as a researcher in the area of physics misconceptions. I believe that the distinction that he draws between "theory" and "knowledge in pieces" is useful, powerful, and possibly valid. As a teacher, I feel very strongly that one of our greatest and most important challenges is developing students' concern for consistency. But experience has convinced me that this objective cannot be reached rapidly. Piaget has shown us that it can be a serious mistake to assume that other peoples' reasoning is driven by the same logic as our own, and I fear that both teachers and researchers of physics conceptions have been too quick to assume that coherence is a goal for students. The knowledge-in-pieces view suggests that consistency may not only be lacking, it may in reality be unattainable, at least initially.

The examples of piecemeal knowledge I offer all come from competent college students, who are better than average novices in a variety of different topics. I intend to stress that the piecemeal theoretic approach is not just a characteristic of early development but a common aspect of learning any novel situation. It may even be good science (Smith & Millan, 1987).

Our first cases come from the topic of circular motion. McClosky, Caramazza, and Green (1980) showed that many students seem to apply different P-prims to situations that physicists would consider equivalent. Barowy and Lochhead (1980) found an even greater diversity in student responses. Barowy asked questions about a fictitious crisis on the Civil War battleship *Monitor* (see Figure 5.1a). The boat had a single turret that could be rotated in any direction; in this scenario something went wrong and the sailors were unable to stop the rotation of the turret. He asked students to draw in the path of a bullet fired so that it would hit the target ship *B*. Students had to indicate when to fire the cannon during the rotation of the gun, and then show the path of the bullet. In some cases students chose to fire the cannon before it was aimed at the target, and the bullet curved in (Figure 5.1b). In others, it was fired after the target had been passed, probably relating to a p-prim based on an experience with a garden hose (Figure 5.1c). The last two responses (Figure 5.2) were motivated by the question: "What would happen if the turret were turning more rapidly?" All these answers were given *after* students had studied the appropriate physics; nevertheless, no student noticed the incoherence between the curved path they predicted and Newton's laws of motion.

The data on circular motion give dramatic illustration to the way in which people construct predictions without being constrained by other knowledge they have. Thus there is a failure to connect aspects of knowledge that theoretically ought to be highly interrelated. However, there is some reason to question the importance of such a failure, in a context that has little significance in everyday life. Of course everyday experiences rarely call for coherent theoretical understanding, but school experiences do (at least in theory). For science students the reading and writing of simple mathematical formulae is a common experience of considerable importance. It is also an activity that most entering college students have been practicing for four or five years.

Table 5.1 shows selected problems from a written test that was given to 150 freshman engineering students. Problems 4, 5, and 6 test the ability to read written English and translate it into a representation suitable for simple numerical calculations; in each case over 90 percent of the students were successful. Items 7 and 8 test the ability to perform translations from English statements into algebraic statements; 73 percent failed item 8 whereas 37 percent failed the easier example (#5, item 7). The startling drop in performance from 90 percent

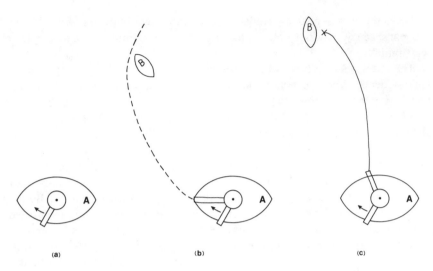

FIGURE 5.1. The *Monitor* question showing boat with rotating turret (a) and two sample responses (b and c)

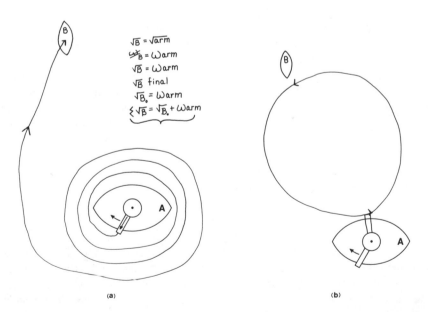

FIGURE 5.2. Sample responses to *Monitor* problem in response to question: "What would happen if the turret were moving more rapidly?"

success on numerical word problems to less than 60 percent and 30 percent suggest that the students' difficulty can be attributed specifically to the translation process. The errors made on problems 7 and 8 were largely of one kind; in both cases most errors were reversals: $6S = P$ instead of $S = 6P$, and $4C = 5S$ instead of $5C = 4S$.

TABLE 5.1
Test Questions ($n = 150$)

	Correct Answer	% Correct	Typical Wrong Answer
1. Solve for x: $5x = 50$	$x = 10$	99	
2. Solve for x: $\dfrac{6}{4} = \dfrac{30}{x}$	$x = 20$	95	
3.* Solve for x in terms of a: $9a = 10x$	$x = \dfrac{9a}{10}$	91	
4.* There are 8 times as many men as women at a particular school. 50 women go to the school. How many men go to the school?	400	94	
5. Jones sometimes goes to visit his friend Lubhoft driving 60 miles and using 3 gallons of gas. When he visits his friend Schwartz, he drives 90 miles and uses _____? gallons of gas. (Assume the same driving conditions in both cases.)	$4\frac{1}{2}$	93	
6. At a Red Sox game there are 3 hotdog sellers for every 2 soft drink sellers. There are 40 soft drink sellers in all. How many hotdog sellers are there at this game?	60	93	
7. Write an equation using the variables S and P to represent the following statement: "There are 6 times as many students as professors at this university." Use S for the number of students and P for the number of professors.	$S = 6P$	63	$6S = P$
8. Write an equation using the variables C and S to represent the following statement: "At Mindy's restaurant, for every 4 people who order cheesecake, there are 5 people who order strudel." Let C represent the number of cheesecake and S represent the number of strudels ordered.	$5C = 4S$	27	$4C = 5S$

*$n = 34$ for these problems

Several different levels of incoherence are revealed in this data. First by correctly solving problems 1–3 students demonstrated an understanding of algebraic syntax that then seemed to vanish in problems 7 and 8. In problems 4, 5, and 6, students show themselves to be quite skilled in the translation between

English and numerical calculations. This translation and the knowledge of algebraic syntax just demonstrated are, theoretically, all that is required to solve problems 7 and 8. Yet for many students these skills are not enough. This is strong evidence for lack of coherence, for even if one grants that students may have difficulty writing a correct algebraic expression, they clearly have demonstrated the skills needed to check and disconfirm their equation. The fact that few students actually do check their work demonstrates, once more, a lack of concern for consistency. The additional fact that they continue to avoid checking even when it is made an explicit course requirement shows that they do not perceive it to be a meaningful aspect of their knowledge. But in cases such as equation writing it is possible to make an even stronger statement. When "mathematically sophisticated" engineering students are made to check their incorrect answers to problem 8 they often find them to be correct (Rosnick & Clement, 1980). This is because they perform their check by applying rules for algebraic syntax that are inconsistent with those they apply in normal situations, such as problems 1, 2, and 3. For example, in the case of $4c = 5s$ a student may check the equation by saying that if there were 16 cheesecakes, there would be 20 strudels. This answer is seen as correct because it satisfies the expected ratio (4 to 5 is the same as 16 to 20); and it is obtained from the equation by substituting 4 for c and 4 for s to yield $16 = 20$. The c and s in this interpretation stand for the number of lots of cheesecake and strudel where a lot of cheesecake has four pieces and a lot of strudel five. Note that this interpretation of c and s is not only inconsistent with the interpretation of variables used in problems 1, 2, and 3, but it also depends on a most unusual use of the equals sign. Nonetheless, this type of interpretation is very common even among calculus-level students.

But there is also coherence to students' incoherence. Most of the incorrect answers to problems 7 and 8 are identical in form. The similarity is striking because it is extremely unlikely that any of the students have ever been taught to write the reversed equations they produce. This is not the place to consider the powerful perceptual and linguistic factors that induce students to make such errors (Clement, 1982; Kaput & Sims-Knight, 1983). It is sufficient to state that in many cases students consistently choose the reversed equation in preference to a correct equation even when very strong cues have been given in favor of the correct solution.

Rosnick (1981) gave the following question to students in a second-semester calculus course designed for the social sciences: At this University, there are six times as many students as professors. This fact is represented by the equation $S = 6P$.

    A) In this equation, what does the letter P stand for?
        i) Professors
       ii) Professor
     iii) Number of Professors
     iv) None of the above

v) More than one of the above (if so, indicate which ones)
vi) Don't know
B) What does the letter *S* stand for?
   i) Professor
   ii) Student
   iii) Students
   iv) Number of students
   v) None of the above
   vi) More than one of the above (if so, indicate which ones)
   vii) Don't know

Over 40% were incapable of picking "Number of Professors" as the only appropriate answer in part A. But what is most striking is that 22% chose "*S* stands for Professor," and every person who chose "Professor" for the answer in part B chose "None of the above" for his or her answer in part A.

This example shows that students are not only inconsistent in their use of variables, but they are consistently and persistently inconsistent. They will pick an incoherent answer even when strong clues are given (*S* ought to stand for Student) in favor of the correct answer. Such behavior results when there are two or more procedures available for handling what we "experts" would like to call the same or at least similar situations. In cases such as those just illustrated, students behave remarkably consistently in that they select the same procedure under the same conditions. Thus, for example, they will treat variables one way if presented with algebraic expression to solve and in quite a different way if asked to generate an algebraic expression from English text. However, there are other types of situations in which it is much less clear that there is a consistent pattern to the manner in which procedures are selected.

For example, the following sections of dialogue were taken from a half-hour interview with a student who was asked to interpret the following equation (Rosnick, 1982):

$$6R + 2B = 40$$

The given information is that records cost $6.00 each and books $2.00; a total of $40.00 was spent altogether. During the interview the student was frequently asked to explain the meaning of the letter *B*:

S: Well, *B* is the number of books, but it—; more importantly—in terms of figuring out how much they cost—, *B* is—is a price, which is $2.00.
I: So you say *B* is the number of books and—
S: at $2.00.
I: at $2.00.
S: Well, no—; *B*—, *B* is. . . . *B* is the—is the, um, the variable that equals the books at $2.00. . . .

At other times during the half-hour the student said:

1. . . . Well, B is one book because it—it—B has something to do with the price of the book. . . .
2. . . . B equals the books. . . .
3. . . . B equals 5 times the price of a book—of the books, which is $2.00. . . .
4. . . . Um, . . . (11 sec) . . . No, I think B is equal to 1 . . . but, um, . . . it—I think you're referring to it right here . . . where you could say B is equal to 5 . . .?

Rosnick (1982) has described behavior of the type illustrated above as being produced through what he calls an undifferentiated conglomerate. By this he means that the letter B in the above example seems to refer at once to anything and everything to do with bookness in the problem—the cost, number, weight, color, and so forth. Thus the inconsistency that we perceive in the student's responses stems from our making distinctions that the student seems not to have considered.

When one understands the origins of these inconsistent responses, it is possible to use them to instructional advantage. For example, in the case of the equation-reversal problem discussed above, the error stems at least in part from a static reading of algebraic equations rather than a dynamic procedural view. Soloway, Lochhead, and Clement (1982) found that when students were asked questions of the form: "Write a computer program that will output the number of cheesecakes given the number of strudels" they were far less likely to write a reversed equation. The context of computer programming seems to access a different p-prim than does the context of algebra. In an interview study, Soloway et al. presented students with a series of these questions, alternating between "Write an equation" and "Write a program." In many cases students would get the algebra reversed but not the program, even when the questions were answered within less than a minute of each other. However, after several such alterations they began to notice the discrepancy. This offers the hope that if algebra can be taught by analogy to programming, students may associate a better set of p-prims with it.

I wish to stress two observations related to this example of the effect of programming. First is how well it fits the knowledge-in-pieces model. A single task—"Write an equation"—is performed in two quite different ways depending on which p-prim is elicited by the context, and the human mental system is normally unaware of the inconsistency. Second, we have here an example of where an analogy to computing works well and as far as I know has no detrimental effect. I point this out because in a little while I will question the benefit of a much more common computer analogy, the one with the human brain.

ORIGINS OF THE MESS

To a certain extent the "knowledge-in-pieces" phenomena should not be the least bit surprising to anyone employing a constructivist perspective on learning. Theories must be constructed, and presumably that is a long process requiring a great deal of trial and error in the form of structuring and restructuring an ever-growing knowledge base. But I am not sure that the examples given in this chapter are entirely natural or inevitable. To a certain extent they may be an artifact of our schools and the current structure of academia. Little that occurs in conventional instruction encourages students to seek global explanations or relate one piece of knowledge to another. I am reminded of a student who was working on a problem concerning an object thrown into the air. He asked his calculus teacher how it was possible for the object to be going up if its acceleration was directed down. (The student's question is a classic example of the type of misconceptions common to physics. In this case, there was a failure to distinguish velocity, which is upward, from acceleration, which is downward, because this object was slowing down.) The teacher's reply was, "I don't know, that is physics, but this is how you do the problem." When such a large gap exists in teachers' minds between two topics that originally were developed simultaneously by a single person, Isaac Newton, is it any wonder that students fail to find coherence in what they learn? Disciplines, departments, and special-interest organizations such as our own Piaget Society, all seem to argue for a "knowledge-in-pieces" perspective. Could it be that the real difference between us and our students is just that our pieces are a little bigger?

WHAT TO DO WITH THE MESS WE HAVE

It is likely that the human knowledge-generation machine is well suited to organizing its experience without resorting to structures we would want to call theories. This may have several important consequences. First, the point made by diSessa: We need to be careful about constructing psychological theories that assume too much coherence on the part of the early learner's knowledge. Here I would like to offer a word of warning about the use of computers as a metaphor for human thinking. Computer hardware (at least until very recently) has not been well suited to the type of inconsistent processing in which humans seem to excel. Computer models of human thought may therefore tend to be overly coherent.

A more speculative point concerns whether we should strive as hard as we have for grand theoretical explanations. If the human mind is designed to cope without resorting to theories to help organize its knowledge, perhaps we should be more willing to avail ourselves of this ability. Theories have proved useful because they allow a vast amount of information to be stored via a few short principles. Now that we have easy access to vast computer information banks, perhaps our need for theories may be reduced. Such a suggestion seems repugnantly inelegant, but it may nevertheless be worthy of consideration. Although many of us are enthralled with the coherence, simplicity, and beauty of physics, I wonder if it may not be misleading. Is reality best understood in these terms, or could the aesthetics of theory building be blinding us to the incomprehensible mess around us? Our confidence in the universality of physical law is based on a wild gamble first made by Galileo. He performed the heresy of assuming the laws of physics found on earth would also be valid on the heavenly bodies. It is an assumption that has proved useful, but there is no earthly reason why it need have. Astronomers today make similar hypotheses about places we can never visit. Is this type of bold assumption of universal consistency a sane way to view our experience? We do not expect extraterrestrials to speak a language found on earth; should we expect them to believe in our physics? In short, is physics the ideal model for scientific thought, or is a less theory-driven and more piecemeal approach more likely to handle the intricacies of ordinary existence?

I am really making two quite different arguments. One is that the "knowledge-in-pieces" approach may indeed be a natural and effective way for people to think. The other is a fear that the concern that diSessa and I have for moving students beyond the "knowledge-in-pieces" approach may be somewhat misplaced. Certainly students need to adopt a more theory-oriented perspective if they are to successfully master physics, as it is understood today. But perhaps such an orientation is peculiar to physics and a few other fields and far less useful in the majority of cases. If that is so, then it would be helpful to point that out to our students. Although I hope my concern is ill-founded and that we can continue to use physics as a model for how science should look, it is certainly true that it will be quite some time before disciplines as complex as the behavioral sciences can even hope for that level of coherence.

As constructivists in the computer age we should be looking for ways that this new technology can help us reconstruct constructivism. Theories and the construct of theory are human constructions, tools that helped us construct knowledge in the precomputer age. We are slowly beginning to recognize that theory building is not the only way to acquire knowledge. In fact, it is not very difficult to see that if theories are constructed, then something nontheoretic must preceed them (Johnson-Laird, 1985). It is time we began to explore ways in which computers can help students build knowledge at the pretheory level, and ways in which computers can model learning at the pretheory level. But we really ought to go one step further and ask whether computers preclude the need for theory.

DiSessa has shown how we have been too quick to assume that all useful knowledge is theory driven. Let me now push the argument to ask if theories are always worth the effort it takes to construct them? Is skill at theory building a necessary prerequisite for all academic work? The fact that these questions seem a little ridiculous merely shows the extent to which our thinking has been based on the assumption that all useful knowledge is theory driven. It may be time we had a better piece.

ACKNOWLEDGMENTS

Parts of this work were supported by a grant from the Exxon Education Foundation.

REFERENCES

Barowy, W., & Lochhead, J. (1980, June). *Abstract reasoning in rotational physics* (Tech. Rep.). American Association of Physics Teachers.

Clement, J. (1982, January). Algebraic word problem solutions: Thought processes underlying a common misconception. *Journal of Research in Mathematics Education, 13* (1), 16–30.

Johnson-Laird, P. N. (1985). *Logical thinking: Does it occur in daily life? Can it be taught?* Hillsdale, NJ: Lawrence Erlbaum Associates.

Kaput, J. J., & Sims-Knight, J. E. (1983, Summer/Fall). Errors in translations to algebraic equations: Roots and Implications. In M. Behr & G. Bright, (Eds.), *Special issue of focus on learning problems in mathematics* (Vol. V, No. 3, 4, pp. 63–78).

McClosky, M., Caramazza, A., & Green, B. (1980, December). Curvilinear motion in the absence of external forces: Naive beliefs about the motion of objects, *Science, 210,* 1139–1141.

Rosnick, P. (1981). Some misconceptions concerning the concept of variable, *The Mathematics Teacher, 74* (6), 418–421.

Rosnick, P. (1982, January). *Student conceptions of semantically laden letters in algebra.* Cognitive Processes Research Technical Report, Amherst: University of Massachusetts.

Rosnick, P., & Clement, J. (1980). Learning without understanding: The effect of tutoring strategies on algebra misconceptions. *Journal of Mathematical Behavior, 3* (1), pp. 3–27.

Smith, C. L., & Millan, A. B. (1987). Understanding conceptual structures: A case study of Darwin's early thinking. In D. N. Perkins, J. Lochhead, & J. C. Bishop (Eds.), *Thinking: The second international conference* (pp. 197–211). Hillsdale, NJ: Lawrence Erlbaum Associates.

Soloway, E., Lochhead, J., & Clement, J. (1982). Does computer programming enhance problem-solving ability? Some positive evidence on algebra word problems. In R. J. Seidel, R. E. Anderson, & B. Hunter (Eds.), *Computer Literacy: Issues and directions for 1985.* New York: Academic Press.

Vygotsky, L. S. (1962). *Thought and language.* Cambridge, MA: MIT Press.

Chapter 6

Making Intuitive Knowledge Explicit Through Future Technology

George Forman
University of Massachusetts/Amherst

INTRODUCTION

At some time during most courses in research design, graduate students have heard this advice: Do not design your research around lab equipment. In spite of this warning, hundreds of dissertations were done with the memory drum, thousands with the Skinner box, and now equal numbers of students are coding video tapes. Are we designing a cognitive science based on the convenience of the equipment we have available? Perhaps graduate students should spend at least one year designing research that should be done, regardless of whether the technology is there to do it. In this spirit the current chapter is written. The emphasis falls on what should be built, rather than what has been built. Call it "Future Tech."

FUTURE TECH

Several excellent examples exist of research that has been driven by wonderful ideas. At the Palo Alto Research Center (PARC) of Xerox, particularly in the 1970s when Alan Kay was there, a team of computer scientists simulated the personal computer using the then-current mainframe technology. Here was born the idea of the Dynabook, a small computer with a flat screen on which children could draw, a keyboard for text input, and a memory capacity and speed that are only now part of microtechnology. Once this environment was created, other projects flourished, for example, the creation of menu-driven software using the now familiar "windows," an object-oriented programming language called

SmallTalk that allows the programmer to treat conceptual entities as objects to be moved and connected in space, and graphic software that smooths out the lines and curves to better represent the intentions of the drafter.

About the same time in Cambridge at the MIT Artificial Intelligence Lab, Seymour Papert, Andy diSessa, and Hal Abelson were among a group of computer scientists who saw the value of combining vector geometry and the language *LISP.* We know the result. The language *LOGO* was developed for school-age children. The LOGO group was continually besieged by criticism that computers are not available to schoolchildren. Papert's steadfast retort was that if the culture appreciates the value of computers, they will become as available as the pencil. LOGO is now used by schoolchildren worldwide.

It is interesting that both the PARC group and the LOGO group give strong allegiance to Piaget's constructivism as a guide. Papert was active in his association with Piaget in Geneva, and Alan Kay read Piaget thoroughly. And I dare to say that it was Piaget's boldness, his willingness to let his questions rather than methods drive his research, that attracted these creative scientists. We see a continuation of this creativity in John Seely Brown at PARC and the inauguration of a new unit at MIT: Learning and Epistemology. Constructivism will continue to supply ideas for this new field of educational technology.

Construction, Representation, and Self-Reflection

Certain concepts of constructivism should be highlighted here as an introduction. Look at three: construction, representation, and self-reflection. The phrase "knowledge is constructed" needs to be understood in the Piaget sense. Think of the child moving from not understanding some system, such as the game of baseball, to understanding that system. Knowing the entire list of rules would not be credited as knowledge, to Piaget. Knowing how to navigate the rules, to infer why it makes sense to hit the ball lightly, to figure out why the rules allow you to run past first base but not second—these examples of a generative use of the rules give evidence that the list has been constructed into a whole system. The learner enriches the rules with inferences that go beyond the givens.

The constructive enrichment is more than remembering what was seen or heard. To construct an integrated system of relations, the learner applies logic operators such as affirmation, negation, and class inclusion as a means to check for consistency or contradiction among the elements of the system. It does not matter that the individual rules are culturally transmitted. The constructivism enters when the person assimilates rule to rule (syntactic relations, if you will) into a coherent system by the use of these general logic operators. Thus attention and memory play only supportive roles in Piaget's work. His approach to knowledge and learning requires us to think beyond how much the player can notice or remember. In like manner, instruction based on Piaget's work seeks to provoke these logical operators in reasoning, inferring, and putting things into relations.

Representation certainly helps the learner put things into relations. An image can be a placeholder for a previous state, for example, the image of the clay as round previous to being flattened. The word can be used to assess old schemes of thinking that the learner considers relevant in a new situation. But representation, in Piaget's theory, takes on a new meaning, because the referent is so often the relation itself, rather than an object or vividly remembered event. The extended vertical palm of the two-year old means "no." The palm stands for the relation between what is about to happen and what is desired. It is neither, say, the friend nor the favorite toy, but the anticipated relation between the two (friend takes toy). In fact, the vertical palm represents the negation of that relation. It is easy to oversimplify the child's gesture as an abbreviated push. To Piaget the referent is a relation rather than an image. This more cognitive view of representation becomes significant in the following discussion of the use of computer graphics in Future Tech.

The third concept, reflection, is particularly interesting to Future Tech. Piaget assumes that a system of understanding improves in its coherence as the knower reflects more and more on the relation between the knower and the known. I may judge a vertical line to be longer than its (objectively equal) perpendicular. But then again, it could be that I spend more time looking at the vertical line, which biases my judgment. The more I reflect on myself as an information processor (the knower), the better I can construct coherence in the world (the known). Again, from a Piaget perspective, instruction provokes the learner to be more self-reflective. In the example above, rotating the paper so that first one line is vertical and then the other should provoke the learner to reflect on the relation between the self and the object. When this is done, first one line appears longer, then the other. This variability violates other assumptions, more strongly held, about the physical world. Thus the student reconstructs the relation between self and object. The illusion can be understood, even if it never disappears.

Self-reflection can be enhanced by Future Tech. The computer, for example, is particularly adept at making transformations that challenge the learner to reconsider his or her perspective to the "facts." At a minimum the computer could provide the rotations in the above example that challenge the student to think about how he or she "looks." The schoolroom dictum, "look more closely" is changed to "look at your looking." Future Tech, as presented below, can have a major role in changing the old dictum.

The Tone and the Note

Although it is true that symbols, to Piaget, reference relations, we can say much more about the nature of these relations. Some relations are continuous (the tone) and some are discrete (the note). An ascending tone causes us to project its continuation upward. We sense the direction of the pitch. An ascending scale causes us not only to project its continuation upward, but also to expect an absolute pitch within an absolute interval of time. Subjectively, we say that the first has a holistic flow and the second a stepwise precision.

If we consider the tone and note as symbols, then the notes stand for successive states and the rising tone stands for the transformation. In the former, the next state is extrapolated; in the latter, the contour is extrapolated. Composers can create patterns of notes and rhythm that titillate the paradox of the discontinued continuation (e.g., syncopated harmony). The listener seeks the certainty in the discrete and the unity in the continuous. The discrete symbol anchors; the continuous symbol supports.

And so it is with symbolic development of the child. Symbolic development has its most significant gains during the age two to seven year period. Piaget (1985) has refined his analysis of this stage of symbolic development. The developmental process can be described as a reconciliation between discrete categories and continuous functions. In the beginning of this stage the child has difficulty integrating states and transformations. A ball of clay rolled out into a sausage shape could just as well be a new piece of clay. Soon the child understands that the clay is the same (e.g., would have the same tastes as before), only its, say, height has been changed. The child thinks that the ball is now tall, whereas before it was short. The attribute "tall" serves as a predication to the continuing object "ball," but a change from "short" to "tall" does not change the object existentially. Still later the child invents middle terms, such as "a little tall" in order to deal with states that are in between tall and short. But "a little tall" is only a new category, a third, where before there had only been the two extremes. These categories occupy a position in a sequence, what may be called *discrete degrees* (Forman, 1981). These states are not yet understood as arbitrary points on a continuum of change.

The construction of the continuum comes in the next substage, and children begin to understand a variable as a continuous change. Tall becomes height, where height is understood as a variable with an indefinite number of values. The continuum is a necessary construction to resolve conflict. The conflict is caused by trying to give opposite names to an in-between state ("not tall" and "tall"). The child does all right for a while, with "a little tall," but the variable is the necessary synthesis when the child tries to add "sort of a little tall" and so forth. Therefore, the child of kindergarten age will invent the variable.

Once the child constructs the variable, he or she begins to combine variables into functions. Changes in the clay's height cause changes in width. Some functions are direct, some inverse. The relation in the clay example is inverse: the greater the width the less the height. As children approach the end of this stage, just before the onset of concrete operations, they can predict the direction of change between pairs of variables. But they can not yet understand what, if anything, remains invariant as variables A and B change together. This concept, known as conservation, defines the onset of concrete operational intelligence. The quantity of the clay is invariant even as a reduced height makes the width increase. (See Forman, 1981 or Forman & Hill, 1984, for a more complete presentation of these substages.) This process is recapitulated as the child moves from the concrete operational stage to the formal operational stage. The categories become classes, and the functions become combinatorial matrixes.

In summary, the child constructs an understanding of symbols by integrating the bounded category (the discrete) with an operator that transforms the content from one category to another (the continuous). Symbols that refer only to categories make the knowledge structure too listlike and brittle; symbols that refer only to transformations make the knowledge structure too redundant and fluid. Without categories we could never know where we are. Without transformations we could never know how we arrived, which in turn makes us ignorant about how to get back. Knowing how we arrived helps us distinguish the apparent from the real. If you arrive at the category "tall ball" by adding clay to a short ball, then you have not arrived simultaneously at the category "same amount." The integration of the discrete and continuous is essential.

The integration of the discrete and continuous, as a goal of cognitive development, can also be a guide for Future Tech. Computer-generated images can be digits (discrete) or analogs (continuous). But more important, they can be somewhere in between, something that I have called elsewhere *kinetic print* (Forman, 1985). Imagine a symbol, such as the word *fear*, printed on the computer screen. The word will change its shape by crouching down slowly as you read it. The word itself gives the denotative meaning; the crouching adds connotative meaning that can vary continuously with slight changes in the movement that the word makes. Certainly our new technology will make possible an incredible interplay between analog and digital representations. Some of these possibilities are presented in the sections that follow.

Audrey's Magic Chalk

Remember the syndicated cartoon of the little girl Audrey. She could draw an object in the air with her magic chalk and the object would become real. What would be the advantage of designing computer software that simulates this power for children? The modern-day child can use a light pen to draw a face on the computer screen. Then she can transform that unique face into a happy, sad, or angry look, or make the head turn around, or put on a hat she has drawn. The child can use keyboard commands provided by the software to activate the drawing. Alternatively, the child can even create her own "verbs" by first moving the drawn object with a light pen and then assigning that movement a number or name. She may rotate the whole figure and store this in her action dictionary under the label "tumble." The child can either create her own sequence of actions, such as walking, or use the menu of actions in the software. She may at any time look "inside" a canned action to see a list of its components. Thus the child has the option of constructing actions through an analog input (the light pen moves) or through a digital input (the keys pressed to access the actions stored in computer memory). She can even see the list of component actions, say, in a running jump, scroll under the image of her person as it moves on the screen. For example, the child draws a stick figure and decides she wants it to bounce a ball across the screen. She hits the key "R" and her figure runs from left to right. She realizes that running does not allow the figure to bounce a ball, because the arms are moving wrong. She takes her light pen, presses it to the right hand of her stick figure, clicks a button on the light pen, and moves the arm up and down in a manner more exaggerated than in the plain run. She then pushes a "do" button and the new arm movement is automatically integrated into the run movement. If she likes the arm movement she gives it a name (say, "dribble") and stores it in computer memory. This allows her to use the "dribble" arm movement as a component of other actions without having to redraw it with the light pen. Next she advances the integrated movement in slow motion, freezes the action when the right hand is high, and uses her light pen to draw in the ball. Henceforth, the computer will treat the drawn circle as a real object and will automatically simulate bouncing as the child activates the run routine again. Consequently, if the circle is actually elliptical, the "ball" will bounce unpredictably, as would a real ellipse. The child can edit the drawing easily, or, if overly frustrated, can use a perfect circle drawn by the computer software.

This technology can be evaluated from the constructivist perspective presented earlier. Drawing would be expanded from representing states to also representing transformations. The child draws a figure in some canonical state and then uses her invented vocabulary of keyboard verbs to make it move. The figure bouncing the ball is constructed by an integration of digital and analogical thinking. The visual image of the entire animation allows the child to work from the goal backwards (top down) by fine-tuning the animation. The key strokes for component acts let the child build from the means forward (bottom up) and experiment with effects she did not expect. The successive states of the animation would be understood as a sequence of well-defined acts (e.g., run-crouch-leap-roll). Each component action is packaged into a discrete category, giving it "an address" that can be called with reliability. It is important to remember that the discontinuous category is a conversion of the analog input, the child's own hand movements with the light pen. This analog input is possible both for drawing shapes (faces, bodies, balls) and drawing action paths (the exaggerated excursion of the stick figure's arm).

Such an art medium will require sophisticated graphics, great speed of computation, and a large computer memory for rewriting the screens during animation. Therefore it is relevant to ask: What is the advantage of giving the child this control over both the shape of the object and the shape of the object's movements? No doubt existing personal computers could handle programs with a menu of geometric shapes and canned actions. The answer lies far beyond the obvious increase in the child's interest. Imagine a child who draws a rectangle, thinking that she has made a good rendering of a house. Now she wants to walk around the side of the house so she pushes a button that she already knows will rotate her figure 90°. To her amazement she discovers that her "house" diminishes into a vertical line after the rotation. Had she given the drawing some perspective in the original, the computer would have had the information necessary to conserve the third dimension. What the child discovers is that a purely frontal view is ambiguous regarding depth.

Constructive conflict would be less likely had the child used a computer-supplied rectangle. It would be easy for the child not to reflect on her intention to represent a three-dimensional house when the computer-supplied rectangle diminished into a vertical line. She could blame the computer's rectangle. However, if she had drawn the rectangle herself, thinking, as she drew it, "I am drawing the front of a house," she would more likely reflect on her intended meaning when the rectangle surprisingly rotated to a vertical line. She may at least consider that she had drawn it wrong. She would consider the relation between self and symbol, a first step toward a reconstruction of the relation between symbol and referent. Constructivist education places great importance on making sure that the learner "owns" his or her performance as what was intended. Constructive conflict occurs only when the learner blames his or her prior assumptions. We want to avoid making it too easy for the learner to blame the medium (see Forman, Fosnot, & Hoffman, 1982).

Mirrors Who Scream

Let us develop this notion of highlighting the intentionality of a person's performance. Technology should make it less likely for us to excuse our poor performance as a "slip." Given that the task does not exceed our physical prowess, a poor performance is better understood as not knowing what to do, a conscious miscalculation of timing or distance. Currently there is a computer revolution going in the science of athletics. This revolution is based in part on the simple premise that poor performance is a case of poor thinking. Athletes are using computerized displays of their action to improve the way they think about their performance. Here is a Future Tech extension of this trend.

A male athlete picks up speed to throw the javelin. A video camera tracks the athlete on a parallel course, digitizes his image, and feeds the real time flow into a computer. The athlete also wears tiny remote sensors on key muscle groups. These sensors measure the waves of tension and relaxation as the athlete moves. The athlete receives feedback from a light-weight headset. The headset gives him aural feedback through the earphones aned visual feedback from a small flat screen (LCD) slightly larger than the human eye. The screen is displaced from foveal vision sufficiently for the athlete to view both the screen and the javelin. The screen displays a side-perspective silhouette in motion, the changing position of his body as he runs. The earphones give the athlete updated messages in English or in clicks for more instantaneous feedback.

The computer compares the flow of tension and relaxation from the athlete with the physical optimum for acceleration and release of the javelin. The optimal parameters are specific to each particular run and are upgraded each msec as the run continues. The athlete can see exactly when his movements depart from the physical optimum calculated by the computer. The screen can isolate body parts, such as the wrist, and the earphones tell the athlete when to bring his movements within the optimal values. The LCD screen helps him integrate these discrete commands from the earphones with the holistic flow of the run.

This example has some features previously mentioned for constructivist education. First, the athlete cannot easily escape ownership of the performance. The sensors are on-line as he runs. The execution is a simple extension of the athlete's intentions. Second, the digital commands from the earphones are supported by the analogical symbols on the screen, and vice versa. Third, the entire run can be replayed as the athlete sits and watches his last run. The computer can compare the last 10 runs and abstract patterns of inefficiency. Here again, the athlete must own the performance as a case of bad thinking. If a glitch occurs repeatedly at the same juncture, it is not reasonable to believe the bad throws result from lapses in concentration.

The small screen is the most controversial element in this system. Imagine an athlete trying to divide attention between the screen and his body. Let us assume that an alert young athlete could learn to deploy attention with practice and eventually resume peak performance. Still there is the question: Why is concurrent feedback more educational than postperformance feedback? Why not have the athlete watch this replay of the analog and digital channels some minutes after each run? The answer again rests on the learner's attribution of meaning. Knowledge is not enough, it must be applied during appropriate states. Suppose the athlete knows he is to hyperextend his wrist one step from the throw. Assume that the athlete misreads the kinesthetic feedback for a partial extension as a hyperextension. If technology can bring the corrective feedback forward in time to be concurrent with the athlete's own kinesthetic feedback, the kinesthetic feedback could be given a more accurate meaning. The technology could teach the athlete to read himself better. The knower-known relation is improved.[1]

Why both the analogical and digital display? The analogical display facilitates imaging the goal, which is the configuration of the whole system in projected time. This allows the learner to work backwards from the anticipated goal to the current means in progress (top down). The digital display helps the learner isolate and address the components so they can be attenuated more quickly and efficiently (bottom up). The analog display facilitates integration; the digital display, differentiation; and the two together facilitate execution and control in real time.

Shadows Who Lead

Let us take this idea of top-down thinking one step farther. In the above example the athlete sees a kinetic image moving concurrent with his own, as in a mirror. We also can program a computer to display an image that is the optimal NEXT state, say, one-quarter of a sec in advance of where the performer is now. Take the case of a female dancer learning a newly choreographed sequence. The sensors feed information to the computer about the dancer's current position. Instead of giving her corrective feedback after a mistake, the computer gives the dancer feedforward by displaying the next configuration the body should assume by $N + 250$ msec.

Again we ask: Wouldn't a tutor dancing parallel with the student be equally effective? Probably not, because in the case of feedforward from the self, the message is clear. No student could read the message from the human tutor as well as a message calculated at one step ahead of the self. The student has a phenomenological shift. Instead of following a tutor, she is led by an extrapolation of her own intentions. The phenomenological shift occurs because the computer image is contingent on the dancer's current state. The human teacher makes no such calculation. Obviously, the computer image needs to do more than to mirror to be educational; thus we program it to lead the dancer. It is

---

[1]The power of concurrent computer feedback can be found in a contemporary example. Dr. Samuel Fletcher at the University of Alabama in Birmingham has fitted deaf adults with an electronic palate. This device measures tongue placement and contour as the deaf try to pronounce words. The computer displays this information as a changing pattern of 96 dots on a monitor. With this immediate biofeedback, deaf people have shown remarkable progress in articulation, even for difficult sounds like "sh" and "ch." The computer feedback enhances their ability to reflect and self correct. They do this in two ways. One, they try to produce articulate sounds that are cued by lip reading and feeling another's throat. Two, they try to make the computer graphics of their voice match a standard graphic pattern seen on an adjacent monitor. The combination of real-world guidance (lip reading) and computer-enhanced guidance (graphic display) assures that the deaf person will move from skill to fluency, from knowing how, to knowing when. Or, to use Dr. Fletcher's words about a young boy's progress, "All the (conventional) instruction he'd been receiving suddenly made sense to him." (*Wall Street Journal,* December 19, 1986, p. 25).

reasonable to classify this example as self-regulated learning, because the teacher and student are, if you will, in the same shoes.

A word should be said about digital versus analogical processes in decision making. Without sounding too Zen about "shadows who lead," the student being led by the computer should enter a seamless flow of decisions. Each movement would be the completion of the previous preparation and the preparation for the next movement. The dancer would not count steps but would yield to the feedforward on the monitor. In effect, we would be improving performance without improving the dancer's conscious representation of that performance. [This follows from the premise that naming a digitized component *is* consciousness.] The latter would come from freeze-frame replays to give the dancer a vehicle for talking about the performance. The frames, the digitized flow, would be named, compared, and summarized in a formal symbol system, such as choreography. Writing the formal symbol system calls for the translation of the analogical into the digital. Reading the formal symbol system calls for the reverse translation. If the digital representation itself is derived from self-executed excellence (the freeze frames), then attributing meaning to the choreograph should be greatly facilitated. Therein lies the power of the Shadow Who Leads.

Trainable Trains and Teddies

We know that a two-dimension (video) replay can improve self-reflection. For example, Fosnot, Forman, Edwards, and Goldhaber (1987) had seven-year old children watch an instant video replay of themselves trying to balance long blocks (some with hidden weights inside) on a fulcrum. They were able to reflect on their errors and improve their performance. But note that the video image is a two-dimensional representation of some recent action. What if the feedback display could be the very objects that the child had manipulated some minutes earlier? It is technically possible to produce a three-dimensional replay with robotic objects.

A child moves a small train over an input board flat on the table. The input board is a matrix of microswitches that relay information to the computer. The child then presses the "replay" button at the edge of this board. A light flashes on the board to indicate where the train should be placed, the exact place the child started the action on the training run. Once the board senses that the train is in that position, the computer sends commands to the train, via an infrared signal, that repeats the exact path that the child had executed. The child has trained the train to move through a prescribed path. The child can simultaneously watch a computer screen that flashes a new arrow, in the current orientation of the train, every time the train passes through an arc of, say, more than 5°.

Input could come from objects other than trains. The child could manipulate a small mannequin wired with rheostat sensors at each joint. The child could move the limbs physically to simulate sitting, or walking, perhaps. The sensors will relay information to the computer about each limb's movement. Once again, the child could push the replay button, place the small mannequin on the starting position, and watch the robotic motors animate the doll through the same sequence the child had just "programmed." As in the example shown in Figure 6.1, the computer screen can flash discrete symbols to show the changing position of the robot as movements pass through an arc of 5°.

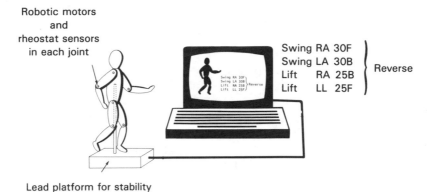

FIGURE 6.1   Object manipulation as input: The articulated mannequin serves as both an input device, via sensors; and an output device, through robotic motors. The screen automatically displays both icons and code.

Even with present technology children can program toy robots to move by interfacing the robots to a computer and using a computer language such as BASIC or LOGO. So what is the pedagogical advantage of giving children this analogical input (physical movement of the replica toy) compared to the digital input of LOGO? And, for that matter, what is the advantage of toys that remember versus plain old dime-store trains and teddy bears? Let us take the first question.

We want the child to begin with what she already knows. She already knows how to make a toy look like it is walking. At least she knows it as expressed in physical, pragmatic play with the toy. But she lacks an adequate representation of her success (see Piaget, 1978). The holistic, analogical, flow of play is not digitized into components that allow the child to reflect on a sequence of acts. This deficit is best indicated when one child tries to tell another child how to make a toy move (Forman & Heller, 1986), or how to assemble a block structure (Robinson, 1981).

If she tries to make this conversion of the analogical into the digital by hitting keys on the keyboard, the young child is placed at a disadvantage. She must bootstrap herself from her pragmatic and intuitive knowledge up to the level of the LOGO code. This difficulty explains why teachers often have children walk in a square and then have the children try to convert their physical acts into the

LOGO code. But the pedagogy is all wrong here. The computer should make this conversion automatically for the young child, like a teacher taking dictation of the child's natural language. Then the child can read the digital notation with the understanding that comes from remembering her own intentions during sensorimotor play. The exact form of this digital notation, successive pictures of the toy or more abstract symbols and quantifiers, can be determined by developmental research.

Now to the second question: Why use toys that remember, as opposed to plain old dime-store trains and teddy bears? What pedagogical advantage do trainable trains and teddies offer? Children play very well with toy trains and trucks now. They put these toys through incredible paces of going through pretend tunnels, around corners, and toward pretend landmarks. As children move a toy their thoughts are centered on the immediate position of the toy with peripherial attention on a nearby goal. The concept of a serpentine path versus a simple curve is not likely to be encoded even if the children make these variations. However, once the computer executes the children's action, and the children are free of executive decisions, the holistic quality of the path should be encodable. The children can shift from a local perspective to a more global perspective. The flow of control is reduced to a control structure. Instead of thinking "Where is this object going?" the child has more free time to think about the configuration of the path.

We are asking children to shift their perspective. Instead of thinking about the single position of multiple points (static shape), we are asking them to think about the multiple positions of a single point (action path). This shift from stationary-points to moving-point is not encouraged in our culture. Teachers too often ask children to name or draw an object, rather than to name or draw its path of action. However, children can encode an action path when appropriate representations are used (Forman & Hill, 1984). A whole new mode of process thinking can be added to the curriculum.

LOGO may be one such representation, but it has the problem mentioned earlier. To begin the play, the child has to key in the alphanumeric code to create the action, rather than having the computer create the code from intuitive actions of self on object. Furthermore, the alphanumeric code may be too abstract. Something more pictorial, such as icons that represent momentary positions of the object's limbs, might be better for the young child. The child could then edit the icons on the screen by changing their sequence, for example, with a joystick or light pen. The icon sequence is both the output code from the direct manipulations of the object and the input code for revising the object's movement. The replica object itself, during its replay, does not codify or digitize the action. But replay of the object itself does allow high-level reflection, because the child is freed from executive decisions. We expect that a child would attempt to make the mannequin move in particular ways, (e.g., walk, crawl, sit).

The net result of this act-read-write sequence should be an explicit understanding of how component events can be resequenced to form new events.

Living Graphs

Future Tech will allow us to make better use of our intuitive knowledge. It will help us explicate what we already know, yet give us tools to edit our knowledge structures and reach a higher level of understanding. In this volume the chapters by diSessa (Chapter 4) and by Lochhead (Chapter 5) are efforts to identify the breakdown between intuitive and formal knowledge. These efforts are directed at understanding the intuitive knowledge of the novice sufficiently to help the novice reconstruct the intuitive into the formal. The constructivist is committed to doing more for the student than getting the student to forget his or her intuition. Learning something new is not enough; the student must assimilate the old.

We could start with the bold premise that intuitive knowledge should not be replaced. We could even argue that intuitive knowledge is not wrong, at least not wrong in any absolute way. Intuitive knowledge is quite correct within its own rule-based system. This means that our objective as constructivist educators is to improve the representations for intuitive knowledge and have faith that the system, once made to bow to the new representations, will self-correct faulty rules. For example, our intuition tells us that heavy objects fall faster than light ones. We already know a related fact, that a heavy object will hit the ground harder than a light one. If this itself is an intuition, we probably make it because we know from experience that heavy objects hurt more when they fall on us than do light objects. We also know that objects thrown fast hurt more than objects thrown slowly. So we reason that heavy objects fall faster than light ones.

The problem is not simply that our intuitive knowledge is wrong. The problem is that our experience is not well represented and does not allow better inferences. Our representation for weight (pressure on a scale) is confused with our representation for impact (pressure on the ground). Because we think of impact as a force, we represent gravity as a force. A new representation of gravity would have us think of gravity as the differential between two speeds, the stone and the Earth, or the book and the table. But our school child images of falling stones or resting books do not include the relative motion of the Earth or table. We do not consider that the Earth is merely moving more slowly than the stone (along the stone's line of fall). But we could include moving points of impact in our new representations, particularly on computers, thereby seeing weight as a differential in speed. So, rather than replacing intuitive knowledge with formal knowledge, it should be possible to edit the intuitive structure with better tools of representation. One could have an intuitive understanding of acceleration once the temporal, spatial, and reciprocal relations are well represented. The learner would pass through the constructive stages of conflict and conflict resolution as he or she posed questions to his or her new representations. The living graphs in the example that follow portray how young children might interact with new tools of representation.

Two children make a seesaw rise and fall. Movement and pressure sensors relay information from the seesaw to a nearby computer. The children can observe a graphic representation of the acceleration/deceleration of the seesaw in action. When the child on the right pushes against the floor, the monitor displays a spike in the pressure graph for the right floor. When the left most child's feet first touch the ground, another graph displays a deceleration of speed, concurrent with an increase in pressure on the left floor. These three streams of data, in simple polygraph form, help the children use higher ordered representations to understand a system heretofore intuitive. Pressure-pad transducers could be added to each seat to display five channels all together: acceleration of the seesaw, pressure on floor right, on floor left, on seat right, and on seat left.

If children had daily access to these types of displays, one could expect them to become more fluent in reading and understanding graphs. To develop this fluency the children should work in two directions. They should try to produce particularly graphic effects by experimenting with the seesaw, and they should try to produce particularly seesaw actions by reading runs of the graphic displays of other children. That is, they should move from action to representation and from representation to action.

The pedagogical objective here has very little to do with teaching children how to operate a seesaw. The higher objective is to make them literate in graphs that plot change. Change itself is a high-order concept. It is not a value, as fast or slow, but rather a comparison of two values within a prescribed interval. The technology of putting the computer inside the seesaw (or balance beam, or lever, etc.) gives the child an opportunity to see these high-order representations in real time with changes in the physical system. Mapping of the representation to the physical system should improve.

Graphs are often given a literal interpretation. Even high school students get confused. If a student is looking at the acceleration curve of a baseball hurled toward home plate, the student quite often treats the drop in the curve as the path of the ball toward the ground. The student has mapped the curve to a spatial system rather than a higher order system of change. The "drop" of the acceleration curve is a reduction in the rate of change, not a reduction in the distance from the ground. A similar curve would be generated by a ball slowing down as it rolls in a level groove. If the groove were wired to a computer, the student could "see" the deceleration represented as a "drop" in the graph as the ball slowed.

Perhaps such Future Tech graphing will cause us to redefine what we mean by intuitive understanding. Our ability to understand rate of change might take on the apperception that is characteristic of first-order percepts. Discrimination of fast versus slow acceleration eventually could be perceived as easily as fast versus slow speed.

If computers allow this type of scaffolding for higher order concepts, the mental manipulation of the higher order concepts will be greatly improved. For example, computer-generated displays could help us anticipate the covariation of higher order concepts. We can look to the chapters by diSessa and by Lochhead (Chapters 4 and 5, respectively, this volume) for excellent examples of where covariation is a problem for physics students.

After reading diSessa's chapter (Chapter 4) one could well ask: Why wire the physical objects with sensors? Is it not enough to simulate the movement of objects in microworlds? My prediction, and of course this research needs to be done, is that the novice could come away from the microworld play without assimilating that knowledge to his intuitive knowledge. And I suspect that the separation between intuitive knowledge and the microworld would occur even for adult students if they too are new to a problem domain. But if the novice were allowed to send information to the computer by experimenting with real objects, more of the questions the novice asked of the computer graphics would come from his previous knowledge base. And it is that idiosyncratic, personal knowledge base that we want the student to reconstruct. The issue is whether the student will generate interesting questions about the real world, not whether the student has the general competence to deal with formal operations.

These examples of living graphs have emphasized fluency with the medium. I have not yet highlighted the type of coherence that can result when students can study covariation in a kinetic graph. Let us take the example of a dancer trying to understand the technique of graceful form. The dancer must think about the relation between actions and compensations, a version of what Piaget calls the coordination of affirmations and negations. The dramatic tension in dance comes from a performance in which mutually exclusive acts appear to co-occur—for example, a leap with a pause at its height. The illusion is created by a slight movement of the hands at the beginning and the end of the leap, but none at the middle. The suspended pause results from the contrast between the moving body and the stationary hands. The reciprocal relation between the two creates the dramatic tension between the invariance (the pause) and the variation (the leap). The movement and nonmovement are integrated into a coherent illusion.

The computer helps the dancer study the timing of action onset in parallel with continuous action in order to improve the illusion. Binary feedback from threshold transducers on the wrists is displayed over continuous feedback from a movement potentiometer on the torso. The digit and analog inform each other. The dancer can review by watching a replay of his or her torso action as a sine wave and his or hand action as an on-off histogram. The dancer can recognize in the video itself which leaps do and which do not create the illusion. Recognition is not a problem. The problem is reliable replication of the illusion. The dancer notices that the hand movements stop somewhat later in the leaps that create the illusion. His or her living graph, of wave and histogram, have represented the dancer's decisions in a manner that he or she can better interpret. The dancer then learns to strike an optimal tension between the affirmation and negation of movement.

Composing and Performing

Symbol systems help us construct complex relations. Music notation is a perfect example. The composer makes a draft, reflects on the notation, observes an imperfection, edits, and moves on. Harmony, climax, resolve, rounds, and counterpoint are all aided by the composer's ability to see the temporal flow of the music externalized from his or her mind's ear and held whole and stationary before his or her eyes in the musical score. A repeated phrase, in notation, looks exactly and precisely the same as before. The composer is forced by the constraints of the notation syntax to explicate even subtle variations. The composer may edit because of something he or she sees in the notation or hears in the performance at the keyboard. In either case, the composer is limited by the technical skills of translating an imagined phrase into notation or performing a notated phrase on the keyboard. The art cannot be solely conceptual if we are to replay our inventions. The limits of technical skill will be greatly reduced as a result of computers and music synthesizers.

A child sings into a microphone and watches the computer screen as it creates a music score spontaneously. Then the child can press the replay button and hear the music as the notation scrolls by on the screen. If the child wants to change the song, he or she can either sing the revision into the microphone or move the notes around on the screen with a light pen. The child can even clone phrases in the music score, or change meter, key, and timbre by choosing appropriate icons on the menu. The child can sing his or her own harmony by dubbing a previous soundtrack with a second input from voice or light pen.

As in many of the previous examples, we allow the child to move from referent to symbol and from symbol to referent. The referent is the system known with great fluency—singing, in this case. The symbol is the music notation. The child can explicate an intuitive system and add meaning to a formal system. Once the formal system is vested with meaning, it can be used to improve performance. The formal system helps the child reflect on the structure of the performance.

This principle of two-way traffic between symbol systems and intuitive systems can be extended to other examples. Imagine a voice-recognition system that prints every word that the child says and says every word that the child prints. Imagine a video digitizer that choreographs every step the dancer makes and has an image that dances every choreograph the dancer writes. The student's fluency with the notation system would be accelerated as well as his or her sense of structure in performance. The intuitive system is more likely to be coded in an analog form (whole and unique phrases of music, dance, and speech), whereas the notation system is itself digital (a syntactical system of a small number of elements). The student can invent the notation system by manipulating the intuitive system. Invented spelling, invented choreography, invented music notation all build from the known performance to a more explicit awareness of the knower-known relation as convention and motifs are formulated.

CONSTRUCTION, REPRESENTATION, AND REFLECTION REVISITED

At the beginning of this chapter I stated that construction, representation, and reflection are central Piaget themes. Construction works by building a representation that reconciles the differences between an intuitive system of understanding and some perturbation in that understanding. Representation helps the learner read the facts and put them into relations. The learner must go beyond the old and new facts to make the integration. In many cases the representation signifies the relation itself—for example, the transformation from one state to another. In order to gain purchase on the higher order system the learner needs to reflect on the origin of these relations. The learner reflects on what he or she, as the knower, added to the facts, what operators were applied, that gave meaning to the facts.

The Future Tech examples above encourage the learner to (a) construct formal knowledge from intuitive knowledge, (b) use computer-generated symbols to yield both digital and analog representations of intuitive knowledge, and (c) reflect on intuitive concepts where categorical propositions begin to conflict. A consolidation of these principles yields the following prescription of educational technology: Begin with the learner's naive understanding, help the learner represent that naive understanding with such articulation that conflict can be induced, and give the learner tools that will improve the reflection necessary to reconstruct the naive understanding. Technology can help at each step. The interface between the computer and the learner will only get better.

From Movement to Code.   Computer programs will be developed that can read the structure of intuitive knowledge. Once such programs exist, the computer will code input from the learner's intuitive system without demands on the learner for a special vocabulary. The analog input devices are good examples, such as coding the javelin thrower's movement, coding the placement of real objects in three-dimensional space, and printing the spoken word instantaneously. The computer will display the result of a person's decisions as both analog and digital output. For young children, it would be best to begin with analog output to preserve meaning. This method will assure that the children will sense the rhythm of their performance before they try to understand its component structure. The component structure of the states and their transformation can come by an overlay of digital and analogical displays. For example, in the living graph of a seesaw, the computer can turn an icon on or off to indicate exact balance, as well as present a streaming wave form for all positions above and below equilibrium. The computer screen helps the child convert the rhythmic flow into discrete propositions.

From Code to Conflict.   This conversion of the rhythmic flow of information into polar opposites is necessary for the child to experience cognitive conflict. Cognitive conflict occurs when some event is treated as a member of two classes which are themselves known to be opposites (see earlier section on "the Tone and the Note"). Thus bifurcations are initially useful for the child to reconstruct rhythm on a higher level of understanding. This is a shift from rhythm to opposites to discrete degrees to variables (see Forman, 1981). The concept of *variable* exists when the child knows that the values on a continuum do not occupy discrete locations. The values are simply pointers for the amount (more or less) of the attribute that varies. This reflective abstraction results from a conflict between adjacent categories, say, big and little. The in-between ("sort of big") is created as a necessary state, and then indefinite in-betweens are an extension of this necessity that yields the concept of the variable.

From Conflict to Coherence.   The conflict results when discrete categories are confused with continuous functions. The pause in the dancer's leap is coded both as motion and position. An understanding that the dancer's pause is an indefinite transition between rest and motion makes it art, makes it coherent. Understanding the weight of a resting object as the result of its motion, relative to another surface, gives weight and acceleration a coherence previously lacking. With Audrey's Magic Chalk the child is first conflicted when she sees the square rotate and diminish into a vertical line; she had expected the side view of her house. Gradually the child constructs a new system that includes state information about depth so it can be preserved in a transformation.

In summary, the computer will become more and more sophisticated in its ability to explicate our intuitive knowledge. It will do this through a combination of digital and analogical representations. The tension between the two sources of information will create a type of constructive conflict. The conflict will be resolved through a process of reflective abstraction. The abstraction will be a coherence at a higher level of understanding. These dynamics of learning can apply to any domain, as long as we know where to find the intuitive systems that are their origins. Reading comes from speaking, speaking from nonverbal communication. Understanding others probably begins with understanding ourselves. Math could have its origins in reconfiguring small objects (Piaget & Inhelder, 1969) or playing with gears (Papert, 1980). Drawing could have its intuitive origins in making shadows, pressing and etching the sand, rolling in the snow. The adult artist has access to a vast intuitive knowledge about light, movement, and balance. One hopes our future technology will bring all of us closer to these sophisticated systems of personal knowledge.

REFERENCES

Forman, G. E. (1981). The power of negative thinking: Equilibration in the preschool. In I. E. Sigel, R. M. Golinkoff, & D. Brodzinsky (Eds.), *Piagetian theory and research* (pp. 345–352). Hillsdale, NJ: Lawrence Erlbaum Associates.

Forman, G. E. (1985). The value of kinetic print in computer graphics for young children. In E. Klein (Ed.), *Computers and children* (pp. 19–35). San Francisco: Jossey-Bass.

Forman, G. E., Fosnot, C. T., & Hoffman, M. (1982). *The child's understanding of absolute constraints in three-dimensional graphic media: I can't vs. it won't.* Paper presented at the American Educational Research Association national convention, New York.

Forman, G. E., & Heller, E. (1986). *Paired problem solving of young children with robots.* Paper presented at the American Educational Research Association annual convention, San Francisco, CA.

Forman, G. E., & Hill, F. (1984). *Constructive play: Applying Piaget in the preschool.* Menlo Park, CA: Addison-Wesley.

Fosnot, C. T., Forman, G. E., Goldhaber, J., & Edwards, C. (In press). The development of an understanding of balance and the effect of training via stop action video. *Journal of Applied Developmental Psychology.*

Papert, S. (1980). *Mindstorms: Children, computers, and powerful ideas.* New York: Basic Books.

Piaget, J. (1978). *Success and understanding.* Cambridge, MA: Harvard University Press.

Piaget, J. (1985). *The equilibration of cognitive structures: The central problem of intellectual development.* Chicago: University of Chicago Press.

Piaget, J., & Inhelder, B. (1969). *The psychology of the child.* New York: Basic Books.

Robinson, E. J. (1981). The child's understanding of inadequate messages and communication failure: A problem of ignorance or egocentrism? In W. P. Dickson (Ed.), *Children's oral communication skills,* (167–188). New York: Academic Press.

Structural and Individual
Development
in Computer Worlds

Chapter 7

Computing Space:
A Conceptual and Developmental
Analysis of LOGO

Greta G. Fein, Ellin Kofsky Scholnick,
Patricia Forsythe Campbell,
Shirley S. Schwartz, and Rita Frank
University of Maryland, College Park

There is a sense of urgency about research in computer literacy. The invention of the computer may yield a revolution in thinking as broad as that resulting from the invention of the printed word. We must capture the moment before each child is computer literate, lest we lose forever the opportunity to study the impact of a new technology on human thought. But before everyone dashes off to study the consequences of computer literacy, we would urge a few stragglers to pose a different set of questions. There are various forms of computer literacy, from inserting a game disk into a drive to writing a sophisticated program. There are various programming languages. The question is: Which form of interaction and which language will produce consequences of theoretical and functional importance?

Even though the possible consequences of computer programming have preoccupied educational researchers, the assessment of consequences may be premature. We cannot evaluate the consequences of mastery until we know what the individual masters and how this mastery is attained. Additionally, certain entry conditions or precursor skills may influence acquisition and constrain its consequences (see, e.g., Sternberg, 1984). If these precursor skills are absent, little may be gained from exposure to a computer language. Most likely, the process of learning will differ in different individuals or in different instructional settings, and different consequences will follow from these variations. Before we invest too much energy in the study of consequences, three sets of preliminary questions must be addressed. First: What are the psychological demands of a particular computer language? Second: What are the prerequisite skills needed to master some or all of these demands? Finally: How can we describe the process of learning?

This chapter is organized around these three questions because, independent of the particular computer language taught or acquired, the conceptual analysis called for by the questions provides a conceptual basis for distinguishing consequences that are important from those that are trivial, and consequences that are likely from those that are wildly improbable. These are familiar, sensible questions, similar to those we ask about other educational innovations and about the process of acquisition in general. We pose them here not merely to redress the neglect of antecedents and processes in regard to computer learning—a careful examination of acquisition in the computer context might also illuminate the acquisition process in broader realms of conceptual development.

Our examination yielded two proposals that appear in this paper: a model describing the acquisition of a computer language, and an evaluation of the advantages of using this domain to explore cognitive development. Because these aims are ambitious, we limit ourselves to one computer language, LOGO, and to stages of its initial mastery.

CONCEPTUAL DEMANDS OF LOGO

When Seymour Papert (1980) proclaimed that LOGO created *"mindstorms"* of powerful ideas about mathematics and procedural thinking in children, he tempted us to look at the consequences of programming with LOGO graphics. However, LOGO provides an expandable and specified problem space consisting of modest ideas as well as powerful ones. This problem space can be introduced to children at different levels according to our best guesses about their conceptual capabilities. Because LOGO is a well-defined conceptual domain, it provides a tool of remarkable depth and flexibility for studying stages and sequences in the acquisition and application of knowledge. For example, LOGO is a spatial language with a hierarchical structure suggesting that what we know about spatial, linguistic, and category development can be applied to building a model of LOGO learning. Perhaps what children know about space, language, and categories helps them to master LOGO. Because in using LOGO graphics, children create a visible record of ideas they are exploring; their progress is accessible to the investigator. Thus, we can look at what children know about space and language before they enter this domain and then how children transfer this knowledge to a new medium.

When Papert was in Geneva he absorbed the Piagetian philosophy of learning as an active process. The computer language he created provides us with a powerful tool for examining children actively acquiring powerful ideas. The purpose of our chapter is to examine what this acquisition process might look like. Following the structuralist tradition, we begin by considering the nature of LOGO's conceptual domain defined in terms of the primitive commands used to move the cursor. Two questions are central in this discussion. First: What prior knowledge is needed for a child to comprehend the conceptual, spatial, and linguistic context of these elementary cursor commands? Second: What kind of conceptual model of the domain must the child acquire in order to coordinate these primitive graphic components into a flexible system? Then we proceed to describe how the child arrives at this model, illustrating the issues with data drawn from a study of the initial stages of LOGO learning in a group of kindergarten children. We hope this tentative model of the structure and process of LOGO acquisition will persuade you not only that the study of LOGO can illuminate the child's encounter with a new technology, but also that LOGO offers a technology for studying the child's cognitive and linguistic development.

The Nature of Logo

Among those interested in Artificial Intelligence, it is common to create limited domains of discourse, make-believe worlds within which fanciful events can be represented. One well-known invented domain is the block world inhabited by a robot named Robbie (see Winston, 1977, for a concise discussion of this program). Robbie has at his disposal a limited number of sensorimotor schemes (e.g., grasp-ungrasp, pick up-put down) for manipulating a limited number of objects (e.g., blocks of different shapes and colors), in a space consisting of a limited number of topological/projective relations (e.g., in front of, on top of, supported by). Even though Robbie is the presumed agent within his world, he lacks a unique spatial position in it. Robbie's spatial perspective is exactly that of the human operator; spatial relations such as "in front of" are interpreted from the operator's perspective as if the monitor screen were a window into a three-dimensional environment. In Robbie's world, objects and relations are predetermined. In order to communicate with Robbie, it is necessary to appreciate the semantic categories of entities within his world and the grammar controlling his behavior, which, as it turns out, has many properties of natural language. However, unlike natural language and the intelligent systems from which it emerges, Robbie's language is not generative. Although the language of the block world permits the user to discover what Robbie knows how to do, it does not require the user to comprehend a different spatial perspective, or ask the user to construct new components of action, or permit the user to learn powerful principles from the exchange.

The microworld of LOGO graphics is also an invented, limited-discourse domain dealing with spatial relations. However, there are several notable differences. In LOGO, one takes the perspective of the cursor, not the operator. The surface of the monitor screen is treated as it is, a two-dimensional plane. Rather than predefined objects, objects are constructed on this plane using a few primitive, path-making commands. Thus the conceptual domain of LOGO graphics describes the organization and appearance of paths through space. The commands themselves portray Newtonian vectors that, when combined, may yield the objects and spatial relations of Robbie's world or of some other world we choose.

What is the LOGO domain? At its most tangible level, it consists of a conventional keyboard and a caret on the screen called a "turtle" (Figure 7.1). When certain keys are pressed, the turtle's position changes, moving forward or back, or turning left or right. Mastering LOGO requires learning the precise

FIGURE 7.1.   The "turtle"

and predictable contingencies between actions on the keyboard and observable events on the screen expressed in primitive commands such as forward, back, left, and right. LOGO learning is aided by understanding that one's personal knowledge of movement through space applies to the movement of the cursor on the screen.

Next, LOGO learning involves mastery of syntactic rules for combining these primitive elements into ordered sequences. Then the turtle can be made to travel anywhere on the screen. In Figure 7.2, the turtle has been turned 90° to the left and moved 50 paces forward. Figure 7.3 shows the same commands in a different order: first forward 50 paces and then 90° to the left. When the order is changed, the turtle travels a different path. In Figure 7.4 the turtle has rotated 90° to the right and moved 50 paces back. Whereas different LOGO primitives are used in Figures 7.2 and 7.4, the cursor has traveled the same path. Relations among these visible movements are the source of the conceptual structure the child will eventually infer.

FIGURE 7.2.

?LEFT 90 FORWARD 50
?

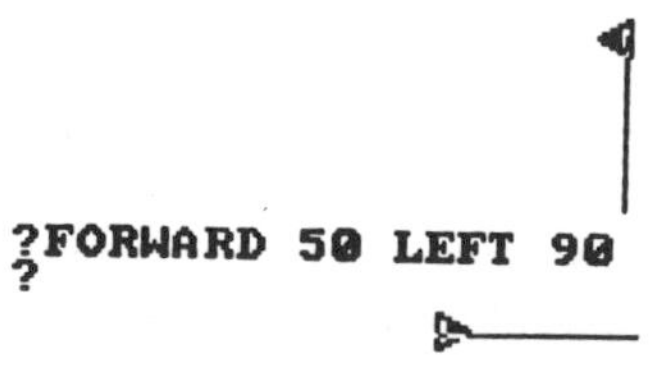

FIGURE 7.3.

?FORWARD 50 LEFT 90
?

FIGURE 7.4.

?RIGHT 90 BACK 50
?

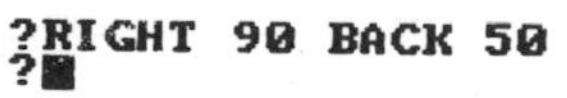

Once having grasped the four primitive commands and how to combine them, the child can design a sequence to achieve some goal such as drawing a squiggle or a house. When the goal is achieved, the sequence can be stored in the system as a procedure. The turtle now "knows" how to squiggle or how to "house." Unlike Robbie's world, the turtle's world is expandable. The child's interaction with Turtle Graphics progressively changes from the management of spatial movements, to the construction of graphic objects, to the modularized components of a procedural language. Our analysis focuses only on the beginnings, the child's comprehension of the semantic and syntactic organization of primitive LOGO movement commands.

PREREQUISITES TO LEARNING LOGO

Entry Conditions

From the beginning, LOGO graphics invite children to imagine a world, somewhat like the ordinary, mundane world they know so well, but different from it in important ways. Children must select from their knowledge of spatial movements and language those things that apply to this new domain, rejecting those that do not apply. This analysis of the similarities and differences between old and new culminates in the detection of relevant knowledge and creation of its appropriate transformation. This relevant and transformed knowledge enables entry into the LOGO environment.

The child must realize that LOGO is an invented world in which the turtle is the agent, the only entity that can do anything. The human at the keyboard is the one for whom actions are done. The instrument of action is the turtle's body, an isosceles triangle whose smallest angle is its nose, and whose smallest side is its back. Much as the expression, "Follow your nose" means to move in the direction your nose is facing, so the turtle's nose gives its heading. Even though left and right are not graphically marked on the turtle's body (as they are not marked on your own), it is necessary to interpret these spatial orientations from the perspective of the turtle's nose. A central aspect of LOGO learning is the human operators' understanding that despite this difference in perspective, their personal knowledge of movement through space applies to the turtle's actions. The difference is that when you move in space, you follow your own nose, but when you command a turtle to move, you follow its nose, not your own. The child's problem is to imagine an independent but controllable agent with familiar spatial properties and its own distinctive perspective.

Perspectives in the microworld differ from those in the real world in other ways as well. We usually move on a horizontal plane, but, from an operator's perspective, the turtle moves on a vertical plane. Thus when the turtle is in home position, a forward command moves the turtle up, and a back command moves it down. Not only is the plane of action transformed in this space, but what appears subjectively as a physical continuum is now described in terms of units of measurement. Turtles move in units that determine the magnitude of the distance and direction traveled. Among other things, the child setting out to master LOGO must treat a triangular shape as if it had agency and its own perspective with respect to left-right orientation, plane of action, and span of movement.

There is also a language of commands that, although arbitrary, resembles English enough to feel friendly. All language is based on semantic and syntactic relations, and LOGO is no exception. But there are some crucial differences. Unlike natural languages, where some degree of imprecision is tolerated, computer languages require precision. The turtle will do only what it is told to do and only in the language it understands. However, the most intriguing aspect of LOGO is that it requires what few other spatial tasks require, namely a linguistic analysis of spatial movements. In LOGO, the operator is not drawing; the operator is telling the turtle how to draw. If one wishes merely to draw beautiful designs, choose another language, because LOGO is cumbersome. However, LOGO's commands make explicit the spatial principles behind the graphics, and if these principles are of interest, LOGO has special advantages.

Spatial navigation and linguistic mapping are not new tasks to the child. Presumably, in navigating the natural spatial environment, the child forms some kind of a spatial representation of the external world. LOGO asks the child to use a language to produce spatial representations in a microworld where the spatial constraints are somewhat different from those in the real world and the language is more precise and stable. For these reasons, LOGO allows the developmental psychologist to examine how children transfer real-world knowledge of space and representation to a new domain. If spatial knowledge is an essential precursor to LOGO mastery, one would expect an assessment of spatial knowledge to predict the course of LOGO learning. In our own work with kindergarteners, we found a close relationship between LOGO mastery and children's ability to coordinate perspectives and use a map to navigate a terrain (Campbell, Fein, Scholnick, Schwartz, & Frank, 1985). Similar relationships have been reported for high school students (Webb, 1984). Thus some aspects of spatial knowledge may facilitate understanding of the LOGO environment. Whether some aspects of semantic or syntactic knowledge also transfer remains to be determined.

The Infrastructure

From understanding how a cursor moves on a screen to programming is a large step. To view LOGO only in terms of grand ideas such as procedures or modules is to underestimate its elegance and its potential for illuminating children's thinking. LOGO's grand ideas emerge from an infrastructure of interconnected, modest ideas from which more powerful ones are derived. One set of modest ideas is found in the semantics of LOGO, that is, in the meaning of single commands. Another is found in its syntax, or the way commands are sequenced. Yet a third set is found in the integrated operations whereby the semantics and syntax become coordinated into a system of cognitive-spatial relations.

Discussions of children's learning of LOGO ultimately depend on analyses of the conceptual structure of the microworld itself and children's ability to marshall their understanding of that structure to command the turtle to achieve some goal. First we turn to a description of that structure and then to the child's construction of it.

A Taxonomy of Actions. It is useful to think of the command structure of Turtle Graphics in terms of a conceptual hierarchy like that shown in Figure 7.5. At first glance, the lowest levels of the hierarchy seem to represent action schemes that produce distinctive events on the screen. Much as shaking a rattle produces sound, so the press of certain keys produces a forward movement of the turtle.

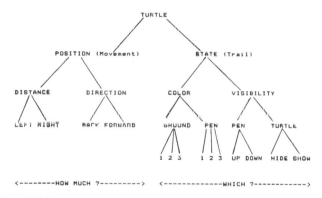

FIGURE 7.5.   LOGO taxonomy

However, if the turtle is understood as the agent of the action, a better analogy is that of a child making a doll walk. Viewed this way, the taxonomy represents a system of agent-action-object relations in which the child controls the turtle, who as agent acts to produce event-objects on a two-dimensional monitor. Thus there is a double-layered, interconnecting causal system in which "I" cause the "turtle" to cause an event on the screen by issuing a set of commands. What follows is an analysis of the structure of these commands.

Quantitative and Qualitative Properties. We can describe the turtle's path in quantitative terms such as direction and distance, and in qualitative terms such as the color and shape of its trail. To give movement commands, you must specify how much, and to give state or trail commands, you must specify which. As shown in Figure 7.5, action schemes that move the turtle to new positions do so by controlling quantitative properties of its movement. Other schemes control qualitative properties of the appearance of the turtle and its trail. Thus the semantics of LOGO rest on a distinction between spatial properties of the turtle's movement portrayed as a Newtonian vector, and qualitative properties of the display produced by that movement. Spatial properties can be further specified in terms of the direction and distance traveled. There are two directions, left and right turns, each of which must be described by degree of rotation. Similarly, distances may be forward or back, specified by the number of steps taken.

Qualitative aspects of the trail also have two variations: visibility and color. State commands determine whether or not the turtle leaves a trail behind it (PU or PD), the color of the turtle and its trail (PC), the color of the background (BC), or whether or not the turtle itself is visible (HT or ST). In this branch of the hierarchy, states are either on or off, and when number is used to control color, it specifies which color, not how many.

Complementary and Reciprocal Relations. Because this taxonomy describes actions, a forward command followed by a back command of the same magnitude returns the turtle to its original position. A similar relation holds between left and right. A turn of 90° to the left followed by a turn of 90° to the right returns the cursor to its original heading. These relations mean that the turtle can travel several straight-line paths to the same goal.

Suppose a child wishes to hit a target at the top center of the screen and the turtle is at home position pointing upward. There are three ways to do it: (a) the turtle can simply move forward; (b) it can turn left 180° and move back, or (c) it can turn right 180° and move back. Perhaps one of these strategies is more efficient, but they all get to the same goal. The child who knows these strategies are possible understands the functional equivalence of left and right, or forward and back. Two sets of powerful ideas are inherent in these relations, those dealing with how space and drawing operate, and those enabling the child to use relations that promote flexibility and new capacities for self-correction.

LOGO Syntax

The Nature of the Unit and Default Values. The semantic structure of these commands defines the basis of LOGO syntax in two ways. First, the structure identifies what a command must specify, and second, it creates the problem of sequencing these specifications. A basic problem in any language, including LOGO, is the definition of a sentence and the way the ideas inherent in a sentence should be expressed. Every LOGO sentence must specify the direction and distance of the movement, the appearance of the turtle, and the appearance of the line relative to the background. Therefore each command has an explicit and an implicit referent. If you tell the turtle to move forward 20 steps, only distance is changed. However, you have implied that other essential attributes are unchanged from their previous values. Usually, the system initially assumes a direction of 0°, white pen color, black background, a visible turtle, and the potential for a visible path. Once a move is made, the system updates those implicit values. If you give the commands, "Pen up, Forward 20," and then "Pencolor 2, Forward 20," you will not see a colored line on the screen because you have not put the pen down. In this sense, LOGO meanings have a historical context. Once having told the turtle "pen up," that earlier state will determine the appearance of the line in the present and in the future unless the pen command is explicitly changed. Assumptions about implicit or default values are important in commanding turtle movements. They are the constituents of command strings, and their ordering is the basis for the syntax of LOGO.

Enablement Rules. The taxonomy in Figure 7.5 refers to the turtle's actions and to the states that result from these actions. Natural language gives us considerable latitude in describing actions and states of appearance. We can describe the appearance of a mark as "a line that is oblique and red," or as "a line that is red and oblique," as well as "a red, oblique line." In the real world, a mark is simultaneously red, oblique, and a line. However, if we wish to make such a line, we must first choose a pen and paper, lower our hand to the page, point our hand in the correct direction and then move hand and pen across the surface. In order to understand LOGO, we must think of the appearance of a line as the product of a sequence of actions.

In LOGO graphics the language executes components of the sentence in the order they are typed. However, the logic of natural movement dictates the order of typing. Consequently, the sequence in which commands are chosen matters, and different sequences of the two commands may yield different effects: forward and then right is not the same thing as right and then forward.

The underlying enablement sequence is as follows:

(State) → (Direction) → (Distance)

In summary, the hierarchically organized category structure of primitive commands describes a limited domain of human actions and the spatial events these actions yield. Added to the hierarchy is a logic of action that describes the sequence in which commands must be entered, along with the implications of nonentry. Comprehending the infrastructure of LOGO thus engages the child in mastering a symbolic system of graphic production based in interesting ways on concrete experience.

AN ACQUISITION MODEL

How do children master this system? We assume that the child starts by building up a conceptual hierarchy of commands. Elaboration of the hierarchy naturally leads to induction of the syntax of LOGO with its implicit default values and enablement sequences. Therefore we begin with a theory of the child's learning of the taxonomy. We present the three-step model shown in Figure 7.6 so as to specify what might be important in LOGO learning and how the learning might be ordered.

```
--------------------------------------------------------------
STEP 1 COMMANDS
F     R
STEP 1 SYNTAX
SEPARATE SINGLE COMMANDS
--------------------------------------------------------------
STEP 2
F <------>B        R <------> L
STEP 2 SYNTAX
RT 90 FD 15 IS NOT THE SAME AS FD 15 RT 90
--------------------------------------------------------------
STEP 3
RT 90 FD 15 = LT 270  FD 15= LT 90 BK 15 = RT 270 BK 15
STEP 3 SYNTAX
RECOGNITION OF DEFAULT VALUES
MULTIPLE WAYS OF ACHIEVING SAME ENDS
--------------------------------------------------------------
```

FIGURE 7.6.   The proposed developmental progression

The Three-Step Sequence

Step 1: Any conceptual hierarchy lends itself to a developmental model of differentiation and integration. Our view of differentiation is borrowed from Piaget's (1980) discussions of equilibration and from an early version of Eve Clark's (1973) theory of semantic development. Thus initially a restricted range of dimensions will be sampled; within each dimension one pole will be favored. We speculate on which dimensions and poles will have greater salience.

The first step involves learning to differentiate commands. When first encountering the turtle, the child is attracted by its dynamic properties because of their direct analogue in actual body movements. However, the child does not begin with all of the movement commands and their relationships. Rather, the child has a single global concept, turtle, defined in terms of undifferentiated movement. Once the turtle's trail begins to fill the space, the child quickly grasps the distinction between the cursor and the line it produces, a distinction between agent and object. But turtles move to different locales, and so the child must begin to differentiate movement commands from one another.

Asymmetry appears at this point. Distance will have priority over direction because if the child writes only a distance command without stipulating a direction, the turtle leaves a trail. A direction command by itself only produces a rotation of the turtle, a movement that must be seen as it is happening. Moreover, for young children, a directional command is confusing because of their incomplete mastery of right and left and the need to judge right and left from the turtle's perspective. Within distance commands, there is also asymmetry. Forward has priority over back, in part because conceptually and spatially, the nose favors a forward trajectory. Additionally, children usually change their locations by moving forward. Thus the child has an idea of movement, but defines movement as forward. The child has an idea of line but merely as a product of forward movement. Limitations on travel in one direction (forward) quickly lead the child to differentiate angular directions. Within directional commands, right is favored over left. This pattern of differentiation means that cursor movements now consist of forward progress and right turns. In summary, the child initially will produce more distance than direction commands and will use distance commands more efficiently. Additionally, there will be a bias toward right and forward commands, but the child conceptualizes these as two separate commands strung together haphazardly.

Differentiation of back and left prompt further progress. The impetus for differentiation is practical; if the child wishes to go 15° to the left, it is cumbersome to rotate 345° to the right. Properties of the space along with problems confronted while maneuvering in it lead the child to use less-preferred commands. Once these commands are identified, the child is ready to move to step 2, in which the nature of command relations and the logic of enablement orders are discovered.

Step 2: The differentiation of four commands creates a need for syntax. At first, the child knows that some combination of forward and right will move the turtle, but has yet to realize the enablement structure in which one order produces an outcome different from the other. The child simply has a set of four strings: right alone, forward alone, right and then forward, and forward and then right. The child recognizes the results of single strings without yet grasping the fundamental enablement relationship that produces a different outcome for each combination.

In step 2, the child is able to synthesize the fragments into what Piaget would call an operative hierarchy, in which the dimensions are organized and syntactic principles are constructed. Several kinds of experience with real-world movement and drawing may prompt the child to construct this taxonomy of relational terms. The use of LOGO commands may also provoke direct experiences of inverse functions. Any right move can be reversed by an appropriate move to the left. Any forward move can be reversed by a move back. These relations permit self-correction and flexibility, especially when combined with state commands that produce erasure. Lower levels of the command hierarchy are related not just because they are different descriptions of distances and directions but also because, within each branch, commands are inversely related to one another.

Several important consequences result from understanding relations among commands. The child can now explore all combinations of the four quantitative commands and learn their graphic consequences. The child understands why right and forward is not the same as forward and right. Thus the child understands the logic of the enablement structure and can marshall a variety of commands to produce a desired design such as the one shown in Figure 7.7. At this point there will be very few violations of syntax, and movements of the turtle will be used intentionally to produce planned configurations. One indicator of intentional control is the appearance of efficient repairs of mistakes.

FIGURE 7.7.   A LOGO design

Step 3:   The realization that left-right and forward-back are inverse relations leads to the third step in the learning sequence. Step 3 involves a progressive reinterpretation of relations among upper branches in the hierarchy. Children discover the relation between angles and distances. Back is equivalent to a 180° turn followed by a forward, hence it can turn a left into a right turn. Thus, there can be as many as four ways to reach the same target and many more ways to draw the same two-legged figure. The remarkable power of the microworld is that spatial properties of the system encourage differentiation of its conceptual properties. Thus the child will show flexible strategies for achieving a goal.

Three sets of powerful ideas are inherent in the semantics and syntax of primitive LOGO commands: ideas about Newtonian space, ideas about syntax derived from the preconditions for drawing, and ideas about semantic relations that promote increasing flexibility and more avenues for self-correction. Spatial attributes are discerned in the first step. Relations and syntax emerge in the second. Notions of paraphrase, or combinatorial flexibility, and further hierarchic integration appear in the third. Clearly, these ideas are not unique to LOGO. Descriptions of the discovery of flexibility and combinatorial properties abound in Piaget's theory. In a highly motivating setting, LOGO provides a constrained microworld in which classical problems central to congitive and linguistic development can be studied. Thus it is possible to ask how the child's knowledge of the real spatial environment and of natural language structure affects the acquisition of LOGO concepts, to examine how the latter are acquired, and, eventually, to determine whether learning in a microworld affects spatial and linguistic understanding in the real world.

SOME SUPPORTIVE FINDINGS

The Kindergarten Study

Our theory of how children construct the LOGO infrastructure was inspired by our observations of 20 kindergarten children attending the University of Maryland's Center for Young Children. These children were exposed to a curriculum designed by June Wright, director of the Computer Discovery Project. The children were taught a version of Instant LOGO in which each press of "F" and "B" moved the turtle 10 steps, whereas each press of "R" or "L" turned the turtle 15°. Before working with the turtle, they spent five weeks in the classroom learning how to make a computer-driven robot move and playing games emphasizing similar movements of their own bodies. Thus even before they entered the microworld, they encountered a series of spatial experiences that may have prepared them for LOGO learning. In the first 30 minutes of individualized instruction using the turtle, the children were encouraged to explore the four position commands, and in the second 20 minutes state commands were introduced.

In order to tap what the children were learning, a battery of three tasks was administered after 30 and 50 minutes of instruction. The test battery, which focused mainly on mastery of the position commands and syntactic-sequential relations, was based on our analysis of the LOGO infrastructure. In the AIM task, the children were asked to move the turtle from the center of the monitor to different target positions on the periphery in the fewest number of moves. The problems were designed so that the best solution required different combinations of the four basic movement commands in a single enablement sequence. We were interested in three issues: (a) the nature of command biases, (b) the incidence of corrective strategies, and (c) the degree to which children used either optimally efficient combinations of direction and turn commands, or less efficient but formally equivalent combinations. Thus the AIM task examined children's mastery of single enablement sequences in which only direction and distance need be considered. In presenting this task, the turtle was described as a rocket ship. A line, described as a space station, was presented some 70 steps from the center of the screen at some angular rotation. The children were asked to pilot the rocket ship to the space station as efficiently as possible, because the ship was low on fuel. In the first assessment, the rocket-turtle was at the home position, midscreen and pointed up. The targets could be reached optimally with turns of 45° right, 90° right, back and 90°, and 45° to the left. The same turns were optimal in probe 2, but the turtle was now rotated off home. Figure 7.8 illustrates the task.

The REPRODUCE task required the child to copy a two-legged figure from one monitor to another one, placing it in the same quadrant and orientation with the same angular separation between the legs as the model. In probe 1, the four

FIGURE 7.8.   The AIM task

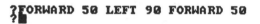

FIGURE 7.9.   Two examples of the REPRODUCE task

figures represented 90° and 45° angles appearing in the second, third, and fourth quadrants of the monitor screen. In probe 2, figures with 45° and 135° angles appeared in the first, second, and fourth quadrants. After drawing the four figures in each set, the children directed the experimenter in the reproduction of a fifth figure, identical to the third figure in the series. Differences in the accuracy of these two figures was considered a measure of the discrepancy between children's intuitive grasp of the LOGO command structure and their ability to communicate explicitly their understanding. Two sample figures are shown in Figure 7.9. Whereas the AIM task assessed children's control over single enablement sequences, the REPRODUCE task called for accurate reproductions of figures requiring two enablement sequences. In both tasks, it was possible to examine the child's fluency with the four distance and directional commands.

In the COMPLETE task, the child was given a line stem and asked to make it into an easy or hard figure. This probe provided us with some information about the child's theory of programming. Several models of programming were assessed, but we only cite the two that enter into later discussions. In the first model, the child views LOGO as actions on a keyboard; hard figures call for more keystrokes than easy figures. In the second model, the child distinguishes between easy and hard figures according to the type of commands used rather than the numerosity of keystrokes. Children generate the hard figure by changing command types through adding, deleting, or substituting commands. This model assesses a perspective typical of step 3 in our developmental progression, that is, children's views of LOGO as a flexible system in which how an effect is obtained is as interesting as whether it is obtained. The COMPLETE task also lends itself to assessment of biases (a behavior typical of step 1 in development), therefore permitting some aspects of mastery assessed in AIM and REPRODUCE to be assessed here as well.

We will tap data from these tasks to illustrate our developmental theory of LOGO learning. We do so with some cautionary notes, First, our tasks mostly tap the learning of position commands. Second, because these children experienced a supportive curriculum designed to facilitate mastery of LOGO entry conditions, they may be more sophisticated than children who enter LOGO without such preparation (Cuneo, 1985). Third, they worked with Instant LOGO, which required minimal quantitative concepts to define distance and direction.

Perhaps because of the simplicity of Instant LOGO and the spatial experience the children had prior to working with it, they were remarkably skilled in the LOGO tasks we designed for them. On the two AIM probes, targets were eventually hit on 96% and 98% of the trials. On the first probe, the target was hit with one combination of directional distance commands on 71% of the trials, and on the second probe, this figure increased to 89%. On the first REPRODUCE task, children made reasonably accurate reproductions of two-legged figures, although some erred on the angels and quadrant relations.

Because the tasks were simple and the children had learned so rapidly, we have data relevant to all three of the steps we have proposed: (a) asymmetry: restriction and bias in use of commands, (b) repairs: corrections of a false move with its opposite, and (c) the use of combinatorial properties of the system. There is also evidence that practical control was followed by reflective control over the semantic and syntactic structure.

Evidence of Asymmetry (Step 1)

Omission of Commands. We have characterized the initial stage of learning in terms of specific asymmetries, favoring forward and right commands over back and left commands. Because the children were so proficient, one might expect little evidence of response bias. Yet when we looked at the 20 children separately for each AIM probe, some children omitted certain commands. On the first probe, 15% omitted back and another 5% omitted left. None omitted forward or right. The most dramatic difference occurred on the second task where the rotation of the turtle from home position posed a more demanding problem of perspective taking. Then 45% of the children did not use a back command on the AIM task, and an additional 15% omitted both back and left. One child omitted forward. Data from the REPRODUCE task show an identical pattern.

Disproportionate Use of Commands.   Another index of asymmetry is disproportionate use of commands. Table 7.1 contains data on the first directional move to an AIM target displaced to the left or the right. Entries in the table compare the child's move in relation to the direction of the target. Although the majority of children type a command in the appropriate direction of target displacement, there is a greater tendency to go in the opposite direction for left than right displacements; 33% of initial moves go right for left targets but only 8% go left for right targets.

TABLE 7.1
First Directional Move on the Aim Task
(Percentage of Responses)

Target Direction	Move Direction	Probe 1	Probe 2
Right	Right	98	86
Right	Left	2	14
Left	Right	28	35
Left	Left	72	65

TABLE 7.2
Percentage of Usage of Each Command
for Different Aim Targets

Target	Optimal Move	Command Usage			
		Left	Right	Forward	Back
Left	LT + FD	31 (50)	16 (0)	45 (50)	8 (0)
Right	RT + FD	4 (0)	40 (50)	48 (50)	8 (0)
Back	BK	14 (0)	23 (0)	33 (0)	30 (100)
Total		16 (22)	28 (22)	45 (44)	11 (11)

Note: Figures in parentheses are expected percentages if optimal moves are employed.

Table 7.2 summarizes the AIM data across items for every command prior to reaching a target, for items where the direction of the target is to the left, right, forward, or behind the cursor. When targets are to the left of the cursor, the optimal-move sequence is left and forward, and so you would expect 50% of the commands to be left commands and none to be right commands. Rather than none, 16% of the moves are right commands. In contrast, when the target is to the right, only 4% of the commands are to the left. Right is preferred. But the most striking contrasts appear when the optimal move is back. When the target is behind the cursor, there are as many forward commands (usually combined with a directional rotation) as back, but when the target is displaced to the right or left, backward commands are relatively rare. Again the bias is to use a forward move.

There are comparable data from the REPRODUCE task. When the first leg of the figure to be reproduced can be created by just a forward move, 95% of the responses begin with just a forward move. When the first leg can be created by a single back command, that command is used only 35% of the time. When the creation of the first leg necessitates a right turn combined with a forward move, 93% of the protocols show that combination. But when the required combination is left and forward, a left occurs as the first move in only 79% of the protocols.

Definition of Hard Commands. The most persuasive support for the existence of asymmetry comes from children's own judgments of difficulty. As in the previous analyses, when the children are asked to make easy and hard figures, there are fewer uses of back and left commands than forward and right commands. Moreover only the back command is used differentially; more frequently in the hard than in the easy figure. The use of left is also more prevalent in hard than easy tasks on the first probe, but that bias disappears by the second probe. These data appear in Table 7.3.

TABLE 7.3
Percentage of Children Using
Each Command on the Complete Task

Time:	Probe		Probe 2	
Task:	Easy	Hard	Easy	Hard
Command				
Forward	100	100	95	95
Right	65	75	68	68
Back	40	75	40	63
Left	50	70	47	37

Repairs (Step 2)

Efficient correction of errors can be taken as an index of intentional control over the relational system (step 2). We saw evidence of repair behavior. On the initial

AIM probe, where the children were more likely to make errors that needed correction, 60% of the children used a back to undo a forward move or to correct an overshoot of the target. It is interesting that not all the children who used the back command for correction used it on AIM items that called for a back movement. Three patterns occurred with equal frequency. In one, children used back only to reach a target behind the turtle. In another, children used back only to cancel a forward move, and in the third, children used both functions of back. Children who recognized both functions understood the inverse relation between differentiated forward and back commands.

Combinatorial Flexibility (Step 3)

In the second probe session, several children redefined the AIM task in a way that shows evidence of the flexible spatial system characteristic of step 3. They decided to hit each station going backwards. Perhaps because these children could move forward easily, they may have become bored with doing things straightforwardly and added challenge by playing with the system.

Yet another bit of evidence for the development of an integrated system was the response to the COMPLETE task. For instance, in probe 1, 95% of the children marked the distinction between hard and easy figures by giving *more* commands, but only 55% of the children marked the distinction by using *different* commands. By probe 2, these percentages were reversed; now only 55% used keystroke numerosity to mark the distinction between hard and easy figures, whereas 90% changed the kinds of commands they were using. Table 7.4 shows the proportion of children who changed commands to distinguish easy from hard. These data indicate substantial growth in children's combinatorial flexibility, that is, in their ability to modify their choice of commands in response to different descriptions of task difficulty.

TABLE 7.4
Number and Type of Command Changes (Addition, Deletion, Both)
Between Easy–Hard Conditions: Percentage of Children

	Number of Changes				Type of Change		
	0	*1*	*2*	*3+*	*Add*	*Delete*	*Both*
Probe 1	45	40	15	0	91	27	18
Probe 2	10	50	30	10	89	39	28

Reflective Control

Performance on our test battery indicates that these children were able to use the basic LOGO commands to solve a variety of graphic problems. However, there is a difference between solving a problem and being able to represent the solution well enough to communicate it to someone else. In probe 1, children showed little evidence of reflective control, that is, they were able to differen- tiate their perspective from the turtle's but they could not differentiate their perspective from that of another person. Figures in the REPRODUCE task were more accurate when the children directly controlled the keyboard than when the keyboard was controlled by someone else. Telling was much harder than doing.

The children's ability to represent and communicate how to make an accurate reproduction improved by probe 2, and the difference between doing and telling was no longer significant. Perhaps telling someone else how to tell the turtle what to do requires a deeper level of understanding than our three steps describe.

DISCUSSION OF THE ACQUISITION MODEL

Our aim is not to demonstrate that some children quickly learn a simplified LOGO system, even though our five-year olds performed far better than we expected. We certainly make no claims about the profundity of their learning. It is not clear whether these children who used LOGO so flexibly and creatively were conscious of the cognitive principles they used so well, even though even- tually they were able to represent their knowledge well enough to communicate correct command sequences to someone else. Neither do we want to claim the discovery of an invariant sequence of acquisition immediately applicable to all LOGO tasks. Our model is not yet sufficiently refined to warrant testing its sequential properties.

Nor have we determined whether these children could use these principles in other tasks. At present, we are not claiming that the child at step 3 in our system has a general representation of Newtonian properties of space. Even our most insightful children may not have understood the general workings of the graphic system or how the principles of self-correction and combinatorial equivalence apply to other domains. We doubt whether an hour of computer learning (or any learning for that matter) can produce profound change in a cognitive system, although it is entirely possible that as a child faces repeated LOGO challenges, some principled understanding may arise.

Rather, we wish to claim that it is possible to build a model of the structure of LOGO acquisition that will have much in common with other models of cogni- tive development. We presented this model so as to specify what might be important in LOGO learning, to describe how this learning might be ordered, and to identify attributes of performance relevant to the model. We have argued that a model of differentiation and integration can fit the initial stages of LOGO learning, and that the Piagetian emphasis on the discovery of flexible means to achieve a desired goal provides a way of looking at changes in the child's mas- tery of LOGO commands.

What we have said about quantitative branches of the taxonomic tree can also be said about its qualitative branches. The difference is that the child may at first assume that appearance is an unchangeable property of the system, learning only gradually that state properties too can be changed. Generally, the child will prefer the state that initially defines the default condition, such as pen down, or the usual pen color, white. Differentiation of pen up from pen down, pen colors from one another, and pen color from background color occurs first. At the second step, the child may discover the complementary relations implied by the contrast between pen up/pen down, or hide turtle/show turtle. The relation between pen color and background color may be the hardest to establish, because these dimensions have a somewhat different structure. Unlike the simple on-off contrast of pen up/pen down or hide turtle/show turtle, color takes several values. The relation between pen color and background color is therefore a relation between interdependent dimensions rather than a relation between poles of independent dimensions. You cannot see a red line on a red surface.

This insight may lead to the third step in the developmental sequence, constructing relations between different qualitative states that enable their flexible use. You can draw an invisible line in two ways: by using the pen up command, or by making the line color the same as the background color. As important, you can erase an unwanted line by retracing it in the color of the background. Thus quantitative and qualitative branches of the hierarchy converge, because the reversibility of distance commands gains new meaning when combined with the interrelation of foreground-background color. These interdependencies, all of which affect the appearance of the cursor and the line, but not the movement of the cursor, may help the child understand the difference between movement variables and state variables while discerning the organizational principles needed to generate a command sequence that will achieve a desired goal.

Alternative models not inspired by Piagetian theory might work better to describe the child's LOGO progress. For example, models of the development of expertise also incorporate the flexibility and interconnectedness we have described (e.g., Chi, Glaser, & Rees, 1982). Whatever the source, a conceptual model of LOGO acquisition will serve several ends. For one, we will be in a better position to speculate on who might be ready to learn LOGO and how preparation for learning might occur. For another, we might be able to anticipate where problems in understanding are likely to arise, and to design and sequence entry experiences to overcome these problems. Finally, with a sound grasp of the acquisition process, we may be in a position to identify those areas in which transfer might occur from one aspect of LOGO to another aspect, from LOGO to other cognitive problems, or from LOGO to natural spatial and linguistic environments.

WHY INVESTIGATE LOGO?

Why devote so much effort to a microanalysis of a particular computer language, especially when more traditional tasks may address similar issues? Why would anyone be interested in teaching LOGO, in studying the process of learning, and in evaluating the outcome? Our answers to these questions touch matters of content, change, and personal investment.

In content, the ideas LOGO expresses are pervasive in descriptions of cognitive development. We examined children's grasp of spatial properties portrayed in LOGO as Newtonian vectors. Elsewhere we expand this analysis, examining evidence that the spatial system expressed in LOGO and mastered by these young children fits what could be described mathematically as a polar coordinate system (Campbell, Fein, Scholnick, Schwartz, & Frank, 1986). Because LOGO illustrates consequential spatial and mathematical concepts, it is as at least as legitimate a place to study cognition as the Three Mountains or Conservation tasks, if not more. Often these singular tasks form the basis of sophisticated computational theories of various cognitive processes. When these task theories are developed, we then find to our chagrin that various theories are unrelated to one another. But given the singularity of the task domain, how could there be any other outcome? Why should a theory of such a narrow domain have more than a limited bearing on broader, generic cognitive issues?

Future studies of LOGO might examine ideas that have not received much attention from developmental psychologists. Consider, for example, the idea of a procedure, whereby a set of ordered enablement sequences defines a new semantic term capable of being iterated or combined with other terms to produce new graphic objects. Procedural modularization leads to the distinction between repetition and recursion, other ideas of great significance in contemporary mathematical thought. How children acquire these ideas is as interesting as their acquisition of those ideas typically studied by developmental psychologists.

As for change, using LOGO is a dynamic process permitting cumulative and saltatory changes in level of understanding. Like our more traditional tasks, LOGO is a limited domain. But unlike these tasks, the domain is rich and interactive. Therefore the learner has the opportunity to explore the implications of each level of understanding and to restructure that level. Perhaps the spatial and linguistic structure of LOGO is particularly conducive to restructuring and reflection. Consequently the developmental psychologist has a rare opportunity to examine the growth and transformation of knowledge. For example, during the initial phase of acquisition, children could reproduce figures but they could not instruct others to reproduce the designs. When children in our sample gained a flexible and integrated understanding of LOGO's conceptual domain, they gained the kind of control needed to communicate problem solutions to someone else. In examining acquisition of LOGO, we could pinpoint when the gap between mastering a strategy and communicating it was bridged. In more traditional tasks, the time lag between acquisition of a strategy and the ability to communciate that knowledge may be exaggerated by children's lack of a precise, consistent language encompassing both doing and telling.

As for personal investment, one advantage of LOGO is that concepts and skills are instrumental in achieving a goal that children find intriguing. It is difficult to imagine children voluntarily exposing themselves to our traditional tasks, trying to figure out why a given response is inadequate, or using what they understand about a task to design interesting variations for us to study. Our traditional tasks present children with domains that are so highly reduced, so specialized, and so fragmented that the value of the task derives primarily from the theoretical perspective of the developmental psychologist, rather than its appeal to the children who participate in our studies.

Why devote so much attention to LOGO rather than to other programming languages? We know of no other programming language accessible to children so young. Unlike most computer activities designed for children of this age, LOGO expresses a general model of thinking, applied in LOGO graphics to spatial representation. In our view, LOGO is a model of thinking in which categorical and procedural knowledge are intertwined. How to draw a line involves knowing that lines can go in different directions; knowing how to draw a line in different directions involves knowing that commands from different parts of the structure can be combined in different ways. Because LOGO prompts self-reflection and analysis in the child, it provides us a means of examining how the child's analysis shapes the course of acquisition. Whereas some information processing approaches aim at devising a computer model of the acquisition of knowledge, LOGO provides an opportunity to study children's acquisition and application of a sophisticated computer model.

LOGO is more a process than a computer-assisted learning activity. Acquisition and application occur concurrently and reciprocally over time as a result of repeated encounters. Because we know the structure that is to be acquired, we can monitor the process, experiment with different instructional formats, and, perhaps, tease apart invariant relations from those that are context-dependent, or reflect individual learning styles. More powerful, and even friendlier, programming languages in the future may exemplify different models of thinking, may draw upon different aspects of knowledge, and may be equally motivating and accessible to young children. These languages will also merit our attention because they, too, will offer an opportunity to study children interacting with general models of human intelligence.

Although we have focused on one programming language and one view of how it might be acquired by young children, our central message is that LOGO offers an opportunity to study the process of learning rather than the product of learning; to study the intricate bridging structures that permit the transport of old knowledge to yield new configurations, and perhaps, with a theory of transport in hand, to study how these new configurations are transported to yet other new and different problems. The title of this volume is *Constructivism in the Computer Age*. Perhaps we can use acquisition of LOGO to examine problems in the construction of knowledge that have so far eluded us.

ACKNOWLEDGMENTS

Portions of this paper were presented by Ellin Kofsky Scholnick and Greta G. Fein at the Fifteenth Annual Symposium of the Jean Piaget Society, Philadelphia, PA., June, 1985. The authors want to thank June Wright, Director of the Computer Discovery Project at the Center for Young Children, University of Maryland, for her insight, assistance, and support during this research. Funds for data analysis were provided by the Computer Science Center, University of Maryland, College Park.

REFERENCES

Campbell, P. F., Fein, G. G., Scholnick, E. K., Schwartz, S. S. & Frank, R. E. (1985). *Spatial perspectives on LOGO learning*. Paper presented at the meeting of the American Educational Research Association, Chicago, IL.

Campbell, P. F., Fein, G. G., Scholnick, E. K., Schwartz, S. S., & Frank, R. E. (1986). Initial mastery of the syntax and semantics of LOGO positioning commands. *The Journal of Educational Computing Research, 2*, 357–377.

Chi, M. T. H., Glaser, R., & Rees, E. (1982). Expertise in problem solving. In R. J. Sternberg (Ed.), *Advances in the psychology of human intelligence* (Vol. 1, pp. 7–75). Hillsdale, NJ: Lawrence Erlbaum Associates.

Clark, E. V. (1973). What's in a word? On the child's acquisition of semantics in his first language. In T. E. Moore (Ed.), *Cognitive development and the acquisition of language* (pp. 65–110). New York: Academic Press.

Cuneo, D. D. (1985). *Young children and Turtle Graphics programming: Understanding the turtle commands*. Paper presented at the meeting of the Society for Research in Child Development, Toronto, Canada.

Papert, S. (1980). *Mindstorms: Children, computers, and powerful ideas*. New York: Basic Books.

Piaget, J. (1980). *Experiments in contradiction*. Chicago, IL: University of Chicago Press.

Sternberg, R. J. (1984). Mechanisms of cognitive development: A componential approach. In R. J. Sternberg (Ed.), *Mechanisms of cognitive development* (pp. 163–186). New York: Freeman.

Webb, N. (1984). Microcomputer learning in small groups. *Journal of Educational Psychology. 76*, 1076–1088.

Winston, P. H. (1977). *Artificial intelligence*. Reading, MA: Addison-Wesley.

Chapter 8

Artistic Imagination During the "Latency Period," Revealed Through Computer Graphics

Joachim F. Wohlwill
Pennsylvania State University

INTRODUCTION

As microcomputers increasingly pervade the classroom, suggestions for their use and software for instructional purposes proliferate. For the most part these applications consist of tutorials, in which the computer is used to drill the pupil in this or that subject matter, much as the teaching machines of old, although the more imaginative kinds of software do provide for a degree of interactiveness rarely encountered in the era of programmed instruction. There is, furthermore, an increasing volume of research on children's use of and response to computers, to which the present volume, as some others that have preceded it (e.g., Klein, 1985a), gives effective testimony. In particular, computer graphics—which is the focus of the work being reported in this chapter has been applied by Klein (1985b), Forman (1985a, 1985b), and a few others, to determine its value in furthering children's comprehension of spatial relations, and their symbolic development, as well as their response to computer-generated feedback. Less attention, however, has been given to applications of the computer for more open-ended responses, where the *child* chooses and defines the problem.

The Computer as a Facilitator of Artistic Creativity

Such an open-ended approach is, of course, of the essence in any type of creative endeavor, particularly in the realm of the arts. Even though applications of microcomputers in this domain are still infrequent, at least with school-age children, they appear promising for several reasons. First, the microcomputer permits us to capture the creative process through which children construct some particular product of their own imagination, and to undertake a fine-grained analysis of the steps of that process, at least when it takes the form of constructing a program. In a more substantive sense, furthermore, this medium may shed light on the basis for the alleged decline in children's imaginative and artistic productivity during the school years (e.g., Gardner & Winner, 1982; Lowenfeld & Brittain, 1970) and perhaps offer a strategy to counteract it.

The microcomputer is ideally suited to this purpose, because the medium of computer graphics allows the child to create a design that is more determinate in its form than a product achieved through freehand drawing. This greater determinacy results from the fact that the design is created by writing a *program,* typically made up of an extended series of statements. This process thus involves breaking the component parts of a design up into a set of elements (e.g., points and lines, or, in the case of the language LOGO, segments of lines and angles). This is a medium, then, that is marked by a rather high degree of structure. And therein may lie its potential appeal for children during the years of elementary school, in comparison with the relatively unstructured forms of ordinary art work.

To put it in more psychological terms, the process of programming a design provides children with the sort of cognitive control over their creations, with ample opportunity for elaboration and change, that may be optimally adapted to the mentality of children caught in the throes of "concrete operational" thought—children, that is, who value reasoning and problem solving more than affect-driven forms of self-expression.

The Relationship Between Cognitive Development and Artistic Creativity

Here we come up against the issue of the relation between cognitive development, in the sense in which it has been studied by Piaget and his legion of followers, and the development of creative thought and activity. To date, this question has been considered primarily in terms of the relationship between convergent and divergent thinking, as part of the issue of the independence, or lack of it, between creativity and intelligence (Kogan, 1983l; Wallach, 1970). As such, it has been treated predominantly from a differential rather than a developmental perspective. The question of the developmental course of creative activity and its relationship to cognitive development has, with very few exceptions, been left untouched.

Certainly this has been true of Piagetian theory. Piaget's model of cognitive development is that of the epistemologist concerned with the formation of logical, mathematical, and scientific thought. Thus activities that do not originate from a question or problem given the child by some outsider, and that are not directed at arriving at the correct answer or solution, are problematical for Piaget's system, just as was true of the category of behavior termed *play.* In his treatment of that topic, Piaget (1962) saw play as involving a mix between processes of accommodation and assimilation that was greatly biased toward the latter, in contrast to functional intelligence, which for Piaget entails an effective balance between the two. This appeared to be a sufficient reason for Piaget to consider play as being at best of peripheral relevance for the child's cognitive development, and indeed he never returned to the topic of play subsequently.

Under the circumstances it is hardly surprising that Piaget did not show any more interest in artistic development (see his brief statement concerning children's drawings, Piaget, 1953), or in creativity more generally. And the same has been true of his followers, including those like Papert (1980) who have in fact gone considerably beyond the epistemological realm, as in the latter's work with the computer language LOGO, which might seem to invite attention to the creative process.

The Gardner-Winner View

We are thus left with a condition marked by a sort of vacuum as regards the relation between cognitive development and the development of creative thought and activity—a vacuum that has, however, been filled more recently by the work of Gardner, Winner, and their colleagues of "Project Zero." Yet their analysis of the situation (Gardner, 1973, 1980; Gardner & Winner, 1982; Winner, 1983— see Wohlwill, 1985, for a critical review) suggests an *inverse* relationship, rather than a positive one. For these writers postulate that both the interest in and the creativity of children's artistic production (notably in the realm of drawing and of the visual arts more generally) undergoes a marked decline between the preschool period and the years of middle childhood. Their explanation for this decline is not very extensively argued or elaborated, but appears to be grounded in a belief that during this period, in which children's intellectual powers are becoming more fully developed, they are progressively more dominated by a concern for reality and objectivity, and are assimilating the conventions of their sociocultural setting. As a result, the drawings that they do produce are marked by a heightened realism and literalism, at the expense of freeness of expression and flow of imagination (see in particular Gardner, 1980).[1] This view is buttressed by reference to the artistic work during the years of childhood of some individuals who were destined to become major creative artists—notably Paul Klee and, rather less convincingly, Pablo Picasso.

This conception parallels closely the views of leading figures in art education such as Lowenfeld (Lowenfeld & Brittain, 1970), Lark-Horovitz (Lark-Horovitz, Lewis, & Luca, 1967), and Read (1958); in some of these writings it is reinforced by reference to the child's growing reliance on language as the

---

[1] It seems plausible to argue Gardner's view is influenced by Piaget's analysis of concrete-operational development during this period in terms of proper balance between accommodation and assimilation, as noted above. In any event, it is noteworthy that the notion of a decline in artistic creativity through the middle-childhood years is contained in Piaget's (1953) own very brief note concerning this topic.

primary vehicle for expression, which is thought to inhibit further the school-age child's creativity in a graphic medium. Yet this negative assessment of children's creative bent during this period has not been without its critics. Foremost among these have been the Wilsons (Wilson & Wilson, 1977, 1982), who argue that the supposed decline in the quality of children's art during the school years is more a product of cultural and societal influences than an intrinsic consequence of some deep-rooted developmental process. Duncum (1986), endorsing these objections, has most recently subjected the thesis of Gardner and Winner to further searching examination, noting that the postulated decline is not in fact central to their overall account of artistic development. That account lays primary stress on the acquisition of the conventions of our culture as regards the graphic representation of reality, but does not in itself demand a view of artistic creativity as declining from the preschool period. Duncum is inclined to attribute Gardner's belief in this regard rather to a romanticized, Dionysian view of artistic expression that reflects his values concerning the nature of creativity more than any verifiable characteristics of the developing child.

Further, going beyond Gardner's position, Duncum drew attention to a particular problem with statements concerning the supposed decline in artistic production with age, namely the diversity of criteria utilized by different writers on this topic. He noted in addition the lack of agreement with regard to the precise age period at which this process of decline is thought to reach its nadir, according to the various statements that postulate a U-shaped function characterizing development in this realm. (This postulate becomes even more problematical when the postulated increasing phase suggested at adolescence is restricted to individual cases of artistic talent—e.g., Gardner & Winner, 1982.)

Duncum's critique is all the more cogent, given that empirical evidence supporting the supposed decline in artistic creativity during the school age period—much less the U-shaped function between early childhood and adolescence—is rather harder to come by than the frequent assertions about it might lead one to expect. As Duncum pointed out, the sources on which Gardner (1973) has relied in this regard offer far from convincing support for any decline. Indeed, in terms of sheer ability—for example, in dealing with spatial relations, compositional features such as grouping, and the like—there is rather evidence of a monotonic increase with age between early and later childhood (e.g., Lark-Horovitz & Norton, 1959), just as one might expect. Where decline occurs, it is, interestingly enough, more typically found in adolescence (e.g., Kerr, 1937). The suggestion of a decline in artistic *creativity*, on the other hand, is supported mainly by a few highly impressionistic, nonquantitative accounts of children's drawings (e.g., Malrieu, 1950). The Malrieu paper provided almost the sole support for assertions to the same effect by Boutonier (1953), whose work in turn was relied on heavily by Lark-Horovitz, Lewis, and Luca (1967), in their account of the decline of artistic creativity during the childhood years. It is apparent that much more systematic data, based on reasonable criteria of imagination and creativity, are needed to settle this question. These are simply not available at present.

An Alternative Interpretation

But let us suppose, if only as devil's advocates, that the decline during the school-age period is in fact a real one, in regard to both the child's interest and the creativity manifested in its work, as Gardner and Winner believe to be the case. The interpretation of the basis for any such decline remains very much in question.

Note to begin with that interest and ability, or quality of output, need not of course change correlatively. For a variety of reasons, including the downplaying and devaluing of drawing and similar activity during the school years conveyed by parents, teachers, and peers, interest in the creation of art may well undergo a real decline. If so, it should prove possible to reawaken that interest through some new set of rewards or the introduction of a new motivating agent (e.g., the computer).

The alleged decline in creativity attributed to children during this period, and the supposed growing tendency for realistic, conventional form and content, at the expense of the spontaneity and expressiveness that characterized the pre-school child's art, may be a relatively superficial consequence of the changing external demands and rewards emanating from the society, or may reflect a more fundamental developmental process, as Gardner and Winner (1982) seem to believe. But, still on the assumption that we are talking about a real, documentable phenomenon, it seems possible to suggest yet a different explanation for it.

Rather than postulating some intrinsic drop in artistic creativity, a different way of looking at the problem lays greater stress on the role of the medium typically involved in children's artistic productions. Specifically, we may suggest that the problem for the school-age child invited to make a drawing, for example, with crayons and paper, is the lack of control that the child can exert over his or her productions in this medium. The medium may be rather too amorphous, too deficient in its determinate responsiveness to the child's intentions, to be optimally suited for the child at this age level (e.g., during the latter half of the period of elementary school), at which children demand a greater degree of cognitive control over their activities.

Note that in this view there is nothing intrinsically incompatible between artistic creativity and a mode of approach to art that emphasizes operative over figural intelligence (to use Piaget's terms—cf. Piaget, 1970), or that entails a dominance of intuitive as opposed to analytic processes (cf. Edwards', 1979, speculative distinction between these processes, in terms of left- versus right-hemisphere functioning). This distinction should, in any case, not be overdrawn; there is reason to believe that we are generally dealing with a mix of these two contrasting processes in any cognitively involving performance. Thus, for many mathematicians, graphic representation and visualization play a major role; conversely, the realm of music gives testimony to the place of controlled planning and thought in an artistic medium. What I should like to propose, however, is that for a typical 10- to 12-year old child the discreteness, precision, and clear definition that characterizes the digitally structured process of computer programming may be most congenial; such a child tends, by the same token, to be uncomfortable with an analogically structured form of artistic expression such as freehand drawing.

I am postulating that one readily applicable approach attuned to children at this age is to ask them to create designs in the form of mosaics. I am not aware of any systematic research on children's artistic creations in this type of medium, in spite of its likely appeal to them. But the programming of computer graphics, particularly in the language BASIC, entails a process not unlike the creation of a mosaic design, because it entails dividing the computer screen into an N x N matrix, and filling in a subset of cells of that matrix with a particular color, chosen by the computer-graphics artist, so as to create patterns of dots and lines. (The lines consist of a set of cells arranged in a straight line, with a thickness equivalent to the size of the cell.)

It should be noted that this feature of programmed computer graphics is a double-edged sword, because it imposes a relatively severe degree of discreteness on the design, the degree depending on the coarseness of the grain of the matrix utilized. In the work to be described presently, which involved low-resolution BASIC entailing a 40 x 40 matrix of cells, this represented a particularly notable limitation, which became apparent whenever a child attempted to construct a curvilinear pattern, or even a diagonal line (which exhibited a pronounced stair-step character). But this restriction appeared to be a price worth paying for the sake of the cognitive control that such a programming approach provided the child.

In this respect, the use of the "Turtle-geometry" making use of the computer language LOGO, specifically developed for use with children (Lawler, 1985; Papert, 1980), might seem preferable, because it involves a much more fine-grained matrix, 280 x 240 units in size. In practice, however, it turns out not to be very readily applicable to the generation of complex visual patterns or designs, particularly of a representational kind, that are not composed of combinations of relatively simple shapes and configurations. The main difficulty in using LOGO for more elaborate designs is the problem of exerting proper control over angular values and extents when constructing a shape through an unbroken succession of lines. The proper placement of the discrete elements of a design turns out to demand a rather refined sense of spatial relations, which many if not most children at this age level have difficulty in mastering.[2] For instance, the figure equivalent to the "Tree" prototype in Figure 8.1 (page 138)

---

[2]This writer attempted to obtain designs from fourth- and fifth-grade children with a knowledge of LOGO, but the results were meager indeed, reflecting the difficulties the children encountered in controlling the medium for this purpose. A more potentially interesting use of LOGO in the realm of the arts may be that of the study of children's aesthetic sensitivity. This is because LOGO allows one readily to create a family of relatively intricate prototype configurations, such as spirals, by systematically varying one or more parameters of the core program, resulting in highly salient concomitant variations in the visual appeal of the figure created.

requires the following program in LOGO:

```
TO TREE: RT 90, FD 3; LT 90, FD 30; RT 90, FD 18; LT 90, FD 1; REPEAT 2
[RT 90 FD 3 LT 90 FD 1]; RT 90 FD 3; BK 3 LT 90 FD 3; REPEAT 5 [LT 90 FD 3
RT 90 FD 3]; RT 90 FD 5; REPEAT 2 [LT 90 FD 2 RT 90 FD 5], BK 3 LT 90 FD 3;
REPEAT 4 [LT 90 FD 5 RT 90 FD 2]; LT 90 FD 2; RT 90 FD 3; LT 90 FD 1; RT 90
FD 2 BK 5; REPEAT 5 [RT 90 BK 5 LT 90 BK 2]; BK 1 LT 90 FD 2 BK 5; RT 90 BK
2 LT 90 BK 5; RT 90 BK 2; LT 90 BK 5 RT 180; REPEAT 5 [BK 3 LT 90 BK 3 RT
90] BK 3 FD 5 RT 90 FD 1]; REPEAT 3 [LT 90 FD 3; RT 90 FD 1]; LT 90 FD 3; RT
        90 FD 2; LT 90 FD 14; RT 90 FD 30; RT 90 FD 1; RT 90 FD 30; END.
```

In contrast, the BASIC program involved in generating the TREE prototype in Figure 8.1 consists of the following:

```
(10) VLIN 13, 23 AT 11; (20) HLIN 10, 12 AT 14; (30)HLIN 9, 13 AT 15;
(40) HLIN 10, 12 AT 16; (50) HLIN 9, 13 AT 17; (60) HLIN 9, 13 AT 17;
        (70) HLIN 8, 14 AT 18 (80) VLIN 19, 23 AT 11.
```

Note that the difference between these two programs does not reside only in the much shorter length of the latter, which is in part a consequence of the lesser degree of detail that low-resolution graphics permits; thus the BASIC prototype in Figure 8.1 is in fact less complex than the equivalent LOGO one. The more critical difference is that the programming itself is considerably simplified under BASIC, as each line of the program stands autonomously, and can be corrected or modified independently of the rest of the program. In contrast, under LOGO, a change at any point, because it affects the position and direction of the cursor, will result in a change in all subsequent portions of the figure—LOGO, in other words, is a highly sequential process, requiring therefore a much superior level of control over the spatial relations entailed in the drawing of the figure.

In brief, then, let us entertain the possibility that programming a design does provide children with the kind of cognitive control over their work that they find most congenial during the later years of elementary school, that is, during the "latency period" that is supposed to characterize that phase of their artistic development. This served as the guiding premise that underlay a previous study by this writer, with the collaboration of Suzanne Wills (Wohlwill & Wills, in press). Basically descriptive in nature, it involved an analysis of a set of 61 designs created in low-resolution graphics, programmed in BASIC on an Apple IIe computer, by children between the ages of 10 and 12 who had had a month-long unit of instruction in BASIC in their school. In this study we correlated a variety of objective measures and ratings obtained from these designs with information concerning the children's experience with computers and their interests in relevant subjects and activities, obtained through interviews with both parents and the children themselves.

The study showed convincingly that many children at this age level are able to make use of this medium to generate designs characterized by imaginativeness and indeed flights of fancy, belying the lack of creativity and the penchant for highly conventional, literal productions considered typical of children during this period. This ability was unrelated, not only to these children's interest or involvement in art or music, but even to their experience with computers; more relevant to the quality of children's computer graphics productions was an interest in activities of a problem-solving or a cognitive nature, such as puzzles and games like chess or checkers. Incidental evidence from the protocols of the children's verbalizations and behavior while developing their programs similarly indicated that for many of these children a problem-solving mental set dominated their approach to this task.

A COMPARATIVE STUDY
OF PROGRAMMING VERSUS FREEHAND DRAWING

Because of its descriptive nature, the previous study did not establish definitively that programming was, in fact, the factor responsible for the overall rather positive results obtained. A second study (to be reported in greater detail in a forthcoming publication) was designed to explore this question further, by comparing the computer-graphics designs generated by children between grades 4 and 6 via programming in BASIC with those obtained through a freehand drawing procedure. For the latter we employed the KOALA PAD (a touch tablet on which line patterns can be traced with a stylus and directly transferred to the monitor screen). According to the premise that children during this age period require cognitive control for optimal graphics performance, the BASIC-derived designs should prove superior to those obtained via the KOALA PAD, especially in the case of sixth-grade children.[3]

Note that the emphasis here is on *cognitive* control, a term meant to refer to the role of deliberate, logically guided planning in the execution of a design. Making a drawing with the KOALA PAD is certainly not devoid of some form of control—no more than the execution of an ordinary freehand drawing via pencil

[3]The author is pleased to acknowledge the splendid cooperation in the conduct of this study of the Melrose, Massachusetts Schools, and in particular of the assistant superintendent of that school system, as well as the principal, Mr. Robert Fancy, and the several teachers from whose classes the participating children were drawn. The attitude of support and encouragement all of them provided turned the conduct of this study into an exceptionally rewarding and enjoyable experience for us.

and paper. The KOALA PAD perhaps provides some additional measure of control, because it takes but a simple choice on the menu provided as part of the software to fill a given area in a particular color, to make changes in the background color, and so forth. (See the fuller description of this device below.) But there remains a fundamental difference between it and the programmed drawings via BASIC, which require the child to decide in a precise, mathematically defined fashion on the exact placement of each component of the drawing, that is, points and vertical and horizontal lines.

I will limit myself here to a brief account of this study. In contrast to the earlier study, where the children were free to invent any design whatever—thus creating some difficulties in making comparisons among them—we decided in the present study to impose some constraints on the content of the designs. Thus we specified one of two types of content to which the design was to conform, and provided the children with a "prototype" at the outset that we believed would assist them in generating feasible designs. This constraint was employed in part for pragmatic reasons: The children in this study had no prior experience in computer graphics, and the time we had available to teach them was very limited. Thus we felt that some increase in the structuredness of the task would be beneficial in helping the children with the process of initiating a design. In addition, this procedure ensured a greater degree of comparability in the resulting designs, to facilitate comparison between the designs constructed in BASIC and via the KOALA PAD, as well as among several different types of prototypes employed.

For the programmed designs the children participated in two sessions of approximately 90 minutes each. In the first, two children at a time were taught the elements of low-resolution computer graphics in BASIC, that is, the use of HLIN and VLIN commands to draw horizontal and vertical lines, and of PLOT to fill in individual cells of the 40 x 40 matrix on the computer screen. (Specifically, we instructed them in drawing a cross, via a horizontal line, HLIN 10, 20 at 20, and a vertical line, VLIN 15, 25 at 15. This was followed by a program for a square (HLIN 25, 33 at 30; VLIN 30, 38 at 25; VLIN 30, 38 at 33; HLIN 25, 33 at 38, and the insertion of a dot in the middle of the square PLOT 29, 34). As part of the same instruction, the children were taught commands for changing colors, for running the program, for switching from the GRAPHICS mode back to the TEXT mode, and for listing a program. At the end of this instructional session, each child was given an opportunity to sketch out a simple design, such as a house, or one or more of his or her initials, on the screen via BASIC.[4]

The second session, which generally followed the first after an interval of one or two days, was devoted to the child's programming a design of his or her own

---

[4]The author wishes to note that the KOALA PAD assembly was developed by the State College, Pennsylvania, public schools, although the school system did not participate in this research.

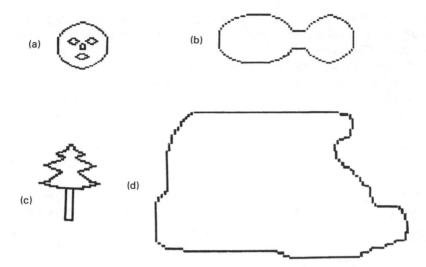

FIGURE 8.1 The four prototypes employed in Studies 1, 2, and 3, shown in the versions used with the KOALA PAD in Study 2. (See Figure 8.2 for the equivalents constructed in BASIC, shown in the context of illustrative designs created by the children in Study 1.) Top left: HEAD; top right: FIGURE; bottom left: TREE; bottom right: POND. (The two top prototypes were used with the "Creature" instruction; the two bottom ones with the "Place in the Country" instruction.

The second session, which generally followed the first after an interval of one or two days, was devoted to the child's programming a design of his or her own choosing, with the constraint that it represent either a "creature" (one that might actually exist, or one that was purely make-believe), or "some place in the country" (either some real place, or a make-believe place). Each child was presented with one of four prototypes (see Figure 8.1), two of which (a and b in Figure 8.1) were associated with the "creature" instruction, whereas the other two (c and d in Figure 8.1) were presented with the "place in the country" instruction. These prototypes appeared on the screen at the start of the session, as well as on a sheet of graph paper divided up into a 40 x 40 matrix, with rows and columns numbered from 0 to 39. This sheet served as a template on which the children sketched out their ideas for their designs before they started programming. (The children were given as much time as they wished to work on their designs. In some cases they worked for two or even three sessions, separated by midmorning or lunch recesses.)

The procedure for the designs constructed via the KOALA PAD was more streamlined, as a relatively brief familiarization and practice period with this tool appeared to suffice, and children were generally able to complete their drawing within a single session. This device consists of a small, square touch tablet on which the child traces a line pattern with a stylus that is directly transferred onto the screen. Additional features, available for selection from a menu, included choice of color both of line and of background, as well as different background textures, and a "filler" option that allowed the child to fill in any closed figure with a color of his or her choosing.

The prototypes used with the BASIC designs were employed for the KOALA PAD drawings as well. Only the children from Grades 4 and 6 were asked to construct KOALA PAD drawings. (Those from Grade 5 were asked instead to create a second design in BASIC, but under somewhat different programming conditions. This variable will not be considered further in the present abbreviated report of this study.)

Three sets of measures were utilized to assess the children's productions. The first set consisted of objective measures based on the programs generated by the child and on objectively measurable characteristics of the designs. The second consisted of ratings of the designs made by independent judges. The third involved process-type measures derived from the program for each design as it developed, and from a comparison between the design and the original sketch drawn by the child. Only the second one of these was applicable to the KOALA PAD designs, and it was relied on for the test of the primary hypotheses involving comparisons between the designs produced via programming in BASIC and those constructed via the KOALA PAD.

The rating scales tapped the following aspects of the designs:

1. *Mastery.* This was a composite of seven-point scales, directed at the child's mastery of the medium, in regard to particular attributes of the graphic designs, that is, use of color, use of straight lines, of diagonals in particular, fluidity of line, sense of proportion (in terms of sizes of major components), use of the total space of the screen, and overall coherence.
2. *Complexity.* This rating was based on a single seven-point scale, which was explicated to the raters as referring to the number and diversity of the separable elements of the design, and the elaboration of internal detail within an element.
3. *Imaginativeness.* This was a composite of two seven-point ratings, one directed at the imagination or creativity invested in the design as such, and the other at the inventiveness displayed in the use made of the prototype.
4. *Pleasingness.* This was a single seven-point rating of the aesthetic appeal or pleasingness of the design.

To determine the reliability of the four rating scales, the designs were rated independently by three judges (graduate students with some experience in children's art). The 12 pairwise interrater correlations ranged from .74 to .43, with a median of .57. The values used in the analyses were obtained by averaging the three sets of ratings from the different judges. (Where one pair of judges exhibited substantially higher agreement than the other two pairs, the average of the first pair only was taken.)

It should be noted that this set of four ratings is far from representing four orthogonal dimensions. The intercorrelations among them are in fact substantial, ranging from .48 between mastery and complexity to .84 between imaginativeness and pleasingness. (The median for the six correlations is .68). There thus appears to be a generalized component of quality or value underlying these ratings. This is unlikely to be an artifact of a direct contamination of the ratings of a given design on one scale by previous ratings of the same design on other scales, because the raters rated all designs on each scale before proceeding to the ratings for the next scale. The pattern of positive intercorrelations that resulted presumably reflects the fact that, at least in the minds of our raters, these dimensions were not mutually independent.

Before considering the main results obtained, a brief examination of two sets of four illustrative designs, each created by the children in the two phases of the study (BASIC and KOALA PAD), should be helpful. Each set consists of one design for each of the four prototypes. These are reproduced in Figures 8.2 and 8.3. They were chosen as designs typical of those developed from each prototype. To start with the BASIC designs (Figure 8.2), note the profusion of limbs or the like, in the form of linear protuberances, in Figure 8.2a; the symmetrization of the figure prototype in Figure 8.2b, the proliferation of small unconnected elements surrounding the Tree prototype in Figure 8.2c, and the elaborate filling in of the area around the Pond in Figure 8.2d. (It should be noted that this design was somewhat exceptional, relative to most of the designs obtained with this prototype, in that the child placed a boat within the perimeter of the prototype, whereas most of the children left the inside of the "pond" empty.)

The KOALA PAD designs, shown in Figure 8.3, are clearly much more similar to freehand drawings that might be created with crayon and paper. As a group, these designs also appeared to be more varied in content and format than was the case for the BASIC-derived designs; thus the ones reproduced here are perhaps not as fully representative of the range of designs obtained for each prototype as the examples shown in Figure 8.2. Again the relative lack of proficiency in the use of BASIC needs to be taken into account in interpreting this difference in the variability of the two sets.

Turning to the results obtained for the ratings, we might note to begin with that the Head and Figure prototypes yielded designs that were scored higher than the other two in imaginativeness, in the case of the BASIC designs, and in pleasingness, in the case of the KOALA PAD designs. These differences appear to be a joint function of the differences in instructions, and in the prototypes themselves. We might note further that sex differences were absent in both sets of ratings, whereas age differences were limited to but a single variable, that of complexity, and were significant only for the KOALA PAD. Nor did experience with computers bear any consistent relationship to these designs. A partial exception to this statement is provided by the extent to which the child used

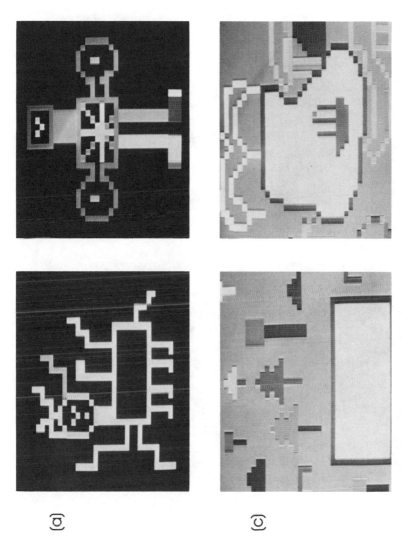

FIGURE 8.2. Examples of the children's designs, employing BASIC programming. Each design uses one of the four prototypes (see Figure 8.1). (a) Smorgasbord (sic), (b) Nicholas, (c) Colorful Forest, (d) Fun Park. The originals are in color.

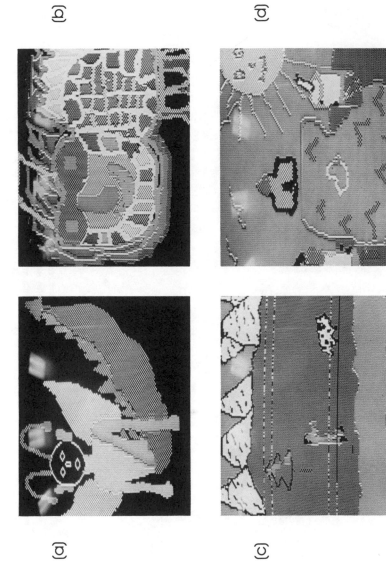

FIGURE 8.3.   Examples of the children's designs, employing the KOALA PAD software. Each design uses one of the four prototypes (see Figure 8.1). (a) Holly, (b) Dracula's Pet (c) untitled, (d) Matthew's Picture. The originals are in color.

computers outside of the home, but that variable correlated *negatively* with several of the ratings—perhaps because it reflected primarily the use of computers for playing video games.

Of greater interest for our purposes are the *differences* between the two types of designs, those created via BASIC, as opposed to those done on the KOALA PAD, because they bear on the role attributed to the programming factor, according to our hypothesis. Because the children in grades 4 and 6 created designs of both types (although working from different prototypes and content instructions), it was possible to make a direct test to determine whether the ratings of the KOALA PAD designs, notably with regard to creativity, differed for the two modes. It should be noted that the research design is deficient for these comparisons, because only 25 children, unevenly distributed across the prototypes, were available for them, and because the order of presentation was counterbalanced only for the grade 4 children. Although the results need to be interpreted with caution, they suggest that there was no across-the-board superiority of the BASIC designs. Only two of the four ratings yielded significant differences between the modes. Of these, one, mastery, favored BASIC, whereas the other, complexity, favored the KOALA PAD. More important, on the most directly pertinent measure, that of imaginativeness, there were *no* significant differences between the two media.

In order to provide some indication of the overall values of these ratings, and the range of these values, the means and standard deviations for them are given in Table 8.1. They indicate that they average ratings were mildly positive for the KOALA pictures, for all but the composite mastery scale, whereas for the BASIC designs the means are concentrated around the neutral point, the mastery scale again deviating somewhat from that common trend. The operation of the well-known central tendency effects to which such ratings are prone needs to be borne in mind in interpreting this outcome.

TABLE 8.1
**Means and Standard Deviations for Ratings
of BASIC and KOALA PAD Designs**

	Means		Standard Deviations	
Ratings	*BASIC*	*KOALA PAD*	*BASIC*	*KOALA PAD*
Mastery (Composite)	4.58*	3.75	1.12	1.14
Complexity	3.79*	4.72	1.28	1.06
Imaginativeness	4.04	4.46	1.06	1.02
Pleasingness	3.86	4.27	1.21	1.16

*Difference significant ($p < .01$)

QUALITATIVE ASPECTS
OF THE CHILDREN'S PERFORMANCE

The children's verbalizations made during the course of their development of the program when working on the BASIC designs, although not as yet subjected to systematic analysis, are enlightening in two respects. First, the verbalizations are preponderantly of a self-monitoring type, addressed to the children themselves rather than to the experimenter, and reflect their reactions to the *result* of a particular addition to their developing program. Comments such as: "Something went wrong there." "That line isn't supposed to be there." "Oh, I messed up." "How did that happen?" "That's where I wanted it." "It looks stupid." "That's right—I know it's right, but it's not the way I imagined it would be." abound. Furthermore, remarks like: "That's right." "It's a little, little tree; it doesn't even look like it." "Right. Geez, that's long!" suggest a predominantly objective, or quasi-objective mental set, even when they were evaluative in tone. Purely subjective, affectively toned expressions, for example: "I like it the way it is." "Yeah! I like it!" "I don't like that green." "Heh, that looks pretty!" were much less frequent. (The two modes are brought interestingly into juxtaposition in the comment: "Hmmm . . . I like it. But this goes up too far!") The impression conveyed by these comments is of an orientation directed primarily at the problem-solving facet of this activity and at the "correctness" (or lack of it) of the child's design, rather than at its aesthetic aspect, or at affectively toned responses to the designs.

The general style of approach manifested by the children during the course of their work on these designs, and individual differences in their approach, merit additional discussion. In the previous investigation (Wohlwill & Wills, in press) we uncovered two contrasting orientations on the part of the child in creating a design in BASIC. One orientation focused the child primarily on the problem-solving aspect of the program itself, the design once completed being evaluated in terms of the success, or lack of it, encountered in solving the problem the child had set for himself or herself. The other approach was focused on the aesthetic quality and meaning of the end-product to the child; the program was thus a means to an end, and less intrinsically interesting to the child. These orientations represent two ideal types, however, into which individual children fitted to varying degrees; varying combinations of these two emphases were encountered in the work of each child. Heuristically the contrast serves a useful purpose nonetheless.

For a variety of reasons the present investigation gave less clear-cut evidence of these two opposing orientations. The lesser degree of experience of these children with BASIC, and particularly with its application to computer graphics, is undoubtedly a primary factor in our failure to validate them. The children were predominantly preoccupied with mastering the fundamentals of the programming, and especially of the spatial coordinate system in which they had to work. Some of the children encountered repeated frustration with the problem of placing the correct values in the functions for HLIN, VLIN, and PLOT; they frequently reversed the horizontal and vertical components, necessitating corrections and constant checks of the program against the evolving design. Thus, if many of the designs still manifest a creditable degree of inventiveness, this represents a tribute to the children's persistence in overcoming obstacles, and in approximating the originally planned end product. Concern for either sophisticated problem-solving or sensitivity to the niceties of design in an aesthetic sense necessarily receded into the background.

The case of a fifth-grader, Steve (a fictitious name), illustrates the points just made. He started out with a remarkably vague and incomplete sketch, which provided a highly inadequate frame of reference for the development of his program. Further, he experienced great difficulty in working out the spatial positions of the elements of his original design, resulting in frequent expressions of disappointment, and even discouragement, at the way the work was progressing. Lack of fit between program and sketch was met as often as not by erasures of relevant portions of the sketch, and substitutions of new ideas, requiring further modifications of the program; alternatively, on occasion Steve simply ignored the sketch. His work is interlaced with such comments as: "Wow, that's way off! I want to get rid of this!" "This is going to be tiring." "Too far down!" "Oh, I wanted it at the bottom!"—but also: "Now let's get to work." "That's just perfect." "I guess we can keep it unusual." After one and one-quarter hours of work on the program, when he had to suspend work on it, he had only completed a limited portion of the design he had planned. Nevertheless, he returned three days later with renewed energy, and in spite of similar continued mistakes and expressions of frustration at them, he produced a design that was rated near the top for imaginativeness and complexity. It is exceptional, among those based on the Figure prototype Figure 8.1b, for going well beyond the immediate confines of the area around the prototype, creating a complex pattern through the addition of elements separated from the prototype. The design is further notable for its arresting title: "Frankenstein's Dream of Hawaii"— probably more of an expression of his ambivalence about the end product, in the light of the pains and effort it caused him, than a reference to a concrete image represented in the design.

Steve's experience was admittedly extreme, but it bears witness to the persistence and self-imposed effort that some children lavished on this work, in spite of patently deficient tools, to realize their intended design.

CONCLUSIONS

The results of the research reported here, however serious its methodological limitations, have a variety of implications for the character of children's artistic imagination during the school-age period, and the place of computer graphics in developing that imagination.

First of all, we find some confirmation of the potential fruitfulness of our chosen approach, that is, through the use of programming in BASIC, for eliciting imaginative productions from school-age children, that the previous investigation (Wohlwill & Wills, in press) had documented. Although a direct comparison between the sets of programmed designs from the two investigations is not feasible, given the very different conditions under which they were produced, those obtained in the present research appeared as a group to be more constrained in their imaginativeness and inventiveness, and certainly less effective in the use made of the medium (e.g., in terms of the complexity of the designs, the use of color and of the available area of the screen, etc.). There are various explanations for this difference, the most plausible one being the much lesser degree of mastery over the programming language achieved by the children in the present investigation. The role played by the prototypes presented to the children, and the constraints these exerted on them (along with the instructions to create either a "creature" or a "place in the country"), must similarly be taken into account.

Of more central relevance to the major aim of our research is the comparison between the designs produced via BASIC versus those obtained with the KOALA PAD. That comparison, however vitiated by the limitations of the design, provides little overall support for the proposition that served as the guiding assumption for this research. Our original hypothesis placed primary emphasis on the role of programming in stimulating imaginative expression on the part of school-age children, based on the control it provided the child in the execution of a visual design. The finding that the designs produced on the KOALA PAD were as a group at least the equal of those constructed via BASIC as regards imaginativeness and aesthetic pleasingness, as well as complexity, is clearly inconsistent with this hypothesis. If this result is taken at face value, one would be led to shift attention to more general aspects of child-computer interaction, including perhaps above all the computer's power to heighten motivation and interest. There may well have been something particularly effective and potent in the sheer vividness and visual impact of the designs that the children were able to generate via the KOALA PAD. That conclusion is borne out by the finding that, when queried at the conclusion of their session with the KOALA PAD, a large majority of the children questioned on this point (15 out of 18) expressed a clear preference for the KOALA PAD over BASIC as a method for creating designs.

Yet, before we abandon the potential value of BASIC (or similar computer-programming languages) for the generation of graphics by school-age children, two points should be borne in mind. First, the children in this investigation working in BASIC were operating at a much lower level of proficiency than that which most of the children in the earlier investigation (Wohlwill & Wills, in press) had attained. In fact, given that circumstance, and the general unpopularity of the method for the children, at least in comparison to the KOALA PAD, as just mentioned, one might argue that one should have expected a significant superiority in the quality of the designs produced by the latter method, rather than the overall equivalence between the two methods actually shown by the ratings. The results might, however, be attributed to the operation of two opposing forces that are counteracting one another in this situation: proficiency in the use of the medium, favoring the KOALA PAD, versus the enhanced degree of cognitive control provided by BASIC. In any event, it is apparent that we are far from having tested the limits of the possibilities of BASIC for generating visual designs. Thus a comparison between BASIC and a system such as the KOALA PAD with children comparable to those used in the original investigation might well provide data more in accordance with our hypothesis.

A second point concerns the developmental side of this question. Because age differences were little in evidence in the research reported here, this aspect has not been stressed. Yet age is undoubtedly a relevant factor: as the children advance in their level of cognitive development, they can be expected to become increasingly attuned to the possibilities provided by BASIC for the elaboration of graphic designs. This should happen, first of all, because the role of cognitive control over the creation of the design should become more pronounced as the child's cognitive level advances, and with the attainment of formal operations in particular. Furthermore, these advances will allow children to master more advanced programming techniques, enabling them to give freer reign to their imagination than was possible for the fourth- and sixth-grade children in this investigation, following the rudimentary training we gave them. For instance, FOR-NEXT and GOTO loops may be used to introduce dynamics and elements of animation into designs (as well as to draw diagonal lines much more economically), thereby extending considerably the possibilities for the children to express their imagination. The designs of several children studied in the earlier investigation, who had just finished either the fifth or sixth grades, and who had learned some of these techniques, give concrete testimony on this point. Yet these procedures are probably learned more effectively by children at the junior high school level. Obviously, only future research can establish the merits of this suggestion.

This brings us back to the central issue of the place of the "digital-intelligence" mode in artistic creativity at this age level, that is, of the controlled, rational, step-by-step approach that goes into writing of a computer-graphics program in BASIC, as opposed to the "analog-intelligence" mode, involving the more intuitive and free-flowing approach that we tend to associate with drawing and artistic creation in a visual medium. To put it succinctly, should we regard the computer, and more particularly the programming of visual designs, as facilitating or as inhibiting the expression of artistic creativity and imagination?

The answer to this question is by no means a simple one, for art is itself far from uniform in regard to the relative roles accorded to the two modes that we have just contrasted. Consider Hofstadter's (1979) provocative analysis of the work of a noted graphic artist, Escher, that of one of the giants of music, J. S. Bach, and that of a major figure from the recent history of mathematics, Goedel, in terms of the use that each made of recursion as a basic device. Here we have examples of visual and musical art that are clearly close to the realm of operative intelligence, and that could, one suspects, be readily simulated, and probably extended, by recourse to computer programming. Just as clearly, the shimmering impressionism of Monet, or Debussy, represents a very different product of the artistic imagination, for which the computer would probably be much of an alien device. There are, in other words, major differences among artists, and among styles of art, precisely as regards the role accorded to processes of analysis and cognitive control—though the latter is surely never entirely absent from any work of art worthy of the name. With the possible exception of such rare special cases as the creation of Coleridge's *The Pleasure Dome of Kubla Khan,* a deliberate suppression of cognitive control, for example, through drugs or hypnosis, is hardly a useful prescription for the creation of works of artistic significance.

This point concerning the diversity of creative art in regard to the relative place of analytic as opposed to intuitive processes appears equally applicable to the more modest accomplishments of the children who participated in our research. As was noted in the brief account of the original study (Wohlwill & Wills, in press), the participating children differed considerably in the mind-set that they brought to their work on the computer, varying from a primary orientation toward the solution of a problem as a cognitive exercise to an opposite one focused on the content and aesthetic qualities of the pictorial end product that they wanted to produce. Although no systematic attempt was made to measure these opposing tendencies, it seemed evident that most children fell somewhere between these two extremes, representing varying mixtures of the two modes. At the same time there is some reason to believe that, once the children had achieved a reasonable level of mastery of the programming involved (i.e., in the original study), programming by computer did serve a facilitative role even for those children operating predominantly in the "analogical," aesthetics-directed mode, providing them with a tool that they may have found is easier to control than the medium of crayon and paper.

In conclusion, then, we may sum up the import of our findings with the following observation. Considered in the aggregate, the graphic designs that the children in both this and the earlier investigation produced, whether through programming in BASIC or direct drawing with the KOALA PAD, are clearly at variance with the generally current view of school-age children as disinterested in artistic expression as well as overly constricted and literal in the rendition of their experiences through graphic media. Even if many of the children we studied may have treated this activity more as a cognitive task than as a vehicle for self-expression, their productions were in many cases notable for much imaginativeness and inventiveness. A more fundamental point, however, is that this fallacious conception of the elementary school years as a sort of latency period with regard to artistic development is predicated on an equally unwarranted view of art as primarily intuitive and opposed to operative thought, and thus incompatible with the mentality of the typical child during this period. We need to recognize the diverse forms that artistic expression can take, and the corresponding differences among children in regard to the kind of balance they achieve between the figurative and the operative, or between the analytical and the intuitive. This remains a central point of debate in aesthetics, to be sure. But it represents an issue of no less importance for both developmental psychologists and art educators to address.

ACKNOWLEDGMENTS

The research presented in this chapter was supported by a grant from the Spencer Foundation. I am pleased to acknowledge the skillful assistance of Margaret C. Clark in the conduct of the major study described, as well as that of Joanne Tosti-Vasey and Judy Hall in the analysis of the data. I am similarly indebted to Suzanne Wills, Peter Pufall, and Lynn Liben for a variety of helpful comments and suggestions given to earlier drafts of this paper, which have benefited it considerably.

REFERENCES

Boutonier, J. (1953). *Les dessins des enfants.* Paris: Editions du Scarabee.
Duncum, P. (1986). Breaking down the alleged "U" curve of artistic development. *Visual Arts Research, 12,* 43–54.
Edwards, B. (1979). *Drawing on the right side of the brain.* Los Angeles, CA: J. P. Tarcher.
Forman, G. (1985a, April). *The child's understanding of record and replay in computer animated graphics.* Paper presented at the annual meeting of the American Educational Research Association, Chicago.
Forman, G. (1985b). The value of kinetic print in computer graphics for young children. In E. L. Klein (Ed.), *Children and computers* (pp. 19–36). San Francisco: Jossey-Bass. (*New Directions for Child Development.* No. 28)
Gardner, H. (1973). *The arts and human development.* New York: John Wiley.
Gardner, H. (1980). *Artful scribbles.* New York: Basic Books.
Gardner, H., & Winner, E. (1982). First intimations of artistry. In S. Strauss (Ed.), *U-shaped behavioral growth* (pp. 147–168). New York: Academic Press.
Hofstadter, D. R. (1979). *Goedel, Escher, Bach: An eternal golden braid,* New York: Basic Books.
Kerr, M. (1937). Child drawings of houses. *British Journal of Medical Psychology, 16.* 206–218.

Klein, E. L. (Ed.). (1985a). *Children and computers*. San Francisco: Jossey-Bass. (*New Directions for Child Development*, No. 28).

Klein, E. L. (1985b). Computer graphics, visual imagery, and spatial thought. In E. Klein (Ed.), *Children and computers* (pp. 19–36). San Francisco, CA: Jossey-Bass. (*New Directions for Child Development*, No. 28).

Kogan, N. (1983). Stylistic variation in childhood and adolescence: Creativity, metaphor, and cognitive styles. In P. H. Mussen (Ed.), *Handbook of child psychology*, (4th ed.): *Vol. 3, Cognitive development* (pp. 630–706). New York: John Wiley.

Lark-Horovitz, B., Lewis, H. P., & Luca, M. (1967). *Understanding children's art for better teaching*. Columbus, OH: Charles E. Merrill.

Lark-Horovitz, B., & Norton, J. (1959). Children's art abilities: Developmental trends of art characteristics. *Child Development, 30,* 433–452.

Lawler, R. W. (1985). *Computer experience and cognitive development: A child's learning in a computer culture*. New York: Halsted Press.

Lowenfeld, V., & Brittain, W. L. (1970). *Creative and mental growth* (5th ed.). New York: Macmillan.

Malrieu, P. (1950). Observations sur quelques dessins libres chez l'enfant. *Journal de Psychology Normale et Pathologique, 42.* 239–244.

Papert, S. (1980). *Mindstorms: Children, computers, and powerful ideas*. New York: Basic Books.

Piaget, J. (1953). Art education and child psychology. In E. Ziegfeld (Ed.), *Education and art.* (pp. 22–23). Paris: UNESCO.

Piaget, J. (1962). *Play, dreams, and imitation in childhood*. New York: Norton.

Piaget, J. (1970). Piaget's theory. In P. H. Mussen (Ed.), *Carmichael's manual of child psychology* (3rd ed., Vol. 1, pp. 703–732). New York: John Wiley.

Read, H. (1958). *Education through art* (3rd ed.). London: Faber & Faber.

Wallach, M. A. (1970). Creativity. In P. H. Mussen (Ed.), *Carmichael's manual of child psychology* (3rd ed., Vol. 1, pp. 1211–1272). New York: John Wiley.

Wilson, B., & Wilson, M. (1977). An iconoclastic view of the imagery sources of young people. *Art Education, 30* (1), 5–11.

Wilson, B., & Wilson, M. (1982). The persistence of the perpendicular principle: Why, when, and where innate factors determine the nature of drawings. *Review of Research in Visual Arts Education, 15.* 1–18.

Winner, E. (1983). *Invented worlds: The psychology of the arts*. Cambridge, MA: Harvard University Press.

Wohlwill, J. F. (1985). The Gardner-Winner view of children's visual-artistic development: Overview, assessment, and critique. *Visual Arts Research, 11.* 1–22.

Wohlwill, J. F., & Wills, S. D. (In press). Programmed paintings: Elementary-school children's computer-generated graphic designs. In F. H. Farley & R. W. Neperud (Eds.), *The Foundations of aesthetics, art, and art education*. New York: Praeger.

Chapter 9

Understanding Individual Differences in the Computer Age

Herbert P. Ginsburg
Teachers College, Columbia University

Susan Zelman
Emmanuel College

This chapter discusses a central but often overlooked aspect of knowledge construction in the computer age: the role of individual differences in computer learning. We show that three types of individual differences—in computer activities, students, and teachers—are crucial for understanding computer learning. The first type involves the nature of the material with which the student is engaged. We must attempt to understand "individual differences" among computer activities. What are the different uses to which the computer (that is, the computer along with the software driving it) can be put? The second type of individual difference involves the student using the computer. What are the different ways in which individuals use a piece of software? Why are some students, but not others, "liberated" by different computer activities? The third type of individual difference involves the nature of the social environment in which computer activities are embedded. How do teachers differ in their approaches to computer education?

We discuss the implications of these individual differences for psychological theory and educational practice. In regard to theory, we argue that the understanding of individual differences in computer use forces psychological theory to deal with issues of performance—questions of personality and motivation. Ironically, the computer, that ultimate intellectual object, highlights the necessity for cognitive developmental theories to deal with nonintellectual factors. In regard to practice, we argue that proper use of the computer in education requires more than a naive faith in technology, more than the magical thinking now current; it requires a psychological approach in which both teachers and students are made sensitive to individual differences in learning. Successful use of personal computers in education depends not only on their "magic"—that is, on our ability to exploit their memory, speed, and intellectual power—but also, and more important, on our understanding of children, teachers, and the nature of education itself.

THE COMPUTER AS CHAMELEON

The computer is not a part of the natural world; it is a human invention. Like other cultural artifacts—for example, the book—it was created to accomplish certain purposes that were otherwise difficult if not impossible to achieve in the natural world. Thus the computer allows for calculations so extensive and rapid that they were previously impossible to complete within the human lifetime. One interesting and essential characteristic of the computer is that it possesses many different types of powers: they are so varied that the computer seems almost to have the character of a chameleon (Sheingold, 1983). Computer software is plastic (Perkins, 1985): It can take different shapes and forms. Of course, the computer is not unique in having a multitude of artificially created powers: Books, too, can be used in different ways, ranging from storage of information to aesthetic expression. But the computer can serve an especially large range of educational functions, some of which books cannot serve. At the younger age levels, these functions include: drill and practice; use of professional tools; exploring microworlds; and, curiously enough, introspection. After presenting a brief overview of current computer practice in the schools, we describe these individual differences in computer functions and conclude with some comments on the relations between technological invention and educational practice.

The Current Reality

On the surface, the computer revolution seems to be thriving. Over the past several years, interest in the educational use of computers for little children has increased dramatically: The majority of school districts now possesses microcomputers (Becker, 1983) and are scrambling to buy more; teachers take summer courses in the educational use of computers; parents are concerned about whether their children are being properly prepared in this area; computer camps are springing up, often appearing on the TV news; new graduate degree programs in computers and education are being developed at our universities; computer clubs are formed by local practitioners; and parent groups in affluent areas are donating computers to the schools.

There is also a somewhat hidden side that contrasts with the official optimism and public excitement: Poor school districts find it hard to get computers, so that we are developing yet another class distinction in education; local teachers start software companies to get rich quick; and even some nursery schools are getting into the act by offering computer curricula that are claimed to be essential for later educational success. The actual use of computers in most schools is minimal: in a typical school, there are only two or three computers for the first six grades; there is one specialist (perhaps the special education teacher, or the librarian, or the math teacher) and one classroom teacher trained in the use of computers; there are only a few software packages available for classroom use; and each *class* gets to use the computers only several hours a week, which means that at best each *child* may use the computer some 5 to 10 minutes a week on the average. And perhaps worst of all, teachers often do not know what to do with the computers when they are available: the official line is that computers are a panacea, but some teachers fail to see their value.

There are at least two reactions to this situation. One is optimistic. We can believe that despite the problems described, the extent to which personal computers have assumed an important role in education is remarkable. After all, it was only a few years ago that the Apple IIe was released; and the IBM and Macintosh were introduced even later. Indeed, four or five years ago there was virtually *no* use of personal computers in the schools. Clearly they are beginning to make inroads, and perhaps the serious problems described are only transient growing pains.

The pessimistic view is that computers are on their way to becoming a fad like many others in American education. In introducing computers, educators and psychologists engaged in a kind of magical thinking that promised yet another revolution in the schools. This has not occurred: the actual benefits of computers have been much smaller than anticipated. A similar situation has occurred in the general marketplace. People have begun to realize that they do not need computers in the home for purposes like balancing checkbooks or storing recipes; the result has been a sharp drop in microcomputer sales. Will the overselling of computers lead to a similar demise in educational circles? We hope that this will not occur, because the computer is capable of serving many educational functions, which we now consider.

Drill and Practice

A brief look at computer software catalogues or observation of classrooms reveals that the most frequent use of computers in education involves "drill and practice." Here is an example. In "Math Basketball," the child is given a choice of the arithmetic operations he wants to study and the difficulty level at which practice will be undertaken. The lesson is put in the form of a game, so that he can compete with a friend, doing math as he is "playing basketball." The situation is set up to identify wrong answers and provide correct ones, so that the child is never in the dark as to the existence and identity of right and wrong. In many programs the "reinforcements" are often future-oriented, spectacular, and perhaps amusing. For example, according to a recent software catalogue describing Galaxy Games: "Your students are stranded in deepest space. To get home, they have to dodge black holes, slip through dangerous star fields, and fight off alien Klingons. The only way they can tap the necessary energy and ammunition is by recalling math facts correctly."

Newer versions of drill and practice will be more exciting than the current rather unimaginative forms. As the memory capacity of personal computers increases, drill-and-practice programs may draw on huge data banks of material for their subject matter. And as devices involving speech synthesis and voice recognition are perfected, drill and practice can involve computers talking to students and responding to their vocal commands. We have come a long way from McGuffey's readers!

There are several ways one can look at this. The standard Piagetian argument is that drill and practice leads only to learning in the narrow sense. Drill and practice usually involves merely remembering information (e.g., the names of the states) or practicing algorithmic procedures (e.g., long division) in a clearly structured situation containing predetermined questions and right and wrong answers. Obviously, such "learning in the narrow sense" is not the only kind of learning we wish to promote, although of course it is sometimes necessary. Education should deal with much more than the kinds of specific knowledge and procedures that can be taught through drill and practice. It is hard to see how this technique can foster creative thinking or an attitude of inquiry. Another argument is a moral one: Often drill and practice turns into learning by bribery. This is the ultimate in the television age approach. It is based on the assumption that children have to be bribed, amused, and managed in order to learn. It identifies learning with star wars, with alien invaders, and with the culture of shlock. It perhaps conveys a subtle Madison Avenue message: Why should you learn unless we put on a show for you?

While these criticisms point to some valid issues, we must at the same time recognize that computerized drill and practice (which is essentially a newer version of the teaching machine and its successor, computer assisted instruction [CAI]) can serve some useful functions. Indeed, computerized drill and practice involves several entirely reasonable goals, chief among them individualizing instruction and giving the student a degree of control over the learning process. To a certain degree varying with individual programs, the child can select the lessons to be covered and can review material at will and endlessly, *ad nauseam,* if desired. The computer is very "friendly" or at least tolerant for this purpose. It does not criticize the child but provides nonthreatening feedback concerning the correctness of answers. It may speak to the child, and soon will be able to respond to vocal commands. In principle, then, computer drill and practice could provide an opportunity for efficient learning in the narrow sense. Indeed, Piaget himself (1970) recognized the limited value of this approach when he wrote of the teaching machine: "In cases where it is a matter of acquiring a set body of learning, as in the teaching of languages, the machine does seem to be accepted as of undeniable service, especially as a means of saving time. . . ." although it does fail at the more central goal of education, namely ". . . encouraging the development of inventive and inquisitive minds" (p. 78).

Also, to anticipate a later argument, drill and practice may be particularly useful for certain kinds of students, for example, children who are slow or lacking in confidence. Whereas bright and outgoing children may find drill and practice to be boring, others may see in it at least two useful opportunities: to work alone, at one's own pace, without being hassled by the teacher; to take some degree of control over one's own learning in order to develop small areas of mastery under nonthreatening conditions. For these students, the patient and solitary repetition built into drill and practice may eventually promote competence and build a feeling of confidence.

In brief, even though drill and practice is often used badly, boring many students and conveying false and dangerous messages concerning the nature of learning, this technique has several attractive features, particularly for certain types of students. The power and portability of the new computers and the sophistication of their programming languages provide these students with easy access to a nonthreatening form of the individualized instruction.

Professional Tools

Suppose we begin, as Piaget does, with the belief that all normal children are capable of learning the kind of material taught in elementary schools. How can the personal computer contribute to an environment that can foster their education? The computer can make available to the child powerful, professional tools with which to attack significant problems. One important example is word processing, a tool that was not originally intended as an "educational innovation," but as an efficient device to enable secretaries to transform sloppy writing into a neat form. Soon word processing proved so obviously wonderful and valuable that it was taken over by the people who produced the sloppy writing in the first place (with the result that there may be less of a need for secretaries). Indeed, word processing is now perhaps the most common use of personal computers. Word processing inspires great feelings of affection in writers—even in poets and novelists who are not normally fond of computers—because it allows them to edit text with ease and as frequently as desired without making an illegible mess of the manuscript; to move around chunks of material, trying out a passage first here and then there; to produce neat and even elegant copy; to have their spelling corrected; and even to avoid a good deal of proofreading. Clearly we do not require "research" to teach us that word processing is a magnificent tool for serious writers.

Recognizing its potential for children as well as themselves, educators have developed word processing software for children. The most famous case is Bank Street Writer, a word processing package that is easy to learn, simple, but relatively powerful. The advantage of Bank Street Writer—and of other software that is at least as good—is that it lets the child concentrate on writing as thinking rather than on writing as a mechanical task. One reason children find writing difficult is that they must expend considerable effort on the physical tasks of making neat letters and rewriting material requiring correction. Word processing makes this virtually effortless and allows the child to put most of his or her mental energy instead into *thinking* about what is to be written and how it can be written well. Of course, word processing in itself is not sufficient to teach writing. The child needs above all to read good literature. The child can also benefit from a skilled teacher to encourage the writing and comment on what is produced. Yet word processing does for children exactly what it does for the adult: It provides a powerful tool that permits a focus on the conceptual aspects of writing; it minimizes the need to engage in the traditional occupations of writing as practiced in school, namely the trivia of penmanship, spelling, and copying. Word processing is good for children because it is a real tool, not just something cooked up for school, and can liberate their writing as it does ours. (Similar arguments could be made concerning filing systems, data bases, and computational tools in mathematics.)

Microworlds

Perhaps the most interesting and potentially revolutionary use of computers in schools involves the exploration of "microworlds" developed for educational purposes. These are artificial and self-contained environments for learning; they are generated by computer software, contain their own structure, and afford many opportunities for fruitful intellectual activity.

It is hard to develop microworlds of real educational significance. Successful microworlds seem to have several key features: they are interesting worlds, worth intellectual involvement; they promote a kind of learning by doing, partly by relieving the student of the need to engage in drudgery; they draw on intuitive knowledge; and they may promote certain types of thinking.

Perhaps the first feature of a successful microworld is that it involve a rich underlying structure—that is, a structure worth understanding. The pioneers in this area of work are Papert (1980) and his colleagues, who created the LOGO microworld of "Turtle geometry." This particular microworld involves several "primitives": an object (the "turtle") which can be made to turn in certain directions, move forward or backwards, hide, leave traces of different colors, and the like. Although turtle geometry bears some resemblance to Euclidian geometry, the two are not identical. Yet the apparently simple microworld of turtle geometry contains a good deal of fascinating structure, well worth intensive intellectual effort.

A second feature of a successful microworld is the promotion of a kind of learning by doing. Educational microworlds are intended to offer an alternative to the passive nature of much school learning. Traditional schooling usually involves reading about some topic or listening to someone talk about it. Whereas almost every educator proclaims the value of learning by doing, not much of it occurs in schools at any level. Children are apt to be *told* about a science experiment; they might get to *watch* one; they might possibly *execute* an experiment carefully designed by someone else. But it is unlikely that they will undertake the *exploratory* investigation of some area and then *design and conduct* a series of experiments to resolve issues of interest.

By contrast, computer microworlds have been created to promote a unique form of learning by doing. In a microworld like Turtle geometry, children get deeply involved in activities designed to solve problems that they or teachers may pose. The children are active and learn by doing. Children's explorations of microworlds may encourage them to become "their own epistemologists," and "builders of their own intellectual structures" (Papert, 1980, pp. 5–6). Through the use of microworlds, students may learn facts, but more importantly, they are likely to acquire procedural knowledge ("knowing how rather than knowing that" [Papert, 1980, p. 135]). Further, they are in control of the situation and make important decisions. They try out various constructions, they experiment with geometrical ideas, they see the consequences of their experiments. As Brown (1983, p. 6) expressed it, microworlds ". . . allow students to try out hypotheses, see their entailments, analyze data, find counter-examples to theories, and otherwise perform efficient and effective experiments." The technology is genuinely "inter-active": the student both responds to the computer and makes it respond to him or her.

Active learning of this type is facilitated by an almost unique characteristic of the computer: It relieves the student of much drudgery. There is learning by doing in the sense that the computer does the *doing* so that the student may do the *learning*. In the case of LOGO the student can quickly "draw" hundreds of figures and is not subject to the ordinary constraints of working with paper and pencil. Because the computer is a patient drudge, the student can learn by doing as long as he or she maintains interest in the problem. So the microworld facilitates active learning in a self-contained laboratory in which an unlimited number of experiments can be performed.

A third feature of the microworld is that this kind of learning by doing draws on available informal knowledge. Thus, in Turtle geometry, children use their intuitions concerning movement in space to control the turtle's actions and thereby may eventually achieve an abstract understanding of some key geometric ideas. This stress on informal knowledge as the basis for learning is particularly effective in the case of young children, who often find it difficult to understand formalisms presented in isolation (as unfortunately is often the case in school) but can comprehend them when they can be assimilated into available informal knowledge (a point stressed by both Piaget, 1970, and Vygotsky, 1978).

Fourth, it is claimed that microworlds may also teach thinking. For example, in LOGO the student might learn something about the need and techniques for disconfirming hypotheses. He or she might learn about critical tests that set one hypothesis against another. Papert (1980) in particular has stressed this benefit of his LOGO microworld. At present, the issue is controversial: We do not know how much and what types of thinking can actually be learned in this way. We require a good deal more research to discover whether microworlds can indeed expand the mind in the way Papert suggested.

Finally, there is an obvious limitation on microworlds that bears mention. In the absence of wise adult guidance, free exploration of a rich and potentially stimulating environment may lead only to spinning of the wheels. Teachers are often necessary to guide learning by doing. Brown (1983) has attempted to respond to this need by constructing computer tutors simulating adult guidance. Though useful to a point, computer tutors are far from replacing teachers and probably never will. For one thing, cognitive guidance, done well, is extraordinarily complex and hard to simulate. For another, key aspects of guidance involve offering emotional support, sharing the joy of learning, and empathizing with failure. It is hard to see how the computer tutor can simulate these emotional aspects of adult guidance.

INTROSPECTION

In his pioneering *Mindstorms* (1980), Papert suggested that one major kind of learning that takes place in a microworld environment like Turtle geometry is self-exploration, the acquisition of knowledge concerning one's own learning, a certain type of "metacognition." Such self-knowledge is facilitated by the fact that a microworld like that provided by LOGO forces the student to think in specific ways and to externalize these thought processes. In ordinary problem solving, the student may get away with thinking in a sloppy manner. But, in dealing with a microworld, the student must produce specific and externalized problem-solving routines, or else the computer will not respond. The student must decide, for example, to make the turtle move a certain distance forward and turn a certain degree. And then the student must literally spell out these routines on the screen. Once thinking has been made specific and external, it can be observed. For example, the student observing the consequences of her sloppy programming may realize that her thought lacks the virtues of reflection and attention to detail. The computer forces her to confront and change her cognitive style because procedures are explicit and have concrete effects: To succeed at programming she must pay attention to detail.

Further, the acquisition of such self-knowledge can be facilitated by the structure of the microworld itself. The microworld can be devised so as to store and review the student's attempts at solution. For example, the computer can keep an ongoing diary of the student's learning, "thereby providing the means for him to examine aspects of his own cognition" (Brown, 1983).

Because this work is preliminary, we require research on the role of the computer in introspection. Two issues stand out. First, to what extent can children of different developmental levels engage in and profit from the self-exploration said to be encouraged by work with microworlds? The second issue involves transfer. To what extent does the self-knowledge that may be gained through computer activities transfer to other learning situations?

Summary of Individual Differences in Computer Activities

Computers are in fact seldom used in the elementary schools. The typical student may experience only a few minutes of drill and practice each week. But computers *could* be used more often and for a variety of useful purposes. Drill and practice itself, though often and for good reason maligned as promoting learning in the narrow sense, nevertheless has useful roles to play in assisting certain types of students to achieve mastery under nonthreatening conditions. Computers can also provide students with professional tools genuinely useful for intellectual work. Word processing is a prime example. Perhaps the most innovative use of computers in the elementary classroom is the exploration of specially constructed microworlds. Their aim is to provide an opportunity for the student to engage in a powerful form of learning by doing. Such microworlds may even encourage the student to undertake introspection and acquire self-knowledge.

In the future, we may invent or discover new and sometimes unanticipated educational uses for computers. It is interesting to note that planned inventions may not be employed for the purposes originally intended. Thus, word processing was first designed to facilitate secretaries' work, not to help children learn composition; yet word processing may turn out to be the single most important use of computers in the schools. So we should not necessarily believe computer specialists' inflated claims concerning the potential powers of software or computers: instead we need to examine the actual uses, sometimes unanticipated, to which students put computers in classrooms. We need to take a psychological approach, not a technological one, to the question of individual differences in educational computer activities.

INDIVIDUAL DIFFERENCES IN COMPUTER LEARNERS

We have examined individual differences among computer activities; they can serve many different educational purposes. Now we show that a particular computer activity may be used in different ways by different students. Consider how individual differences in "cognitive style" and motivation affect students' work with computers.

Cognitive Style

Turkle's (1984) informal observations of children using computers show that "different children are touched in remarkably different ways by their experience with the computer" (p. 95) and exhibit different "styles of mastery." In the case of "hard mastery" the individual imposes a preconceived plan on programming activities. The goal is "always getting the computer to realize the plan" (p. 104). By contrast, soft mastery is "more interactive": the individual explores, tries things out, and in a serendipitous fashion discovers the plan as he or she proceeds to interact with the medium. In Turkle's metaphor, hard mastery is a monologue, soft mastery a conversation. Drawing on the insights of Shapiro (1965), Turkle proposed that these styles are extensions of personality into the cognitive realm: ". . . we are the same person whether we are solving an intellectual problem or sorting out a personal difficulty" (p. 107). So we do not all approach even the same piece of software in the same way; we exhibit different styles of mastery reflecting our personalities.

Turkle's work revives in the area of computer activities the old issue of "cognitive style." Although psychologists have long recognized the importance of individual differences in cognitive style, in recent years research in this area has not been especially popular. Investigations of cognitive style have fallen out of favor for at least two reasons. First, Piagetians have concentrated on what are thought to be the universals of cognitive development—the concrete operations and the like—and have tended to slight individual differences within a developmental level (except of course for those involving the age of acquisition of the universals). Second, available measures of cognitive style are unsatisfactory in a variety of ways. The most serious problem is that they tend to trivialize an interesting concept (Zimiles, 1981). Whereas we all know that cognitive style is important in everyday life, there are few if any good ways of measuring individual differences in this area. Fortunately, the zeitgeist is shifting; work like Turkle's, though perhaps suffering from a certain lack of precision and thoroughness in its observational technique, nevertheless points the way towards important issues requiring further investigation and thought. In particular, we need to examine in rich and careful detail how different cognitive styles, conceived of as extensions of the personality, are involved in computer activities, and indeed in all forms of learning.

Motivation

In this section we consider several aspects of motivation. First, we describe the extremes: The computer engages some children, individuals and groups, in an intense form of "involvement," whereas other children display a rigid and un-productive approach to computer activities. The reasons for differences in involvement are not entirely clear. Second, we show how the computer can promote in handicapped children a kind of "intellectual liberation." We conclude by discussing the implications of these phenomena for Piagetian theory.

Involvement.   Informal observations of children in schools, computer camps, and homes show that some children engage in intensive work with computers. Their level of "motivation" is very high. For example, in a computer camp that one of us observed, a 10-year-old decided to develop a program to test knowledge of obscure baseball facts. Who won the third game of the 1947 World's Series? What's the record for the most consecutive games won on the road by an American League team? Trivia like these filled his mind nearly to overflowing and he wished to share this wealth with others. When he started the camp, Albert knew no programming. In the course of a week, he learned enough BASIC to write crude programs to conduct mini-inquisitions on baseball esoterica. Every day, he wrote programs posing new questions; at night, he must have gathered new facts. He did not want to go to lunch or out to play; he wanted to program baseball facts. Albert's case is not atypical. Indeed, some children have been known to lose themselves so completely in computers that they slight their schoolwork, show no interest in sports or other activities usually considered "normal" or even wholesome for children of their age, and in extreme circumstances even grow faint.

A related phenomenon involves the cooperation and hard work displayed by *groups* of children engaged with computers. For example, in the same computer camp, some adolescents chose to engage in programming activities. This often involved using the BASIC or PILOT languages to create interesting graphics in imitation of arcade games. Because this was "camp" and not "school," the adolescents were allowed to work in a group, cooperating in the attempt to solve the programming problems. Under these conditions, they became very task oriented, worked long hours, pooled intellectual resources, discussed the definition of the problem to be solved and possible solutions, and in general operated independently of adults.

Such examples of intense motivation, in either individuals or groups working with computers, are very appealing, particularly because they present a striking contrast with the boredom often prevalent in our schools. But we need to place the observations in proper perspective. First, one should not forget that hard work and dedication are not limited to computers. Some children read books or write or learn about music with as much passion as other children display when working with computers. Second, because research in this area is limited, we do not know how common is the intense motivation involving computers or whether such motivation can be sustained over a long period of time in an educational setting. Presumably further research will shed light on the generality of the phenomenon in question.

Moreover, we know that computers do not motivate all children. Zelman (1985) has observed that some adolescents in an experimental high school did not enjoy programming, did not see the relevance of debugging, and in general wanted nothing to do with computers. The quality of the computer materials and of the instruction given did not seem to be responsible: Many other students in the same classroom were "turned on" by LOGO.

Why do some children become so involved in computer work while others do not? Zelman (1985) used Dweck's (1985) framework to describe different "motivational orientations" in the high school students she observed. According to Dweck's view, some students are "entity theorists" who believe that intelligence is a fixed, global trait that cannot easily be changed through experience. These students are generally less interested in the process of learning than in "looking good" or showing successful overt performance. Other students are "incremental theorists," believing that intelligence is a repertoire of skills that can be improved through effort. These students are generally concerned more with the process of learning than with overt performance. In Zelman's study, students' involvement in programming was related to their motivational orientation. Students holding an incremental theory became deeply involved in learning to program. They were not bothered by their initial poor performance and in fact valued mistakes as informative. By contrast, some entity theorists who held a poor view of their own intelligence doubted from the outset that they could be competent in working with computers. Believing that good programmers are born, not made, they saw initial programming mistakes as indications of low intelligence and were more concerned with avoiding mistakes than with learning to program, which often depends on *finding* mistakes. Hence they chose to work on easy problems and avoided situations that could have resulted both in failure and genuine learning. Though Zelman's research was preliminary and Dweck's distinction between incremental and entity theories is perhaps an oversimplification, the notion of motivational orientations seems to contribute to an explanation of individual differences in computer learning.

Intellectual Liberation.   The computer has also been used to promote intellectual activities in young children suffering from extreme physical and mental handicaps—paraplegic, retarded, autistic, and learning-disabled children. For example, Meyers and Rosegrant (described by Trachtman, 1984) used the computer to help young children experiencing language difficulties. At the beginning of the experiment, many of the children could not speak. "Some of the children don't have the physical control to form words with their mouths; others haven't caught on to the secret of language, the association of sound with meaning" (p. 44). To remedy this situation, the investigator provided the children with a computer-based communication machine—a kind of linguistic prosthesis. This device involved a pressure sensitive panel on which were pictures of common objects and which was connected to a computer. When a picture on the panel was touched with the hand, the computer, "in a low-pitched electronic voice," named the object in the picture, and the child was then given the object named. Under these conditions, many of the handicapped children paid close attention to the linguistic prosthesis, became "alert," and used it to produce various words. And more remarkably, "many children who began to speak through the computer's voice rapidly started speaking themselves" (p. 44).

How general are these remarkable results? Other investigators have made similar observations. For example, Weir reports cases (e.g., Weir & Watt, 1981) in which handicapped children who normally fail in school display remarkable intellectual achievements when they are introduced to LOGO. One of us observed a physically handicapped child, confined to a wheelchair, who came alive intellectually, apparently for the first time, when he was given the opportunity to engage in computer programming.

How can we interpret results like these? According to Meyers, many of the young children with whom she worked began the experiment with feelings of failure:

> They already know they're not talking. They already know that people are disappointed in them. What we can do is immediately give them the ability to talk through the computer. And what happens in many cases is that they start talking with their mouths. At first they thought, "I'm a failure, I can't talk." And all of a sudden they think, "I can." And the words just start to come out. (Trachtman, 1984, p. 48)

Apparently, the young children with whom Meyers and Rosegrant worked began with some knowledge and skills that were not apparent: they had already learned something about language, knew some words, and knew something about what words are for—even if they could not speak. At first, the computer overcame the physical barriers to speech: it let them talk by means of a linguistic prosthesis. It liberated intellectual abilities already present. Once the children were able to use the computer to produce speech—something they could not do before—they felt competent and confident for perhaps the first time. They had a sense of control and accomplishment. Also, the computer gave the handicapped children a way to enlarge on their nascent abilities: they could imitate the computer-synthesized speech and thereby acquire new words. So the computer serves initially as a linguistic prosthesis, an artificial organ of speech. This liberates nascent abilities, inspires confidence, and leads in turn to new learning. Once this process of liberation and learning is under way, the prosthesis itself may in some cases play only a minor role and eventually be abandoned.

According to this interpretation, the computer technology is effective partly because it promotes feelings of efficacy and power. In a good deal of their educational experience, children are passive; they are manipulated and managed by adults. By contrast, in computer work, the child can exert a measure of control and can make the computer do what he or she defines as personally meaningful. The child is the "locus of control," the powerful agent who may even be more skilled at computers than the adult! (The contemporary phenomenon of teen-age programmers who drop out of school to make millions from a cleverly programmed game reinforces the perception of children as potentially more competent than adults in this area.) So some children work very hard at computer activities and display unsuspected abilities because they are in control of a real task, meaningful to them.

Note too that a crucial aspect of the work with the handicapped is a *theory* that motivates the entire enterprise. The theory involves at least the following beliefs: The handicapped child is seen as actively learning about language even if the learning cannot at first be expressed in speech; while suffering from genuine deficits, he nevertheless possesses real intellectual capability that can be expressed and nourished under the proper conditions; he has the capability to learn more and could do so if only he were properly motivated and had an outlet through which to express his learning. These are the beliefs that make the experiment possible.

Perhaps the example of handicapped children learning by computer can serve as a metaphor for education generally. Like the handicapped, poor children, black children, and learning-disabled children possess more knowledge and skill than they are generally given credit for; they are more competent than their typical performance indicates; they can learn more than they usually do. The educational system is unsuccessful in liberating and nourishing their potential, just as it is in the case of the handicapped. The system fails for many reasons; one is that educators often do not believe that the potential exists; they think that the children are deprived or intellectually inadequate—damaged goods. Perhaps inventive use of the computer can help to correct these misconceptions of children and remove the educational handicap.

Conclusion: Individual Differences in Motivation and Cognitive Style Are Crucial for Understanding Computer Learning

We have argued both that computer activities take different forms and that students approach computers in different ways: There are important individual differences in both computer activities and the students learning from them. Students show different styles of mastery, and these cognitive styles are extensions of their personalities. Under favorable conditions, perhaps involving the establishment of feelings of control, some students are "liberated" by computer activities and display often unsuspected intellectual abilities: Thus, children previously mute show that they already know some language and can rapidly learn more. Other students are not motivated by computers and gain as little from them as they do from other aspects of schooling. So observations of computer use once again highlight the role of individual differences in education. In particular, the observations point to the importance of personality and motivational factors in learning from and with computers. One of the remarkable features of computers is their ability to create environments that motivate and liberate some students and serve as a kind of projective test for individual differences in cognitive style among learners.

Of course, virtually identical statements can be made about *any* educational objects or activities. Works of fiction take different forms and so do history lessons. Individuals vary in their approach to Cuisenaire rods and to typewriters. Some students are liberated by conventional educational activities like a book or a lecture; thus Ashton-Warner's (1963) Maori children rapidly learn to read when they are allowed to designate from their own experience the words to be read. Other children deteriorate intellectually in schools. In brief, though computers offer special qualities (just as books do), they are the same as other educational objects in the following respect: They are characterized by individual differences in their functions and elicit individual differences in their users.

Dealing with individual differences is one of the keys to effective education. No doubt competent teaching involves many skills and personal qualities, among them understanding of and feeling for the subject matter, and knowledge of basic intellectual processes shared by virtually all students. But the art of teaching must also be solidly based on an appreciation of individual differences in motivation and cognitive style and on an understanding of how to deal with them. The educator needs to understand why some students show "hard mastery" of programming, and what, if anything, should be done about it; why some students do as poorly with computers as they do with conventional schooling, and how their dormant intellectual abilities can be liberated; and why other students are enthralled by computers, and how that passion can be nurtured. In brief, an effective psychology of education must involve at least two components: One is a theory of how individual differences in motivation and cognitive style affect learning; and a second is techniques for modifying or otherwise dealing with these key individual differences. At the present time, our understanding of both these matters is limited.

How can a Piagetian, constructivist theory contribute to an effective psychology of education? Ginsburg (1981) has argued that though a Piagetian approach has much to offer for understanding education, an appreciation of individual differences has not been its strong point. Piagetian theory has generally been concerned with cognitive universals and with issues of competence. The theory shows that virtually all children possess the intellectual competence necessary for adequate learning of common school subject matter, at least in the elementary grades, if not beyond. The theory also provides a method, the clinical interview, useful for establishing intellectual competence. But Piagetian theory's value in explaining educational phenomena is limited precisely because it is a theory of competence, not performance. The theory deals with what people are capable of doing, not with what they ordinarily do or with the psychological factors, like personality or motivation, that determine what they ordinarily do. Whereas a focus on competence is useful, performance cannot be slighted—at least if the aim is to produce a valuable psychology of education. Yet Piagetian theory is primarily a genetic epistemology and secondarily a psychology. It pays insufficient attention to the effects of personality and motivation on learning. A major reorientation of Piagetian theory is required before it can be relevant for understanding individual differences in education.

Investigations of computer learning can serve a useful role in the reorientation of Piagetian theory. Research focusing on the ways in which students with different cognitive styles interact with varying computer environments may provide useful insights into intellectual performance and hence issues of pedagogy.

THE SOCIAL ENVIRONMENT

In schools, computers are part of a social environment that includes teachers and peers. Although the student may sometimes work relatively independently with the computer, relying little on the teacher's input or on interaction with peers, it is more often the case that the teacher exerts an important influence on the student's computer activities. The teacher may suggest activities to be undertaken, may pose problems to be solved, may offer guidance and assistance, and may evaluate the student's work. We now show that there are important individual differences in the ways teachers influence computer learning.

Individual Differences Among Teachers

Common observation shows that teachers display enormous individual differences in approach and philosophy. How do these differences reveal themselves in computer work? In her preliminary study, Zelman (1985) used Dweck's model of achievement motivation to examine the orientations of teachers using LOGO in the classroom. She found that "entity theorist" teachers (those who believe that intelligence is a fixed trait determining performance) differed in their instructional practices and feedback preferences from "incremental theorist" teachers (those who believe that intelligence and achievement can be improved with effort).

Entity teachers posed problems that could be done quickly, independently, and with immediate success. Entity teachers used published LOGO materials that included worksheets and flash cards. They believed that immediate success experiences were important in motivating students and engaging them in the

LOGO programming process. They felt that it was important to use grades to evaluate student LOGO projects.

By contrast, incremental teachers gave students problems that were difficult and challenging. Rather than using "canned" projects, incremental teachers created activities for students to do or encouraged students to develop projects that might be done in cooperation with peers. Wanting students to learn how to cope with the challenges, frustrations, and ambiguities of the problem-solving process, incremental teachers rewarded students for both successful and unsuccessful efforts: The message was that effort and struggle—not success alone— are key. Incremental teachers intervened only when students were obviously spinning their wheels and did not attempt to exert strong control over the learning process. In brief, teachers' motivational orientations may determine how they approach the teaching of computer activities. Teachers generally instruct with computers in the same manner in which they learn from them.

How easy is it to change teachers' motivational orientations? Recently we conducted miniature "T-groups" with teachers who were attending a workshop on programming in LOGO and using it in the classroom. The teachers had prepared for the workshop by reading Papert's (1980) *Mindstorms* and during the workshop were thoroughly indoctrinated in its philosophy. We observed that although the teachers paid lip service to Papert's approach, many were deeply concerned with maintaining control over their classrooms and evaluating performance in clear-cut ways. Discussions in the group focused on the legitimacy of allowing students to work on different projects and thus learn different things; on the possible disruptive effects of allowing students freedom to determine their learning agenda; and on what they saw as the negative possibility that students might share work with or "steal" ideas form one another. Apparently, participation in the LOGO workshop did little to alter this "entity theory" or authoritarian approach to learning and teaching. We attempted through the T-group to get teachers to examine their own learning processes, but our efforts were tentative and short-lived, so that we do not know how deep-seated in teachers are motivational orientations like these.

For the Future

Obviously, there are important individual differences among teachers. Some differences involve techniques of instruction that may easily be changed if teachers want to change them. But other differences, particularly those involving motivational orientations toward learning and teaching, may be deep-seated and less susceptible to modification. Indeed, some of these differences may be linked in deep ways to personality structure. But our knowledge in this area—as in many involving individual differences—is limited. We need a good deal of research investigating the nature and stability of individual differences in teachers' beliefs and motivational orientations, the ways in which these individual differences affect teaching and learning, and whether and how the individual differences can be modified.

INDIVIDUAL DIFFERENCES ALL AROUND

We have described three types of individual differences—in computer activities, students, and teachers. Obviously, we need to achieve a deeper understanding of all three considered individually. For psychologists, perhaps the most interesting challenge is to investigate intellectual *performance*—the ways in which motivational and personality factors are involved in intellectual development and learning.

We also need to tackle an even more difficult problem, but one central to a useful psychology of education—namely, the ways in which the three types of individual difference interact. Indeed, this may be considered a genuinely ecological problem, involving as it does the individual's learning in an environment comprising educational materials varying in function and teachers varying in orientation. How does a student with a given cognitive style engage in a particular type of computer activity under the guidance of a teacher with a particular orientation to learning? It is conceivable that a specific computer activity (like drill and practice) may work well with students of a particular type (for example, those lacking in confidence) under the guidance of a certain kind of teacher (perhaps one with a performance orientation) but will not prove effective with other kinds of students supervised by other kinds of teachers. Understanding interactions among these individual differences is therefore crucial for education.

We also need to deal with an "applied" problem, namely, how individual differences in students and teachers can be modified. At present, little is known about this, but we can speculate about several possibilities. One is to promote understanding of individual differences among students themselves. As we pointed out earlier, some computer activities may promote introspection and self-awareness. Are there other means for helping students to learn about themselves as learners? We think there are, and we are experimenting with a kind of "intellectual therapy" designed to increase self-knowledge in teachers. A second possibility is to increase self-knowledge in teachers. What do teachers know about their own learning and about the orientations that affect their teaching? We are experimenting with videotape procedures designed to promote this kind of understanding. A third is to increase teachers' knowledge about individual differences in students' approaches to learning. We are experimenting with workshops designed to accomplish this end. Perhaps these kinds of interventions, directed at both teachers and students, will lead to modifications of the individual differences themselves.

CONCLUSIONS

The computer can play a unique role in education. It offers the student several different levels and types of "empowerment," including a means for controlling drill and practice, a prosthetic device for speech and thought, a professional tool for writing and calculating, microworlds in which to engage in learning by doing and to conduct experiments without ordinary constraints, and even the means for self-examination. Individuals differ in their involvement in and motivation for computer activities and in the cognitive styles with which they approach them. Teachers present computer activities in markedly different ways. To exploit the powers of the computer in the educational setting, we therefore cannot rely only on technological "magic" but need to develop a clear understanding of individual differences in computers, students, and teachers, and of the ways in which they interact and can be modified.

ACKNOWLEDGMENTS

The writers express their appreciation to the Spencer Foundation for supporting preparation of this paper and to Jane Knitzer for her valuable review of the paper.

REFERENCES

Ashton-Warner, S. (1963). *Teacher.* New York: Simon & Schuster.

Becker, H. J. (1983, April). *School uses of microcomputers.* Center for Social Organization of Schools, Baltimore: The Johns Hopkins University.

Brown, J. S. (1983). Learning-by-doing revisited for electronic learning environments. In M. A. White, (Ed.), *The future of electronic learning* (pp. 12–26). Hillsdale, NJ: Lawrence Erlbaum Associates.

Dweck, C. (1985). Motivation. In R. Glaser & A. Lesgold (Eds.), *The handbook of psychology and education,* (Vol. I, pp. 83–104). Hillsdale, NJ: Lawrence Erlbaum Associates.

Ginsburg, H. P. (1981). Piaget and education: the contributions and limits of genetic epistemology. In I. E. Sigel, D. M. Brodzinsky, & R. M. Golinkoff (Eds.). *New directions in Piagetian theory and practice* (pp. 315–330). Hillsdale, NJ: Lawrence Erlbaum Associates.

Papert, S. (1980). *Mindstorms: Children, computers, and powerful ideas.* New York: Basic Books.

Perkins, D. N. (1985). The fingertip effect: How information-processing technology effects thinking. *Educational Researcher, 14,* 11–17.

Piaget, J. (1970). *The science of education and the psychology of the child.* New York: Orion Press.

Shapiro, D. (1965). *Neurotic styles.* New York: Basic Books.

Sheingold, K. (1983). *Symposium: Chameleon in the classroom: Developing roles for computers.* (Tech. Rep. 22). New York: Bank Street College of Education.

Trachtman, P. (1984). Putting computers into the hands of children without language. *Smithsonian,* 42–51.

Turkle, S. (1984). *The second self: Computers and the human spirit.* New York: Simon & Shuster.

Vygotsky, L. S. (1978). *Mind in society: The development of higher psychological processes.* Cambridge: Harvard University Press.

Weir, S., & Watt, D. (1981). LOGO: A computer environment for learning disabled students. *The Computer Teacher, 15,* 11–17.

Zelman, S. (1985). Individual differences in the computer learning environment: Motivational constraints to learning LOGO. Paper presented at the American Educational Research Association, Chicago, IL.

Zimiles, H. (1981). Cognitive-affective interaction: A concept that exceeds the researcher's grasp. In E. K. Shapiro & E. K. Weber (Eds.), *Cognitive and affective growth* (pp. 186–201). Hillsdale, NJ: Lawrence Erlbaum Associates.

Section **IV**

Special Applications of Computers and Video-Disc in Education

Chapter 10

The Video Revolution and Its Effects on Development: Some Initial Thoughts

John Bransford, Robert Sherwood,
Ted Hasselbring
George Peabody College,
Vanderbilt University

Many scholars argue that the invention of written language represents a major milestone in human history (e.g., Olson, 1985; Scribner & Cole, 1973). With it, humans achieved the ability to capture information and transport it across time and space. Written language also allows one to return to any segment and reread. This permits contemplation and analysis, including the ability to debug previous comprehension errors.

We believe that inventions available in the 20th century set the stage for two additional milestones in human history. One involves the invention of the computer—especially the microcomputer—and its potential for interaction. Another milestone—and the one that will receive the major share of our attention—involves the use of video technology to capture information in a much richer form than is possible with written language. With videotape, we can now capture linguistic expression *plus* visual and auditory information such as the facial expressions, auditory inflections, and environmental context of the person doing the speaking. With the introduction of computer-controlled, random-access videotapes and videodiscs, we also have the ability to return almost instantaneously to any segment and re-view the events. This permits experiences that could have powerful effects on learning and cognitive development. Our goal is to explore some of these possible effects.

Our discussion will focus on several lines of thought that we have considered as we worked with videodisc technology during the last two years. Our major emphasis has been on ways to use this technology to help students develop important competencies such as knowledge of reading and vocabulary, the ability to think mathematically, and the ability to solve problems. In the discussion below we emphasize the need to consider alternate pathways to the development of important competencies, and we summarize findings from our initial attempts to develop such pathways through the use of videodisc technology.

ALTERNATE PATHWAYS FOR THE DEVELOPMENT OF IMPORTANT COMPETENCIES

In thinking about possible effects of technology on learning, we have found it useful to ask how technology might enable us to create alternative pathways to important competencies such as mathematical and scientific thinking, the ability to read effectively, the ability to critically evaluate evidence, and so forth (e.g., Bransford, Delclos, Vye, Burns, & Hasselbring, 1986).

An article by Burton, J. S. Brown, and Fischer (1984) provided an interesting illustration of the importance of creating alternate pathways. They discuss the goal of helping people learn to ski effectively. The development of the "Graduated Length Method" (GLM) of teaching skiing a number of years ago was a breakthrough that made successful and enjoyable skiing available to thousands of people who had not previously been considered candidates for participation in the sport.

In the GLM method, several elements of the task are carefully and systematically manipulated by a skillful coach so that the learner skis in a series of increasingly complex situations, each requiring an extension of the skills learned in the previous, less complex environment. So, a novice skier is given very short skis, no poles, and is put on a gentle slope. The short skis make turning easier and allow practice in developing rhythm, an essential component of successful control. The lack of poles helps the student to focus on balance and on the movement of the skis. The gentle terrain greatly reduces the frightening speed that novices often experience on steeper slopes.

In the course of training, the GLM coach analyzes the performance of the learner at each level of instruction and makes decisions about when and what to change based on the successes and failures of the student. Gradually, longer skis are introduced; wider, narrower, or steeper slopes are presented; the snow conditions are also varied; poles are added. An important characteristic of the GLM method is that, even at the simplest level of instruction, the student is actually skiing rather than engaging in isolated exercises (e.g., balancing on a wooden beam) that have dubious relevance for the actual performance of complex skilled behavior and that are often not motivating to pursue.

The GLM method also depends on effective teaching. Changes in the types of skis, types of slopes, and so forth are made at points when the coach decides they will help either to advance the student to the next level or to make the student aware of current errors that need to be debugged. The coach might have the student ski in soft, powdery snow so that a lack of rhythmic turning could be clearly visible in the tracks left by the skis, or, if the student was not using the skis properly in negotiating turns, the coach might move them to an icy area, where the proper use of edges of the skis is critical in staying upright. Overall the GLM method is designed to make it easier for instructors to teach.

For present purposes, the important point involves the relationship between (a) people's abilities to develop an important competency (skiing) and (b) cultural practice regarding established methods of teaching. Before the GLM approach, many people had great difficulty learning to ski. It was tempting to conclude that some people simply "had the ability" and many others did not. Given the GLM method, however, thousands of persons who would otherwise have failed were able to succeed. In a very real sense, one could argue that the older context for teaching skiing represented a cultural practice that blocked many persons' chances for success.

It is not difficult to imagine cultural practices that, at least for some individuals, represent barriers to the development of important competencies. As a simple illustration, consider a first grader we know who entered a school system that placed strong emphasis on neat writing. The girl had great difficulty making S's, 3's, 5's, and so forth and, being somewhat of a perfectionist, was very troubled by her poor writing. This led to active resistance to engaging in a number of activities—especially to reading and math lessons that required her to write answers. Soon she did not want to go to school.

The girl was finally helped to overcome her problems, but not without a great deal of effort on the part of her parents and teacher. For other children, a simple problem such as this could cause considerable damage; the child may not be helped to adapt. It seems clear that other ways to teach subjects such as math and reading could eliminate barriers such as children's concern about poor writing. For example, computer-based curricula for reading and mathematics require keyboard skills but not writing skills. Obviously, it is important that children eventually learn to write, but the point is that a computer-based curriculum represents an alternative to one that emphasizes neat handwriting. For some students these alternatives may be needed so that the development of competencies in other areas (reading, mathematics) will not be impaired.

As a more general illustration of how standard cultural practices may make it difficult for many people to develop important competencies, consider the fact that typical school instruction often represents a rather abrupt change from the learning environments of the home, preschool, and daycare (e.g., Bransford & Heldmeyer, 1983; Donaldson, 1978). In school, children are expected to stay on the tasks posed by the teacher, and teaching often presupposes background knowledge that many children have not yet acquired. Similar problems confront many adult learners. In most college courses, the typical cultural practice is to emphasize textbook and lecture-based learning. Many students have not developed the skills necessary to learn effectively in this manner (e.g., Bransford, 1979), but this by no means suggests that they cannot learn. Many learn quite effectively in the more informal learning environments that are found outside of school. These observations suggest that learning might be enhanced if we could capture some of the advantages of informal learning environments and transport them to the formal environments found in schools.

Advantages of Informal Learning Environments

Our initial explorations of advantages of informal learning involved analyses of children's natural learning environments. Several investigators argue that there are two conflicting views about children as learners (e.g., Bransford & Held-meyer, 1983). One is that children are universal novices who consistently perform more poorly than adults. There are several reasons why younger or less mature learners would be expected to perform more poorly than more mature learners. First, younger learners have acquired less knowledge than older learners (e.g. Chi, 1978; Gelman, 1978) and hence have fewer and less well organized knowledge structures for assimilating information. Second, younger learners are less likely to know and use sophisticated strategies (e.g., Brown, 1979; Flavell, Beach, & Chinsky, 1966; Ornstein & Naus, 1978). Some investigators also argue that younger children's working memory is more limited, although the degree to which this is a limitation of "actual" versus "functional" memory is still a matter for debate (e.g., Case, 1974; Chi, 1976). Overall, younger children seem to have a number of *disadvantages* that can hurt their performance in a variety of domains.

In contrast to the proceeding position is one that views children as exceptionally effective learners. Adults often marvel at children's abilities to acquire concepts, language, motor skills, spatial skills, social skills, and so forth. Of course, children do not acquire these concepts and skills instantaneously. In fact they spend a great deal of time learning and practicing. However, they do this in a manner that is more akin to play than work. The play pays off, because most children learn very well. This leads Bransford and Heldmeyer (1983) to ask:

> . . . if we hold this view of "children as exceptional learners" in conjunction with the "child as universal novice" view . . . we are forced to acknowledge that children are amazingly effective learners *despite* their lack of knowledge, *despite* their lack of sophisticated strategies, and *despite* possible limitations on their working memory. How can children be such successful learners in the face of such disadvantages?

We emphasize that assumptions about children's effectiveness as learners generally stem from their performance while learning in everyday contexts rather than from their performance in laboratory tasks. Children's abilities to learn therefore seem to be closely tied to the conditions under which their learning takes place. Important aspects of these conditions are discussed below.

Learning in Context.   One of the advantages of everyday learning is that it usually takes place in the context of meaningful, ongoing activities. When children stack the blocks poorly, the blocks fall over, and they receive feedback from the consequences of their actions. Moreover, in discussions about their own actions, they are able to make use of contextual cues when attempting to understand what others mean. Excellent illustrations of the importance of contextual cues are provided in Chapman's (1978) discussion of children's comprehension strategies. She noted that parents of year-old children frequently report that their children understand everything that is said to them. Furthermore, observations of children's performance in natural language settings provide support for such beliefs. Nevertheless, there is a great deal of information that these children really do not understand.

One of the examples discussed by Chapman is Lewis and Freedle's (1973) analysis of the comprehension abilities of a 13-month-old child. When handed an apple while she was in her high chair and told "eat the apple," the child bit it. When handed an apple while playing in her playpen and told "throw the apple," the child threw it. Lewis and Freedle performed an experiment in order to test whether the child "really" understood words such as *eat* and *throw.* They handed the child an apple while she was in her high chair and asked her to "throw the apple." The child bit it. Later, when the child was in her playpen, she was handed an apple and told "eat the apple." She threw it.

Chapman emphasizes that, in everyday settings, young children have rich opportunities for learning because they can use context to figure out what someone must mean by various sentence structures and words. Unless she was being tested by tricky experimenters, for example, the child discussed above could determine the general meanings of "apple," "eat" and "throw." Similarly, if a mother says "get your shirt" while pointing to the only loose object (a shirt) on the rug, the child begins to understand the meaning of *get* and *shirt.* Chapman (1978) emphasizes that language acquisition cannot take place in the absence of shared social and situational contexts, because the latter provide information about the meanings of words and sentence structures. In MacNamara's (1972) terms, the child "uses meaning as a clue to language rather than language as a clue to meaning." The child who is asked to learn out of context often has little basis for inferring the meanings that speakers intend.

The ability to use contextual information as a cue to language is important not only for young children. It is also important for older children who may not understand all the words used by adults. For example, a statement such as "they sawed the *bics* to make a *vac*" provides very little information about the meaning of *bics* and *vac.* However, in certain contexts this statement can produce new learning, because the context provides many fewer degrees of freedom about what *bics* and *vac* might mean (e.g., Sherwood, Kinzer, Hasselbring, & Bransford, 1987). In addition, even for familiar concepts and statements, appropriate contexts can increase the quality of the elaborations that people are able to make (Anderson, 1983; Anderson & Reder, 1979; Stein & Bransford, 1979).

The Role of Mediators.   Implicit in our discussion of learning in context was the fact that parents, friends, and peers play extremely important roles in cognitive development (e.g., Feuerstein, 1979; Vygotsky, 1978). Their roles are not simply to act as stimuli that provide words, sentences and actions to be modeled by children. Instead, they act as *mediators,* who provide structure to the experiences of the child. Mediators arrange the environment so that children will encounter certain experiences (e.g., toys, books); they help children separate relevant from irrelevant information (e.g., "You can eat on this plate even though it is blue rather than red"); they prompt children to anticipate events (e.g., "After we get up from our nap we will do what?") and they help children connect various parts of their experiences (e.g., "This story mentions a duck. Didn't we see a duck yesterday in the park?").

In addition, effective mediators monitor the performance of their children so that they can encourage as much independent performance as possible yet provide help when it is necessary. In Vygotsky's (1978) terminology, effective mediators are sensitive to their child's "zone of proximal development"—the zone where children can perform *with* prompting in ways that they could not perform without prompting. This sensitivity to the zone of proximal development is assumed to be one of the major factors responsible for children's abilities to learn (e.g., Brown, Bransford, Ferrara, & Campione, 1983; Vygotsky, 1978).

In order to be effective, the mediators need to be aware of various experiences that the child has had that can provide a context for new learning. This is relatively easy for parents who have shared a great number of experiences with their children. For a teacher, however, it can be very difficult to know which sets of experiences will provide support for each child's learning. The task becomes even more difficult when children come from cultural backgrounds that differ from those of the teacher. Under these conditions, children may have special difficulties in their attempts to learn because they lack contextual support.

Some Effects of Video Contexts on Comprehension

Our thoughts about context and comprehension led us to conduct several studies that were designed to incorporate some of the advantages of informal, contextually rich learning environments into more formal educational settings (e.g., Bransford, Sherwood, Kinzer, & Hasselbring, 1985). We used videotapes and computer-controlled videodiscs to create meaningful environments that could be shared by students and mediators, and we compared the effects of learning in these environments with the effects of environments that are often found in schools.

The video segments that we have used involve popular films such as *The Swiss Family Robinson, Raiders of the Lost Ark* and *Star Wars*. One reason for using existing films to create contexts for teaching is that this procedure eliminates the costs of producing high-quality video. In addition, the videos are highly motivating to watch. Furthermore, because the videos do not include instructional segments in them, there is much more opportunity to use them flexibly than is usually the case with typical educational films. The ability to use computer-controlled access to find any segment of a videodisc makes the opportunities for instruction much richer than is possible in typical uses of films.

The purpose of the videos is to provide a context for mediation—a context that is much richer in specifics than is the use of general, verbally based themes. Students who view the video segments in the absence of a mediator are entertained, but they miss most of the opportunities for learning that the video provides. With mediation, the potential for learning becomes clear. As an illustration, consider segments we have worked with from *Raiders of the Lost Ark*. This film provides an excellent context for learning. At one point in the film Indiana Jones wants to fill a bag with sand so that it weighs the same as a golden idol. Assuming that the idol is solid gold, how reasonable is it to suppose that it weighs about the same as a small bag of sand? A number of other aspects of just the first 12 minutes of the movie provide a context for a host of additional problems. The explorers taste the poison on an arrow to see if it is fresh. Is this possible? And where did the natives get the poison and how does it affect the body?

At another point Indiana Jones jumps across a pit. What cues can be used to estimate the length of the pit? Given this information, could a human possibly jump across it (for example, what is the world record in the running long jump?). In addition, if the latter information is not available or needs to be calculated for a particular individual, how does one do so? This problem provides a context for discussing experimentation, averages, variability in performance, and so forth.

Indiana Jones also has a number of spiders on his back after he enters a cave. Are these supposed to be dangerous from the perspective of the film? Would the filmmakers actually put dangerous spiders on their star actor? What kinds of spiders are these? Do they live in South America? In caves? Did they spin the giant webs in the caves?

In one of our experiments we explored the degree to which context facilitated elaboration processes (Bransford, Sherwood, Kinzer, & Hasselbring, 1985). As an illustration, consider the following list of simple statements:

1. Some poisons are so powerful that even a small taste would result in death.
2. A beam of sunlight that shines through a hole in a cave will disappear at night.

3. A solid gold statue the size of a half-gallon milk carton would weigh at least 60 pounds.

Each of these statements is easy to comprehend in isolation. Nevertheless, when the same statements are heard in context they prompt a number of elaborations. For example, in *Raiders* one of the men tastes a poison arrow to see if it is fresh. College students indicated that, when they read statement number 1 above after seeing *Raiders,* they found it to be much more interesting and thought provoking. For example, they realized that the poison on the arrow must not have been extremely deadly because the man did not even get sick.

The statement about the sunlight (number 2 above) is also understood more elaborately when heard in the context of Indiana Jones. It refers to a trap in a cave that is activated when someone breaks the beam of light with any part of their body. Because the beam of light comes from sunlight, shouldn't the trap be set off each night? Can it then reset itself?

The statement about the weight of gold (number 3 above) also becomes much more interesting when read in the context of *Raiders.* While watching the movie, most students do not ask themselves whether a small bag of sand that Indiana Jones tries to substitute for the idol would weigh about the same as the idol if the latter were solid gold. However, when they read sentence 3 they think about a number of implications. Is the idol really gold? If so, how could the people carry it as easily as they do? If not, what value does it have?

We found that college students find facts such as tables of density much more interesting after they have been confronted with the problem of estimating the weight of a solid gold idol that is the size of the one in *Raiders* (Sherwood, Kinzer, Bransford, & Franks, 1987). When information is introduced as an aid to problem solving, it functions as a tool rather than an isolated arbitrary fact (see also Sherwood, Kinzer, Hasselbring, & Bransford, 1987).

Results such as the ones just discussed have important implications for teaching. Teachers know more about their subject matter than their students know. They have a number of experiences that, in effect, function as their own movies. When they make statements, they understand a variety of elaborations because of the contexts that their knowledge base supplies. In contrast, students generally lack the knowledge available to teachers (this is analogous to not having seen the movie). Because of this, they confront sets of seemingly arbitrary facts. Through the use of video-technology, teachers can create learning environments that provide the contextual support necessary to make learning more meaningful. This should be especially helpful for students who lack the background that is often presupposed in schools.

VIDEO CONTEXTS AND PROBLEM SOLVING

In the preceding discussion we focused on the use of video-based contexts to facilitate comprehension. Our approach to problem solving emphasizes the importance of both general skills and attitudes that operate across a variety of areas (e.g., Bransford & Stein, 1984) and specific knowledge that is necessary to solve problems in semantically rich domains (e.g., Bransford, Sherwood, Vye, & Rieser, 1986).

One of the major reasons for emphasizing problem solving involves the issue of gaining access to relevant knowledge. Alfred Whitehead (1929) alluded to the issue of access many years ago when he discussed the problem of inert knowledge—knowledge that is not used even though it is relevant for solving a particular problem. Whitehead also argued that traditional educational practice tended to produce knowledge that remained inert (see also Bereiter & Scardamalia, 1985; Brown, 1985; Brown & Campione, 1981).

An implication of Whitehead's position is that some ways of imparting information result in knowledge that is not especially accessible. As an illustration, consider the following question that was posed to college freshmen (Bransford, Sherwood, Kinzer, & Hasselbring, 1985): "Try to remember what you learned about the concept of logarithms. Can you think of any way that they might make problem solving simpler than it would be if they did not exist?"

The college students who were asked this question were able to remember something about logarithms. However, most viewed them only as exercises in math class rather than as useful inventions that simplify problem solving. These students had not been helped to understand the kinds of problems for which logarithms are useful. It is interesting to contrast their understanding of logarithms with that of English mathematician Henry Briggs who, in 1624, heralded them as welcome inventions: "Logarithms are numbers invented for the more easy working of questions in arithmetic and geometry. By them all troublesome multiplications are avoided and performed by addition. In a word, all questions not only in arithmetic and geometry but in astronomy also are thereby most plainly and easily answered" (cf. Jacobs, 1982, p. 211).

Imagine telling a modern-day Henry Briggs that he will win prizes depending on the number of multiplication problems that he can solve in four hours—problems involving very large numbers. He has no access to calculators or computers, but can take anything else with him. Briggs will probably take a table of logarithms. In contrast, students who have no understanding of the function of logarithms will not think of such a possibility when confronted with the above-mentioned multiplication task. Similarly, many students seem to learn to calculate the answers to physics problems yet fail to apply their formal physics knowledge when encountering everyday phenomena. They need to learn more about the conditions under which their formal knowledge applies (e.g., diSessa, 1982).

Studies of Access.   A number of investigators have begun to conduct controlled studies of relationships between access and the nature and organization of knowledge. Some researchers have focused on the degree to which knowledge of the solution to one set of problems enables students to solve analogous problems. Thus, Simon and Hayes (1977) note that students who learned how to solve the Tower of Hanoi problem do not spontaneously realize that it is structurally isomorphic to the "Tea Ceremony" problem. Similarly, Gick and Holyoak (1980) show that, unless students are explicitly prompted to do so, they do not spontaneously use information that they just learned about the solution to the Fortress problem to solve an analogous problem that they face (Dunker's X-irradiation problem, 1945).

Perfetto, Bransford, and Franks have also explored the issue of access (1983). They provided students with cues that were very closely related to problems to be solved later. The problems to be solved were "insight" problems such as the following:

> Uriah Fuller, the famous Israeli superpsychic, can tell you the score of any baseball game before the game starts. What is his secret?
>
> A man living in a small town in the United States married 20 different women in the same town. All are still living and he has never divorced one of them. Yet, he has broken no law. Can you explain?

Most college students have difficulty answering these questions unless provided with hints or clues. Before solving the problems, some students were given clue information that was obviously relevant to each problem's solution. Thus, these students first received statements such as: "Before it starts, the score of any game is 0 to 0"; and "A minister marries several people each week." The students were then presented with the problems and explicitly prompted to use the clue information to solve them (we call this group the *informed group*). Their problem-solving performance was excellent. Other students were first presented with the clues and then given the problems, but they were not explicitly prompted to use the clues for problem solution (the *uninformed group*). Their problem solving performance was very poor.

The existence of data illustrating access failures has prompted researchers to search for ways to make knowledge less inert (e.g., Adams et al., in press; Gick & Holyoak, 1983). In general, the data indicate that the mere presentation of factual information results in information that generally remains inert. In contrast, the opportunity to understand how information can function as a tool for solving meaningful problems makes it much more likely that that knowledge will be used spontaneously later on (see Bransford, Franks, Vye, & Sherwood, 1986).

Macro-Contexts for Teaching Science Information

A study by Sherwood, Kinzer, Bransford, and Franks (1987) provides one illustration of the effects of various acquisition activities on subsequent access. In that study we investigated the effects of learning information in the context of a general problem-solving situation such as Indiana Jones' need to plan and bring equipment in order to survive in the South American jungle. The trip to the jungle represents what we call a "macro-context." According to our definition, macro-contexts involve a series of specific actions and consequences that revolve around an overall goal (to obtain the Golden Idol). The overall goal requires students to consider a number of subgoals (bring enough food for the journey, find or bring water, avoid traps, plan a means for getting home from the jungle, etc.). We assume that this linking of subgoals helps students integrate knowledge that might otherwise be learned in piecemeal fashion.

The materials for the science experiment involved 13 short passages about topics that might be encountered in middle school and high school science classes. Examples included topics such as: (a) the kinds of high-carbohydrate foods that are healthy versus the less healthy kinds, (b) the use of water as a standard for the density of liquids plus the fact that, on earth, a pint of water weighs approximately one pound, (c) the possibility of solar-powered airplanes, and (d) ways to make a bronze-age lamp using clay and olive oil.

College students in one condition simply read about each of 13 topics with the intent to remember the information. Those in a second condition read the same information, but in the context of problems that might be encountered during Indiana Jones' trip to the South American jungle. For example, students in this second condition were first asked to consider the kinds of foods one should bring on a trip and then asked to read the passage about different types of high-carbohydrate foods. Similarly, the passage about the density and weight of water was read in the context of attempts to estimate the weight of fresh water needed for four people for three days; the possibility of solar-powered airplanes was discussed in the context of finding transportation in areas where fuel was difficult to obtain, and so on. The goal of this type of presentation was to help students understand some of the kinds of problems that the science information could help them solve.

Following acquisition, all participants received one of two types of tests. One-half the students in each group were simply asked to recall the topics of the passages that they had just read. As expected, students who learned in the context of the trip to South America were able to remember a greater number of topics than were students in the "no context" group.

The remaining half of the students in each group received a test designed to assess whether they would spontaneously use information that they had just read to solve a new problem. The test they received was disguised as a filler task to be completed before memory questions would be asked about the previously-read topics. Students were asked to imagine that they were planning a journey to a desert area in the Western part of the United States in order to search for relics in Pueblo caves. They were to suggest at least 10 areas of information—more if possible—that would be important for planning and survival. The students were also asked to be as explicit as possible. For example, rather than say "you would need food and supplies," they were asked to describe the kinds of food and supplies.

The results indicated large differences in students' spontaneous use of information. Students who had simply read facts about high-carbohydrate foods, the weight of water, and so on, almost never mentioned this information when providing their answers. Instead, their answers tended to be quite general such as "take food and take fresh water to drink." In contrast, students in the second acquisition condition made excellent use of the information they had just read. When discussing food, for example, most of them focused on the importance of its nutritional contents. When discussing water, they emphasized the importance of calculating its weight. Similarly, constraints on the availability of gasoline versus solar energy were discussed when the importance of transportation (e.g., an airplane, car) was recalled. Overall, students who received information in the context of problem solving were much more likely to remember what they read and to spontaneously use it as a basis for creating new sets of plans. Similar effects on recall of science information were found in seventh and eighth grade students (Sherwood, Kinzer, Bransford, & Franks, 1987).

Macro-Contexts for Teaching Mathematical Problem Solving

In another study we investigated the effects of macro-contexts on mathematical problem solving (Kulewicz, Barron, Goin, Hasselbring, & Bransford, 1986). For this project we worked with fifth and sixth graders who were approximately one and one-half years behind their peers in math. The environment involved the use of videodiscs to provide a macro-context that helped students formulate meaningful problem-solving goals. To develop this environment we again used the first 12 minutes of the film *Raiders of the Lost Ark* presented on videodisc. This segment enabled us to formulate the following goal: One might want to return to the jungle to explore the region or to get the golden gong that Indiana left behind. If so, it could be important to know dimensions of obstacles such as the size of the pit one would have to jump, the height of the cave, the width of the river and its relationship to the size of the seaplane, and so on. Because this information is on film, it does no good to measure sizes directly (e.g., the pit is only several inches wide on the screen). However, one can use known standards (e.g., Indiana Jones) to estimate sizes and distances that are important to know.

The general goal of learning more about important dimensions of potential obstacles and events guided the selection of mathematically based problems that were formulated on scenes from the 12-minute movie segment. Through the use of random-access videodisc we were able to isolate and quickly access the sequence of frames that specified each problem situation. For example, at one point Indiana comes to a pit and must attempt to get over it. He jumps. How wide is the pit? Could humans possibly jump something that wide?

The width of the pit can be estimated by finding another, earlier scene where Indiana used his bullwhip to swing over the pit. Through the use of videodisc freeze frame we are able to show a scene of Indiana swinging and extending halfway across the pit. Measurement on the screen (either by hand or through the use of computer graphics) allows students to see that the pit is two Indiana's wide. If Indiana is 6 feet tall, the pit is 12 feet wide. Students can be helped to determine this information for themselves and, subsequently, to see if they could jump something that was 12 feet wide.

In our initial studies, the problems that we worked with involved finding the length or width of an object given its proportional relationship to a standard with a known length or width. Our aim was to facilitate children's comprehension of the problem situations and thereby improve their motivation to solve various problems plus increase their understanding of the relations between the known and unknown quantities expressed in the problems. The use of the video provided an especially rich macro-context from which to begin. The video was supplemented with effective teaching (mediation). Students were encouraged to create visual and symbolic representations of problems, and they received individualized feedback about the strengths and weaknesses of their approach to each problem. All instruction was one-on-one.

The results of the experiment were quite strong. Students in a control condition received teaching that was similar to, and actually an improvement upon, the teaching they received in school. For example, in one-on-one sessions that included a great deal of encouragement, students in the control groups worked on problems and were shown correct solution strategies after attempting to solve each problem. Nevertheless, after more than a week of instruction, there was almost no improvement from pretest to posttest. In contrast, the improvement for students who received instruction in the context of the video was extremely impressive. This improvement was not only for problems that referred to the Indiana Jones context, it worked for out-of-context problems as well. We have also observed students who received video instruction spontaneously using what they learned in class to better understand their outside environment; they used themselves and their friends as standards to measure the height of trees, buildings, and so forth. These observations are informal, but they suggest an important goal for instruction. We need to help students realize the value of school-based lessons for increasing the richness of their everyday lives.

Videodiscs and Story Comprehension

A study being conducted at Vanderbilt provides a third illustration of the video to teach important aspects of problem solving (Johnson, 1986). Johnson is working with 4- and 5-year-olds who, because of poor language skills, are at risk for school failure. His goal is to increase their ability to understand stories.

Typically, efforts to increase story understanding involve someone reading a story to children and then asking them questions about what they heard. Ideally, children will learn that stories have structures, and that ideas in a story must be causally connected in order to be understood. However, it is not always easy to instruct children about their misunderstandings of stories. Assume that a teacher asks, "Remember when the ship hit the rocks?" If the child says "no," one must resort to telling the answer. Even if the child says "yes," it is unclear whether the scene is being imagined properly.

With random-access video, it is possible to first show students a video of a story and then ask questions (Johnson is using the first 10 minutes of *The Swiss Family Robinson* as his story). If students cannot answer the questions, it is a simple matter to return to the relevant scene and have the students look at it again. Through this use of scenes, students can be helped to understand the importance of developing causal connections among story elements. Johnson's research is designed to compare the effectiveness of traditional, verbally based instruction with instruction that uses interactive videodiscs. An important goal of the work is to help children develop an awareness of what it means to comprehend adequately versus to need more information. If children fail to identify problems with their own comprehension, they will fail to use "repair" strategies such as asking questions or looking back at a video (e.g. Bransford, Sherwood et al, 1986).

The Importance of Noticing and Perceptual Learning

Taken as a whole, the preceding studies of problem solving and access suggest that students need to understand how concepts and procedures can function as tools for solving relevant problems. Our data suggest that fact-oriented acquisition permits students to remember information when explicitly prompted to do so, but it does not facilitate their ability to spontaneously use this information to solve new problems. In general, our work with macro-contexts has emphasized the goal of providing problem-solving experiences during learning that are similar to those that students will encounter later in their lives (see Bransford, Franks, Vye, & Sherwood, 1986).

The emphasis on preparing students to solve "similar" problems in the future is not new (e.g., Thorndike, 1913). Nevertheless, we have begun to realize that video technology may be especially important for helping students develop perceptual sensitivities that play an important role in later transfer—sensitivities that often are not developed by traditional, verbally based instruction (Bransford, Franks, Vye, & Sherwood, 1986). The issue here involves the degree to which "noticing" is an important component in the development of expertise. In the area of physics, for example, experts categorize problems in ways that differ considerably from those of novices (Chi, Feltovich, & Glaser, 1981).

Many years ago, the philosopher Ernst Cassirer (1923) argued that a major problem with many theories is that they presuppose the existence and salience of particular features. In theories of concept formation, the focus was on discarding dissimilar features and retaining only those that were common to members of a concept; little emphasis was placed on the issue of noticing features in the first place. Cassirer argued that, rather than presuppose their existence, it is the noticing of features that must be explained.

Following the lead of Cassirer (1923), Garner (1974), and the Gibsons (1955), we argue for the importance of focusing on the issue of noticing. Given that experts often notice features of events that escape the attention of novices, how can the learning of novices be enhanced? How can novices be helped to notice relevant features of a current problem that are necessary for recognition of similar problems that they may encounter later on?

Perceptual Contrasts

The ability to notice relevant features of both acquisition and test events is not easy for novices dealing with complex situations. Modern theories of perceptual learning are important for clarifying how noticing can be facilitated. These theories emphasize the importance of contrasts that allow people to notice features that they might otherwise miss (e.g., see Bransford, Franks et al., 1986; Garner, 1974; Gibson & Gibson, 1955). A classic use of contrasts involves the development of expertise in wine tasting. In order to develop a tasting expertise, one does not simply concentrate on a single type of wine; instead, one exposes students to a variety of contrasting flavors and textures (Gibson & Gibson, 1955). These contrasts presumably highlight features of each particular stimulus that the novice might otherwise miss (see especially Garner's chapter on critical realism, 1974).

As noted earlier, this emphasis on contrasts raises the following question: To what extent do typical approaches to instruction and testing help people learn to notice the types of features that will be important in their everyday environments? We argue that even problem-oriented instruction often takes place in contexts that are too dissimilar from those that students will encounter later on.

This latter point can be clarified by noting that a common form of instruction involves attempts to prepare people for the future by telling them what they might experience and how to deal with it. For example, clinical students are often trained to assign diagnoses based on verbal vignettes (Rock, 1986). Thus, a patient might be described as "slightly defensive," "moderately depressed," and so forth, and students might learn to assign a diagnosis. However, once these students enter everyday practice and see real patients, they are often at a loss. They haven't learned to recognize symptoms such as "slightly defensive" and "moderately depressed" on their on. Because of the exclusive reliance on verbal vignettes, the students have received clues that represent *the output of an expert's pattern-recognition process*. In order to perceive the relevant features of wines, clients, and other situations, a great deal of perceptual learning must occur. This requires experiences with a set of contrasts so that the features of particular events become salient by virtue of their differentiation from other possible events (see also Simon, 1980).

Modern videodisc technology makes it possible to use perceptual contrasts to develop new approaches to instruction. As an illustration, consider the goal of teaching teachers about teaching. One method is to ask people to try to remember characteristics of good teachers they have had, poor teachers they have had, and to compare the two (Gage & Berliner, 1984). Whatever memories people have will presumably include only those features that they noticed at earlier points in their lives. There are undoubtedly many subtleties of good versus poor teaching that were not noticed by individuals. By relying only on memories, it is hard for new noticings to occur.

Imagine an alternative approach to teaching about teaching. Assume that we have relatively short video segments of a teacher doing a fair job of teaching something. We then see the teacher doing a worse job, a better job, and so forth. With appropriate contrasts, new insights into components of effective teaching should emerge. For example, a teacher's lag time after asking questions could emerge as a relevant feature given some types of contrasts. Different types of nonverbal communication and their effects on impressions of the teacher could become apparent as well. This invitation to notice new features as a function of contrast sets is quite different from the typical approach that simply lists characteristics of good versus poor teachers. It should result in a greater sensitivity to important characteristics of classroom events.

The use of contrast sets should result in even more powerful learning if students are helped to view them from a multiplicity of perspectives. Many traditional methods of instruction do not encourage students to take multiple perspectives on the same set of events, hence they do not promote multiple access to a variety of relevant concepts. Most texts on educational psychology contain different chapters on motivation, cognitive development, the nature of testing, instruction, processes underlying learning, and so on. Each of the chapters provides examples, but students usually receive *a different example for each concept*. This is very different from the experience of seeing how a variety of different concepts can apply to the same event or set of events.

An emphasis on the application of multiple concepts to the same set of events is a characteristic of case methods of instruction. Beginning in the 1940s (e.g., Gragg, 1940), students at the Harvard Business School were presented with complex cases involving businesses and asked to use a variety of concepts in order to solve important business problems. These methods of instruction are quite different from standard forms of instruction, because the case methods attempt to facilitate multiple access (e.g., Gragg, 1940; Spiro, 1986). The goal is to have students bring a multitude of perspectives to bear on a single case. Even here, however, the instruction has been verbally based rather than verbally plus perceptually based. As noted earlier, verbally based instruction often contains clues that represent the output of experts' pattern recognition processes.

When these verbal clues are removed, novices often fail to perform effectively because they have not developed the perceptual sensitivities necessary to notice important features of complex events.

Overall, the use of videodiscs to facilitate noticing and perceptual learning is designed to help students forge links between formal educational environments and their everyday learning environments. As an illustration, consider the study discussed earlier that used video scenes to teach mathematical problem solving. In that discussion we noted that many children spontaneously began to use available standards to measure interesting aspects of their environment such as trees and buildings. They began to see everyday situations as word problems that were interesting to solve. Similarly, one can imagine using videodiscs to help novices learn to perceive everyday events as illustrations of abstract mathematical concepts such as symmetry and exponential function, inductive versus deductive methods for arriving at general principles and so forth. As students learn to perceive events as instances of important mathematical concepts and procedures, they should be more likely to understand the relevance of these principles for their everyday lives.

GOALS FOR THE FUTURE: SYNERGISTIC DESIGNS

In the studies conducted to date we have focused on individual content areas such as mathematics *or* science *or* reading. The structure of these studies parallel the course structure found in most schools. Students typically receive math during one part of the day, reading during another, science during another, and so forth. An instructional format such as this is not likely to help students integrate their knowledge so that they can take multiple perspectives on the same general problem, neither is it likely to promote the spontaneous utilization of relevant knowledge when confronted with new problems. With videodisc technology and its potential to allow teachers to re-view scenes and provide contrast sets, it may be possible to create learning environments that are much more helpful for developing expertise.

Our ideas about the desirability of changing traditional approaches to instruction were stimulated, in part, by an article entitled *The Shame of American Education* by B. F. Skinner (1984). Skinner made the following claim: "Most current problems could be solved if students learned twice as much in the same time and with the same effort" (p. 947). Skinner argued that this goal can be achieved if teachers are taught to use technology in ways that permit them to teach more effectively. His suggestions for ways to use technology derive from his earlier ideas of teaching machines.

We have found it useful to envision ways to achieve Skinner's goal of learning twice as much in the same amount of time and with the same amount of effort. One method is to try to increase students' time on a task so that more time is spent on instruction. By monitoring student performance, one can also increase the likelihood that students perform correctly when working on a task. Another, complementary method is to develop what we shall call integrated approaches to instruction—approaches that help students learn about areas such as thinking and mathematics while they learn science, and vice versa. Ideally, content from these different areas can be combined synergistically so that the combination produces more effective learning than the isolated parts.

A Demonstration Experiment

The benefits of synergistic approaches to instruction can be illustrated by considering a simple memory experiment conducted with college students (Adams, Kasserman, Bransford, & Franks, in preparation). Students in Group 1 were asked to learn a list of 49 statements that might be made about different topics. For example, 7 of the statements were made about a runner and included "He won without drugs," "That's too much like work," and so on. Other statements were about "a space trip," "a party," and so forth. Overall, there were 7 statements about each of seven different topics, for a total of 49 statements in all.

Students in the preceding condition (Group 1) were read the 49 statements and then asked to recall them. They were provided with the seven topic names as retrieval cues. The students recalled approximately 23% of the sentences (see Table 10.1). They also clustered their answers by topic (i.e., statements about the runner tended to be recalled together, etc.).

Students in a second group received more information to learn than did those in Group 1. In particular, Group 2 students were also told who made each statement. Thus, a lawyer might say about a runner, "He won without drugs." A playboy might say "It's too much like work." For each of the 49 statements, students in the second group received information about who made the statement.

Following acquisition, students were supplied with a list of seven topics (runner, space trip) and a list of seven people (lawyer, playboy). They were able to recall 54% of the statements—approximately twice as many as the first group (see Table 10.1). Furthermore, they were able to state who made the statement (e.g., the lawyer) in almost every instance. Therefore, despite having more to learn in the same about of time, students in Group 2, the "topic plus person" group, did much better than those in Group 1. A control group to assess guessing based on the retrieval cues showed that guessing was not the reason for the increased performance. In addition, the relative advantage of Group 2 over Group 1 was evident in a subsequent experiment that involved free recall rather than cued recall.

TABLE 10.1
Percentage Recall for Three Acquisition Conditions

Topic alone (Group 1)	*23%*
Topic plus person (Group 2)	*54%*
Topic plus picture (Group 3)	*26%*

The preceding experiment also included a third group that illustrates important constraints on the degree to which extra information facilitates learning and remembering. Students in this group, "topic plus picture," also heard the 49 statements about seven different topics. However, rather than being supplied with information about people, such as lawyer, playboy, and minister, they received pictures of seven different people. The pictures were distinctive but did not contain information that could help students understand why a particular person might be more likely to make a statement. Students were therefore unable to generate precise elaborations that clarified the relationships between each type of person and each statement that was made (see Bransford et al. 1982 for a discussion of precision of elaborations).

Students in the "topic plus picture" group were not helped by being supplied with the extra, pictorial information. They recalled only about 26% of the statements from the set of 49. In order for extra information to enhance memory, it must enable students to understand the significance or relevance of the other information to be learned (see Bransford et al., 1982).

SOME ILLUSTRATIONS OF SYNERGISTIC APPROACHES
TO MATERIALS DESIGN

The preceding experiment illustrates some advantages of synergistic approaches to teaching. Nevertheless, the materials used in the experiment are quite unimportant from an educational perspective. It is instructive to consider how similar principles might apply in more academic domains.

One example of attempts to create a synergistic lesson was discussed by Bransford, Stein, Sheldon, and Owings (1980). They note that science instructors often teach about special features of different types of animals. For example, camels have special types of eyelids that allow them to cover their eyes yet still see light; they can close their nose passages; they have dense hair around their cars. Teachers can help students memorize these features about camels, but this is probably not the most useful approach. The information about camels becomes more significant when it is learned in the context of additional information—in this case, information about deserts. Sudden sand storms often occur in deserts, so animals need to be able to cope. The ability to protect their eyes, nose, and ears helps camels in this regard.

The camel example illustrates how information about conditions in deserts can make facts about camels more significant. Conversely, the information about camels clarifies the potential impact of various features of deserts. By learning both areas of knowledge together, students presumably develop integrated knowledge structures that can facilitate subsequent recall and transfer. For example, imagine that students who have learned about camels and deserts later read about desert travelers who wear hats and veils to cover their faces despite the fact that it is very hot. Access to information about the reason for camels' features should help students understand the significance of information about desert travelers. This access should be facilitated by the fact that integrated knowledge structures are usually accessible through multiple retrieval routes (e.g., information about camels may be achieved through cues such as "desert," "sandstorms," "adaptation to harsh climates," as well as through "camels").

Integration Across Traditional Subject Boundaries

The illustration involving camels involves a combination of areas of knowledge (camels, deserts) that both fall within a particular subject such as science. Recently, we have explored the possibility of using video contexts to integrate instruction that generally takes place in different subjects. The examples we have discussed involve an integration of classes that might teach problem solving, science, and math (Bransford, Sherwood, & Hasselbring, 1986). The value of integrating this information can be clarified by beginning with a discussion of mathematics.

Imagine that students receive word problems such as the following in math class: "A water-carrier for a softball team brings one quart of water for each player. If there are nine players, and each quart of water weighs 2 pounds, what is the total weight of the water?" It seems clear that word problems require problem solving. Therefore, one might argue that the typical word-problem format already provides an integration of mathematics and problem solving. We agree that it does, but we also argue that problem solving is emphasized only in a very restricted sense.

Consider how the water-carrier problem could be incorporated into a larger context that provides richer experiences with problem solving. The lesson could focus on the idea of planning for a trip to the South American jungle that is similar to the trip taken by Indiana Jones. In order to plan for the trip, students need to anticipate problems that they might encounter; problems such as the need for food and water. When students attempt to determine the exact amount of food and water needed, they are *generating* word problems that they need to solve. This is quite different from solving problems that other people provide (e.g., Bransford & Stein, 1984).

A problem relevant to the goal of planning for a trip might be analogous to the water-carrier problem discussed above:

Indiana Jones needs to bring enough water to drink. Each person should have at least one quart of water a day, and Indiana needs enough for three people for two days. If water weighs a pound per pint, how many pounds of water will Indiana need?

There are several reasons why the Indiana Jones problem seems preferable to the water-carrier problem. First, the Indiana problem can help students think about information that is useful rather than arbitrary. How much water do we really need per day? What is the weight of water? In the water-carrier problem, one doesn't have the opportunity to learn useful facts such as this.

The Indiana Jones problem also becomes more meaningful because it is related to other problems involved in planning. Thus, problems involving the weight of water can be related to other problems such as the weight of food, the weight of kerosene for the torches, and so forth. Rather than being exposed to only an unrelated set of word problems, students can see each problem as a subproblem related to an overall goal.

Problems oriented around the theme of planning for a trip can also be related to science. For example, an important part of science instruction involves the density of liquids such as water and kerosene. Students who are planning for a trip and who generate word problems involving the weight of supplies can be introduced to density tables as a source of information about weights. This is very different from simply being supplied with information in the word problem itself. Furthermore, by seeing related problems that involve different types of liquids (e.g., water versus kerosene), students can be helped to understand how differences in densities affect how liquids behave (e.g., kerosene floats on water, because it is less dense). Students can also be introduced to alternate strategies for solving a problem like obtaining fresh drinking water. One such strategy is to use a water purifier. How do these work, and how reliable are they?

Vanderbilt University's Learning Technology Center is working on a "Thinker" program that illustrates how videodisc technology can be used to teach science, mathematics, and problem solving in the context of *Raiders* (Goin & Williams, 1986). The program is not designed to be a full-blown curriculum; instead, the goal of the program is to facilitate research on the idea of synergistic design. We assume that students can learn more about each of these areas by having the information introduced in the context of other areas. For example, students should learn more about planning when they are asked to find evidence in the film that Indiana planned ahead for his journey to South America, plus being helped to understand that some types of planning require the quantification of information such as the weight of supplies. Students should also learn more about the value of mathematical thinking when it is introduced in the context of planning. Similarly, when students consult science texts to find information such as densities they are learning information-finding skills that are not

developed when information is simply supplied in the context of a word problem. Furthermore, information about density, water purifiers, and other aspects
of science becomes more significant when students see its implications for important activities such as ensuring survival during a challenging trip (see Sherwood, Kinzer, Bransford, & Franks, 1987).

Overall, the preceding examples provide one illustration of an attempt to
develop synergistic lessons by relating scientific and mathematical thinking to
important areas such as planning and problem solving. Because our Thinker
program is still under development, we have not yet been able to provide explicit
tests of its use as an overall package. Nevertheless, data from several studies
provide evidence for the importance of various components. For example, we
have collected one set of data that shows that, when topics for potential lessons
are all related to a common context, students' abilities to remember what they
learned are much better than when the lessons are presented in a more typical,
unconnected format (Bransford et al., 1985). A study by Jacquelyn Gray and
Robyn Fivush that was recently completed at Emory University shows similar
benefits for children who were approximately two and one-half years old (Gray,
personal communication). Data also indicate that the use of a macro-context—in
conjunction with effective teaching—can greatly facilitate students' abilities to
solve mathematical word problems (Kulewicz et al., 1986) and that science
information learned in the context of problem solving is more likely to be used
to solve subsequent problems than is the same information presented in a factual
format (Sherwood et al., 1987). We also argued that, for the development of
competencies that rely on perceptual learning, the use of video-based contrast
sets during instruction has many advantages over a purely verbal mode (Bransford, Franks, Vye, & Sherwood, 1986).

Evaluations of the benefits of integrated approaches to instruction could take
place at a number of levels. One is simply to compare the effects of an integrated curriculum with traditional curricula. A more precise study is to teach
the same concepts to two different groups of students, but for one group to teach
the concepts in unrelated contexts and, for the other, to integrate different concepts into a single context such as *Raiders* (one way to achieve this integration is
to have one class per day that specifically focuses on this objective). Overall,
research on the effects of integrated knowledge structures is not easy to conduct,
but such research could be very important. We hope to conduct relevant studies
in the near future and hope that others will, too.

ADDITIONAL TECHNOLOGIES THAT SHOULD FACILITATE LEARNING

Before concluding this chapter we discuss two types of technology that should
further enhance the ability to create video-based learning environments that
provide alternate pathways for the development of important competencies. One

involves the Learning Technology Center's Response System (Williams, Sherwood, Hasselbring, & Bransford, 1986). This is an inexpensive system that allows students to use individual key pads to answer sets of multiple choice and true-false questions that can be posed by a teacher who is leading a class. Each student's answer can be immediately displayed on the computer screen; teachers can therefore decide whether to proceed with the lesson or to backtrack and to discuss concepts in more detail. Teachers can also ask opinion questions that yield honest answers because students' responses can be anonymous. In general, the response system makes group instruction much more interactive. When this type of system is used in conjunction with the random access capabilities of videodiscs, we expect that the performance of students in classrooms can be enhanced considerably. For some applications, the response system can also be used to collect individual data from each student, store it, and analyze it for systematic patterns of error. This approach to instruction should help teachers diagnose and remediate misconceptions that students may have about particular domains (e.g., Carey, 1985).

A second use of technology that can enhance learning is a software program that is based on the idea that an excellent way to learn is to teach. Vanderbilt's PRODUCER program (Sturdevant & Weekley, 1986) enables students to create high-quality stories and content-area lessons involving combinations of text and video. Though extremely flexible, the software is designed to be used with students as early as middle school.

The goal of creating computer-based videodisc products is highly motivating for students. One reason is that the product is professional looking because it uses high-quality video from existing videodiscs. Another reason is that the challenge of creating an effective lesson or interactive story that can actually be used by others is much more exciting than the mere goal of handing in an assignment.

A major impetus for creating the PRODUCER program stems from extensive work with students who are learning to program computers in LOGO (Papert, 1980). Our data suggest that, with instruction (mediation) that explicitly emphasizes processes of thinking and problem solving, there is evidence of transfer between LOGO and other tasks (e.g., Kinzer, Littlefield, Delclos, & Bransford, 1985; Littlefield, Delclos, Franks, Clayton, & Bransford, 1986). We have also been struck by the importance of another feature of LOGO: Students have the opportunity to produce designs and programs that are uniquely theirs. This is highly motivating. When a student produces an interesting design or program in class, it almost always captures the attention and admiration of the other students.

LOGO is an excellent medium for learning, but it is also somewhat limited given the general goals we have in mind. For example, if someone wants to create an interesting story, or a lesson on density, or a way to introduce new science vocabulary, LOGO offers few advantages for creating productions that are first-class. We should note, however, that the new software "LOGO Writer" offers more advantages in this regard.

Our analogue to the creation of motivating LOGO designs is our PRO-DUCER program that allows students to create high-quality products. The program is very easy to learn, and it allows students to use video that is professional in quality. This makes the products not only motivating to create, but motivating to watch.

There are a number of possible uses of PRODUCER. An 8-year-old language arts student might want to use scenes from *Star Wars* to illustrate a funny letter to his or her best friend. An 18-year-old aspiring diplomat might want to make her own version of *King Kong* with Russian subtitles. An English teacher might want to introduce a great poem to the class by illustrating it with scenes from a movie. Other potential illustrated products are stories, essays, exercises, lessons, cartoons, games, and journalistic pieces. Our initial experiences with students using PRODUCER have been extremely positive. We have been most struck by the students' creativity and by the degree of commitment they make to the creation of high-quality products. When students work as groups, they also seem to use and develop important social skills.

SUMMARY AND CONCLUSIONS

To summarize we argue that, just as the world is undergoing a computer revolution, we are also in the midst of a video revolution. Thanks to modern videodisc technology we are able to preserve information in a form that includes not only language but also gestures, intonations, and nonlinguistic context, and we are able to re-view this information almost instantaneously. With programs such as PRODUCER we are also able to combine video with computer text and create productions of extremely high quality. It is only during the past several decades that these potentials have become possible. Like the invention of written language, these potentials seem to represent a major landmark in human history. An important challenge is to find effective ways in which this potential can be used.

As one step toward meeting this challenge, we have asked how technology might enable us to create alternate pathways to important competencies such as the acquisition of new vocabulary and the development of mathematical and scientific thinking. We noted that formal educational environments are often quite different from informal learning environments, and we argued that, for many individuals, learning could be enhanced considerably if some of the advantages of these informal environments could be transferred to the classroom. We therefore used video segments to provide contexts for mediation about important concepts. Our initial data suggest that the use of relevant contexts can help students understand the significance of new information (Sherwood et al.,

1987). In addition, our data suggest that students' abilities to solve problems by using science information and by thinking mathematically can be improved considerably.

We also discussed new uses of video such as those involving contrast sets and "case-based" approaches to teaching—approaches that help people experience meaningful problems and learn to notice important features of these problems plus solutions to them. These uses of technology may open up new possibilities for a wide range of individuals. Ideally, these approaches to instruction will be complemented by computer-based technologies that can track student progress and provide diagnosis about strengths and weaknesses (e.g., Brown & Burton, 1978; Hasselbring, Goin, & Bransford, 1985). In addition, the opportunity for students to use programs like PRODUCER—programs that facilitate learning by putting students in the role of teachers—should increase students' abilities to achieve.

It would be exciting if, within the next few years, the typical lecture and text-based approach to teaching courses is replaced by new approaches that make frequent use of short video segments that introduce people to relevant problem situations and then help them see how new ideas and concepts can facilitate their abilities to deal with these situations (e.g., Bransford, Franks et al., 1986). Widespread use of such approaches should lead to new expectations about effective learning environments. As these expectations become commonplace, current modes of instruction may look as outmoded as do the old methods of teaching skiing before the GLM.

We close by considering what we have *not* addressed in this chapter. Our discussion has focused on the development of familiar competencies such as learning about science concepts or learning to solve word problems. We have not addressed the issue of whether the video revolution will produce new types of thinking that hitherto have been unknown. Certainly people who have watched a live football game and continually found themselves anticipating an "instant replay" are aware of the effects of video technology on our everyday thinking and expectations. In addition, the opportunity to work with the Vanderbilt PRODUCER program helps one notice aspects of video that one otherwise might miss. Nevertheless, although the ability to see replays and to create interesting video programs (including contrast sets of video segments) may well increase students "visual literacy" and facilitate the development of expertise in domains such as science and teaching, it is not clear to us that video technology will result in changes in thinking that make it qualitatively different from what we know today. One possible exception to this pattern may stem from the opportunity to see ourselves participating in (and fully attentive to) a variety of situations. This opportunity provides a perspective on our actions that is not possible given "natural" living conditions. Possible effects of this "outside" perspective on cognitive development would seem to be an important topic for future research.

ACKNOWLEDGEMENTS

Research reported in this chapter was supported in part by grant No. G0083C0052 from the U.S. Department of Education, grant No. MDA903-84-C-0218 from the Army Research Institute, and a grant from the IBM Corporation.

REFERENCES

Adams, L., Kasserman, J., Yearwood, A., Perfetto, G., Bransford, J., & Franks, J. (in press). The effects of fact versus problem-oriented acquisition. Memory and Cognition.

Anderson, J. R. (1983). *The architecture of cognition.* Cambridge, MA: Harvard University Press.

Anderson, J. R., & Reder, L. M. (1979). An elaborative processing explanation of depth of processing. In L. S. Cermak & F. I. M. Craik (Eds.), *Levels of processing and human memory.* Hillsdale, NJ: Lawrence Erlbaum Associates.

Bereiter, C., & Scardamalia, M. (1985). Cognitive coping strategies and the problem of "inert" knowledge. In S. Chipman, J. W. Segal, & R. Glaser (Eds.), *Thinking and learning skills: Current research and open questions,* (Vol. 2, pp. 65–80). Hillsdale, NJ: Lawrence Erlbaum Associates.

Bransford, J. D. (1979). *Human cognition: Learning, understanding, and remembering.* Belmont, CA: Wadsworth Publishing Company.

Bransford, J. D., Delclos, V. R., Vye, N. J., Burns, M. S., Hasselbring, T. S. (1986). *Improving the quality of assessment and instruction: Roles for dynamic assessment.* Paper presented at American Psychological Association, Washington, DC.

Bransford, J. D., Franks, J. J., Vye, N. J., & Sherwood, R. D. (1986). New approaches to instruction: Because wisdom can't be told. Paper presented at the Illinois Conference on Similarity and Analogy.

Bransford, J. D., & Heldmeyer, K. (1983). Learning from children learning. In J. Bisanz, G. Bisanz, & R. Kail (Eds.), *Learning in children: Progress in cognitive development research* (pp. 171–190). New York: Springer-Verlag.

Bransford, J. D., Sherwood, R. D., & Hasselbring, T. S. (1986). Computers, videodiscs, and the teaching of thinking. (Tech. Rep. 86.1.1). Nashville, TN: Peabody College of Vanderbilt University.

Bransford, J., Sherwood, R., Kinzer, C., & Hasselbring, T. (1985). *Havens for learning: Toward a framework for developing effective uses of technology* (Learning Technology Center Tech. Rep. 85.1.1). Nashville, TN: Vanderbilt University.

Bransford, J. D., Sherwood, R., Vye, N. J., & Rieser, J. (1986). Teaching thinking and problem solving: Suggestions from research. *American Psychologist, 41*(10), 1078–1089.

Bransford, J. D., Stein, B. S., Sheldon, T. S., & Owings, R. A. (1980). Cognition and adaptation: The importance of learning to learn. In J. Harvey (Ed.), *Cognition, social behavior and the environment.* Hillsdale, NJ: Erlbaum.

Bransford, J. D., Stein, B. S., Vye, N. J., Franks, J. J., Auble, P. M., Mezynski, K. J., & Perfetto, B. A. (1982). Differences in approaches to learning: An overview. *Journal of Experimental Psychology: General, III,* 390–398.

Bransford, J. D., & Stein, B. S. (1984). *The IDEAL problem solver.* New York: W. H. Freeman.

Briggs, H. (1624). *Arithmetica Logarithmica.*

Brown, A. L. (1979). Theories of memory and the problems of development: Activity, growth and knowledge. In L. S. Cermak & F. I. M. Craik (Eds.), *Levels of processing and human memory.* Hillsdale, NJ: Erlbaum.

Brown, A. L. (1985). Metacognition: The development of selective attention strategies for learning from texts. In H. Singer & R. B. Ruddell (Eds.), *Theoretical models and processes of reading* (3rd ed., pp. 501–526). Newark, DE: International Reading Association.

Brown, A. L., & Campione, J. C. (1981). Inducing flexible thinking: A problem of access. In M. Friedman, J. P. Das, and N. O'Connor (Eds.), *Intelligence and learning* (pp. 515–529). New York: Plenum.

Brown, A. L., Bransford, J. D., Ferrara, R. A., & Campione, J. C. (1983). Learning remembering and understanding. In J. H. Flavell & E. M. Markman (Eds.), *Carmichael's manual of child psychology* (Vol. 3, pp. 77–166). New York: Wiley.

Brown, J. S., & Burton, R. R. (1978). Diagnostic models for procedural bugs in basic mathematical skills. *Cognitive Science, 2;* 155–192.

Burton, R. R., Brown, J. S., & Fischer, G. (1984). Skiing as a model of instruction. In B. Rogoff & J. Lave (Eds.), *Everyday cognition.* Cambridge, MA: Harvard University Press.

Carey, S. (1985). Are children fundamentally different kinds of thinkers and learners than adults? In S. F. Chipman, J. W. Segal, & R. Glaser (Eds.), *Thinking and learning skills: Current research and open questions,* (Vol. 2, pp. 485–517). Hillsdale, NJ: Lawrence Erlbaum Associates.

Case, R. (1974). Structures and strictures: Some functional limitations on the course of cognitive growth. *Cognitive Psychology, 6,* 544–573.

Cassirer, E. (1923). *Substance and function.* Chicago: Open Court.

Chapman, R. S. (1978). Comprehension strategies in children. In J. Kavanagh & W. Strange (Eds.), *Speech and language in the laboratory, school, and clinic* (pp. 308–327). Cambridge, MA: MIT Press.

Chi, M. T. H. (1976). Short-term memory limitations in children: Capacity or processing deficits? *Memory and Cognition, 4,* 559–572.

Chi, M. T. H. (1978). Knowledge structures and memory development. In R. S. Siegler (Ed.), *Children's thinking: What develops?* Hillsdale, NJ: Erlbaum.

Chi, M. T. H., Feltovich, P. J., & Glaser, R. (1981). Categorization and representation of physics problems by experts and novices. *Cognitive science, 5,* 121–152.

Donaldson, M. (1978). *Children's minds.* New York: Norton.

diSessa, A. A. (1982). Unlearning Aristotelian physics: A study of knowledge-based learning. *Cognitive science, 6,* 37–75.

Dunker, K. (1945). On problem-solving. *Psychological Monographs, 58*(50), No. 270.

Feuerstein, R. (1979). *Instrumental enrichment.* Baltimore, MD: University Park.

Flavell, J. H., Beach, D. R., & Chinsky, J. M. (1966). Spontaneous verbal rehearsal in a memory task as a function of age. *Child Development, 37,* 238–299.

Gage, N. L., & Berliner, D. C. (1984). *Educational psychology* (3rd ed.). Boston: Houghton-Mifflin.

Garner, W. R. (1974). *The processing of information and structure.* Hillsdale, NJ: Lawrence Erlbaum Associates.

Gelman, R. (1978). Counting in the preschooler: What does and does not develop. In R. S. Seigler (Ed.). *Children's thinking: What develops?* Hillsdale, NJ: Erlbaum.

Gibson, J. & Gibson, E. (1955). Perceptual learning: Differentiation or enrichment? *Psychological Review, 62,* 32–51.

Gick, M. L., & Holyoak, K. J. (1980). Analogical problem solving. *Cognitive Psychology, 12,* 306–365.

Gick, M. L., & Holyoak, K. J. (1983). Schema induction and analogical transfer. *Cognitive Psychology, 15,* 1–38.

Goin, L., & Williams, S. (1986). *Software for teaching teaching.* Computer software. Nashville, TN: Vanderbilt University.

Gragg, C. I. (1940, October 19). *Harvard Alumni Bulletin.* Cambridge, MA: Harvard University.

Hasselbring, T., Goin, L., & Bransford, J. (1985). *Dynamic assessment and mathematics learning.* Paper presented at 109th annual meeting of the American Association of Mental Deficiency, Philadelphia, PA.

Jacobs, H. R. (1982). *Mathematics: A human endeavor.* New York: W. H. Freeman.

Johnson, R. (1986). *Videodiscs and story comprehension.* Unpublished manuscript. Nashville, TN: Vanderbilt Univeristy.

Kinzer, C., Littlefield, J., Delclos, V., & Bransford, J. D. (1985). Different LOGO learning environments and mastery: Relationships between engagement and learning. *Computers in the Schools, 2*(3), 33–43.

Kulewicz, S., Barron, B., Goin, L., Hasselbring, T., & Bransford, J. D. (1986). *The effects of video-context and mediation on mathematical problem solving* (Tech. Rep. 86.1.6). Nashville, TN: Learning Technology Center, Vanderbilt University.

Lewis, M., & Freedle, R. (1973). Mother-infant dyad: The cradle of meaning. In P. Pliner, L. Krames, & T. Alloway (Eds.), *Communication and affect* (pp. 127–155). New York: Academic Press.

Littlefield, J., Delclos, V. R., Franks, J. J., Clayton, K. N., & Bransford, J. D. (1986). *Thinking skills and LOGO: The importance of teaching method.* Paper presented at annual meeting of American Education Research Association, San Francisco, CA.

MacNamara, J. (1972). Cognitive basis of language learning in infants. *Psychological Review, 79,* 1–13.

Olson, D. R. (1985). Computers as tools of the intellect. *Educational Researcher, 14*(5), 5–8.

Ornstein, P. A., & Naus, M. J. (1978). Rehearsal processes in children's memory. In P. A. Ornstein (Eds.), *Memory development in children.* Hillsdale, NJ: Erlbaum.

Papert, S. (1980). *Mindstorms: Children, computers, and powerful ideas.* New York: Basic Books.

Perfetto, B. A., Bransford, J. D., & Franks, J. J. (1983). Constraints on access in a problem solving context. *Memory and cognition, 11,* 24–31.

Rock, D. (1986). Videodiscs and clinical training. Nashville, TN: Vanderbilt University.

Scribner, S., & Cole, M. (1973). Cognitive consequences of formal and informal education. *Science, 182,* 553–559.

Sherwood, R. D., Kinzer, C. K., Bransford, J. D., & Franks, J. J. (1987). Some benefits of creating macro-contexts for science instruction: Initial findings. *Journal of Research in Science Teaching, 24*(5), 417–435.

Sherwood, R., Kinzer, C., Hasselbring, T., & Bransford, D. (1987). Macro-contexts for learning: Initial findings and issues. *Journal of Applied Cognition Psychology, 1,* 93–108.

Simon, H. A. (1980). Problem solving and education. In D. T. Tuma & R. Reif (Eds.), *Problem solving and education: Issues in teaching and research* (pp. 81–96). Hillsdale, NJ: Lawrence Erlbaum Associates.

Simon, H. A., & Hayes, J. R. (1977). Psychological differences among problem isomorphs. In N. J. Castelan, D. B. Pisoni, & G. R. Potts (Eds.), *Cognitive theory* (Vol. 2). Hillsdale, NJ: Lawrence Erlbaum Associates.

Skinner, B. (1984). The shame of American education. *American Psychologist, 39*(9), 947–954.

Spiro, R. (1986). Learning in semantically rich domains. (Personal communication).

Stein, B. S., & Bransford, J. D. (1979). Constraints on effective elaboration: Effects of precision and subject-generation. *Journal of Verbal Learning and Verbal Behavior, 18,* 769–777.

Sturdevant, T., & Weekley, M. (1986). PRODUCER. Computer software. Nashville, TN: Vanderbilt University.

Thorndike, E. L. (1913). *Educational psychology* (Vols. 1 & 2). New York: Columbia University Press.

Vygotsky, L. S. (1978). *Mind in society.* Cambridge, MA: Harvard University Press.
Whitehead, A. N. (1929). *The aims of education.* New York: Macmillan.
Williams, S., Sherwood, R., Hasselbring, T., & Bransford, J. (1986). *The Peabody response system software program.* Nashville, TN: Vanderbilt University.

Chapter 11

The Quality of Interaction: Domain Knowledge, Social Interchange, and Computer Learning

Dennis P. Wolf
Project Zero
Harvard Graduate School of Education

PIAGET'S CONCEPT OF INTERACTION

For many years, researchers and theorists have supposed that it was Piaget's description of a succession of different logics underlying sensorimotor, concrete operational, and formal operational thinking that set his views apart from virtually all previous accounts of human growth. There is no doubt that Piaget's careful examinations taught developmentalists to "see" children's reasoning and problem solving in a new way—not as error-ridden versions of adult thought, but as samples from different *systems* of problem-solving. But paradoxically, it is precisely this investment in the thinking processes of children that has enabled subsequent investigators to learn that if one considers materials, instructions, or motivations, the growth of knowledge is both much more uneven and much more local than original Piagetian descriptions would have it (Fischer & Silvern, 1985). Thus, the enduring legacy of the Piagetian perspective may lie outside of the details of stage theory.

At the center of Piaget's work is a view of knowledge as *constructed through interaction,* or the constant exchange between the knower and known in the act of discovering reality. In fact, Piaget provided us with two powerful, yet different portraits of interaction. On the one hand, Piaget's concept of interaction includes the intense pursuit of knowledge though action on and experiment with material objects as well as thoughts about those objects. His observations taught us to see this pursuit in the infant kicking to make a mobile sway; in the 5-year-old counting stones in one direction, then another; in adolescents (or adults) manipulating pendulums or variables. By contrast, Piaget's second form of interaction is profoundly human and social. It includes the exchanges of ideas, attitudes, and strategies that occur between children, between adult and child, between the acting and observing self.

Part of the power of Piaget's notion of interaction is evident in its longevity. Piaget conceived his views on interaction at a time when the critical factors to take into account included only material objects (clay, sticks, tulips, and roses), other minds, actions, and concepts. He had no need to consider the virtual world of computer-generated "objects" or the partnerships afforded by software programs. Nevertheless, no other concept is more central to development of useful and productive programs than that of interaction. In fact, proponents of computer-based learning argue that its unique power lies precisely in interactivity—a good program is, ideally, highly responsive to its user (Greenfield, 1984; Papert, 1980).

Therefore, it would seem that the legacy of Piagetian theory to computer learning is less a message that learning will occur in stages and more a message that we need to attend closely to the *quality* of the interactions that we design. In this paper, I want to explore how computers can either enhance or suppress the two types of interaction that Piaget thought it important to nurture: (a) provocative encounters with the basic structures of a particular kind of knowledge, which I will refer to as *domain knowledge;* and (b) equally stimulating encounters with other minds. In order to argue for the very general importance of both of these kinds of interactions in computer learning, I will focus on an area quite different from Piaget's reasoning, yet equally sensitive to both types of interaction. Thus, in place of hypothetical-deductive reasoning, I will look at the domain knowledge and the social interchanges that might prove essential to the acquisition of sophisticated reading skills, particularly those demanded by the complex and subtle texts of literature.

Domain Knowledge

Piaget wrote the developmental history of knowing in the most general sense. However, from the center of a current scientific zeitgeist where attention focuses on task demands and the particularity of knowledge in different domains, the meaning or import of Piaget's work on time, space, causality, or logic has shifted. From the newer vantage point, the work can be read as a highly detailed account of the emergence of a *particular* kind of knowledge—the hypothetical-deductive reasoning that underlies much of logic, mathematics, and science. Reconsidered in this way, Piaget's works are highly powerful descriptions of the kinds of materials and experiences that might lead a child to flourish as a young mathematician or scientist: For example, access to manipulable materials like clay, water, and sticks of different lengths; a father more eager to "play" experiment than tea party; and time with adults who raise interesting, but difficult, questions and odd cases; encounters with the core or classic problems of the domain, such as the isolation of variables. Similarly, the Piagetian stages that have often been taken as broad-based revolutions in the very nature of thought itself can be seen as a sequence of steps leading from an initial and relatively shallow understanding of logical thinking toward an in-depth knowledge of what it is to examine evidence and draw well-founded conclusions.

Thus, one lesson from Piaget reconsidered is *not* that interactions with these same ingredients will promote learning of all kinds. Rather, it might be that, like hypothetical-deductive thought, other forms of learning have materials, problems, and interactions that nourish their particular unfolding. Thus, as we move from real-world settings to computer environments, it is crucial to recognize and highlight the unique contents, strategies, and intuitions belonging to the individual domains of human knowledge.

KNOWLEDGE IN A DIFFERENT DOMAIN: KNOWING TEXTS AND LITERATURE

How might the pursuit of a specific set of skills look in a domain quite distant from Piaget's reasoning, one as different as understanding how to read literature? Clearly, at the simplest level, a reader must be able to "make" words from the squiggles on the page, then "take" the meaning out of those words, and—somehow—add those meanings up until the paragraph or novel is understood. But though this kind of decoding and comprehension is certainly necessary, it is far from sufficient. Much more besides matching letters to sounds and sound patterns to meanings is involved in reading. It is not even sufficient to be able to extract meaning from successive sentences. When a sophisticated reader or writer makes sense of a text, he or she is rarely reading just for information (that is for telephone books and street signs). A reader actively builds up meaning *across* sentences by interacting with the text, employing a number of different, *interpretive* strategies.

For example, in order to make full or deep sense of even a relatively simple passage like the opening of Thurber's fable, *The Thirteen Clocks* (Figure 11.1) a reader uses (a) *selecting and organizing strategies;* (b) *expansions;* and (c) *strategies tuned to reading particular kinds of texts.*

> Once upon a time, in a gloomy castle on a lonely hill, where there were thirteen clocks that wouldn't go, there lived a cold, aggressive Duke, and his niece, the princess Saralinda. She was warm in every wind and weather, but he was always cold. His hands were as cold as his smile and almost as cold as his heart. He wore gloves when he was asleep, and he wore gloves when he was awake, which made it difficult for him to pick up pins or coins or the kernels of nuts, or to tear the wings from nightingales. He was six feet four, and forty-six, and even colder than he thought he was. One eye wore a velvet patch, the other glittered through a monocle, which made half his body seem closer to

you than the other half. He had lost one eye when he was twelve, for he was fond of peering into nests and lairs in search of birds and animals to maul. One afternoon, a mother shrike had mauled him first. His nights were spent in evil dreams, and his days were given to wicked schemes.

Wickedly scheming, he would lisp and cackle through the cold corridors of the castle, planning new impossible feats for the suitors of Saralinda to perform. He did not wish to give her hand in marriage, since her hand was the only warm hand in the castle. Even the hands of his watch and the hands of all the thirteen clocks were frozen.

FIGURE 11.1   Excerpt from James Thurber's *The Thirteen Clocks.*

SELECTING AND ORGANIZING STRATEGIES: DYNAMIC TEXTS

An organizing strategy permits a reader to get beneath the surface of the text; to see not what it says, but what it *means.* For example, through what might be called *selective information gathering,* skilled readers dissolve the integrity of the text-as-written, resorting it into information about a number of different topics. Thus, as a reader makes his or her way into the Thurber fable, he or she actively builds up a picture of the "cold, aggressive Duke" by collecting all the clues given about him. By following a chain of *anaphoric references* (a series of terms that refer back to an earlier mentioned referent), the reader learns about *his* niece; that *he* was always cold; that *his* hands were as cold as *his* smile and almost as cold as *his* heart. Because the information about the Duke lies scattered throughout the passage, a reader has to recognize each new reference to the Duke as it appears and weave it into an increasingly detailed understanding of what the Duke is about. Thus, even though a reader may scan the text left to right and line by line, comprehension requires the active dissolution of the original text into relevant lines of information.

Readers interact with the text in additional ways as well. For example, they must often unscramble the text when the "order of mention" does not reflect the "order of occurrence" (Goodman, 1983). Thus, in the middle of the passage about a duke who is 46, the reader learns "that he had lost one eye when he was twelve" when "a mother shrike had mauled him . . ." This freedom to bring relevant thematic material together, in dreams, recollections, flashbacks, and premonitions—indifferent to literal historical occurrence—is a major tool for shaping all kinds of narratives. But it leaves the reader with a dual comprehension task. On the one hand he or she must actively reconstruct the chain of events by unscrambling "the order of mention" to reveal "the order of occurrence." But on the other hand, the reader needs to ask, "Why were these two widely separated events brought together in the text?" coming to the conclusion that the writer is making a point by collecting all the Duke's misdeeds at one moment in the narrative.

Because of the same flexibility that makes word-processing possible (Wolf, 1985; Wolf & Walters, 1986), it is possible to use the computer screen to model or to make visible some of the processes of interacting with texts. In this way print can be made "kinetic"; it can become an essentially plastic substance that can be worked on, transformed, and reassembled much as clay, water, or blocks might be (Forman, 1985). For example, it is possible to demonstrate vividly what it is like to select and organize information from a text. Using the Thurber tale, a cursor moves through the text highlighting the phrases that describe the Duke, thus mimicking the active information gathering and organizing of a skilled reader. Subsequently, it is possible to drop away all the surrounding text from those phrases describing the Duke in order to highlight that line of information within the text. Sentences in a passage can also be numbered and reordered to show the underlying historical sequence. By exercising all of these strategies on the same passage, a reader can visually (and perhaps psychologically) experience what it is like to interact with, rather than to merely decode, a text.

MAKING THE INVISIBLE VISIBLE: ELASTIC AND "X-RAYED" TEXTS

Though we talk about the language of written texts as autonomous or self-sufficient (Olson, 1977), even literary texts, rich as they may be, are something like codes. Throughout any story there are moments when readers must draw inferences, fill in events based on prior knowledge of events or text forms (Schank & Abelson, 1977), supplement the text with details drawn from the "mind's eye." Thus, through a series of *inferences and expansions* a reader supplements what is written with what is implied. For instance, once a reader learns that the Duke keeps his niece Saralinda in his castle, he or she surmises that Saralinda might be an orphan and that some time prior to the onset of the story she either has lost her parents or been kidnapped away from them. In a sense, at that moment, the reader "opens up" the text, inserts that knowledge, and continues reading, having stored a "grudge" against the Duke—based on a likelihood, rather than anything he or she literally read. Similarly, readers also probably imagine Saralinda, not just as captive, but as beautiful—because princesses in fairy tales usually are. So, although Thurber only mentions that Saralinda is warm, the instant he casts her in the role of heroine and princess, we fill in the blanks and supply ringlets, tapering fingers, snowy skin.

There are still other things to appreciate that aren't literally there; for example, the underlying structure of a story or a poem. A large part of being able to comprehend texts fully may lie in recognizing what you are reading—whether the character descriptions you are reading come from a fairy tale, a fable, a history book, or a psychology text. Such knowledge lays down a critical foundation for making predictions, filling in inferences, and drawing conclusions. In fact, one of the ways in which younger and older, unskilled and sophisticated readers differ is the degree to which they can grasp the structures or schemas that underlie the texts they read (Weaver & Dickinson, 1979). For instance, no reader can fully appreciate *The Thirteen Clocks* without recognizing its structure as that of a traditional fairy tale—complete with villain, prince, princess, challenging tasks, a narrow escape, and a happy ending. To grasp fully what Thurber is "up to" involves being able to compare the patterns in *The Thirteen Clocks* (which have to be inferred) with the patterns of a traditional fairy tale (which lies entirely outside of the frame of the book at hand). Only once that kind of comparison is made can a reader chuckle wholeheartedly at the way in which the opening of Thurber's tale is a parody of the way in which fairy tales typically open with a careful description of characters and their traits—whether it be the youngest, kindliest daughter or the wicked stepmother.

Here, too, computer displays can be enormously powerful. An "animated" text can be programmed to open up to "reveal" the kinds of inferences that a skilled reader might make at a particular juncture. Alternatively, the text of Thurber's description of Saralinda can be made to open up to pose a question that prompts the reader to use his or her mind's eye and imagine what the princess looks like. It is equally possible to model the kinds of structures that underlie texts for readers. Many fairy tales trade on a similar set of characters: elder, hero, true love, villain, helper, friend, messenger. In order to reveal this kind of structure, a reader might skim *The Thirteen Clocks* and *Snow White and the Seven Dwarfs*. If the computer then drops out all the text, except that which introduces or describes characters, a reader sees a radically simplified display that highlights the similar cast of characters. Looking across the two resulting displays a reader can begin to appreciate what is the same (the contrasts of good and evil through a series of opposites, the concreteness of the language, etc.) and what Thurber has taken to comic extremes. In this way, the flexibility of computer texts can be harnessed to reveal similarities in the underlying anatomy of different texts. Such "X-rays" can make otherwise quite elusive aspects of texts, like genre or form, suddenly become visible, concrete, and available for reflection.

STRATEGIES TUNED TO PARTICULAR KINDS OF TEXTS: MUTABLE TEXTS

However powerful these and other discourse-processing strategies are, they are also insufficient for accomplished reading. A skilled reader should also have a feel for the difference between *The Thirteen Clocks* and a historical account of

Richard III as a cruel uncle. Making that kind of distinction demands that a reader be able to interact with written text in a variety of ways—for example, from a historical or a literacy stance.

Reading from a particular stance or for a particular purpose demands a specific kind of awareness. For example, an aesthetic response to Thurber's parody certainly involves several sensibilities; among them an awareness of expression, multiple levels of meaning, and repleteness.

Expression: Readers of literature are rarely looking for just the facts. Along with that kind of straightforward information, they take in several other kinds of meaning (Goodman, 1968). Part of being able to read literature includes being or becoming alert to questions of *expression*. What kind of atmosphere, mood, or region do the characters move in and how is that ambiance being conveyed? One of the major ways in which authors convey expression is through controlling the network of images and connotations they create. Thurber provides at least two lines of evidence an active reader might follow simultaneously in an effort to define the mood or atmosphere in *The Thirteen Clocks*. There is a network of cold versus warm imagery that signals the tension between the unforgiving world of the Duke and the generous world of the princess. This is supplemented by a trail of words that point to a gloomy and foreboding world ("gloomy castle," "lonely hill").

Multiple Levels of Meaning: In portraying the Duke, Thurber tells us "his hands were as cold as his smile and almost as cold as his heart." Whereas the Duke may literally have had icy fingers, his heart is only metaphorically frozen. Similarly, when Thurber mentions that the Duke is blind in one eye and limps through the corridors of his castle, he is not just identifying infirmities, he is (probably) using those hallmarks to suggest that the Duke is morally and spiritually handicapped. The fact that the hands of the 13 clocks in the Duke's castle are sympathetically frozen—improbable as that is in the world as we know it—also testifies to the scope of the Duke's cruel malaise. But in order to see these second meanings, a reader must take in not just the literal, but also the figurative meanings being conveyed.

Repleteness: The language in *The Thirteen Clocks* is not transparent, it calls attention to itself through repetition, rhythms, and near rhymes: "she was warm in every wind and weather"; "he wore gloves when he was asleep, he wore gloves when he was awake"; "to pick up pins . . . to tear the wings." In other words, in literature, unlike in grocery lists or warranties or word problems, writers exploit and play with the physical properties of language itself and readers should be alert to them.

Such qualities can be subtle and elusive. However, by using one of the remarkable qualities of computer texts—their mutability—a reader can enter the written stream, play with it, and change it. This allows readers to take on the stance of writers, and through that active involvement, gain a sense for the design of texts. Consider the careful network of cold and warm references that thread through the opening of *The Thirteen Clocks*. In order to get a feeling for the way in which this imagery builds up like a network through the text, a reader could look at how changing those terms would create a totally different feeling. The computer can store sets of alternatives to this language—families of terms that use color or size contrasts to depict the counterpoint between good and evil forces. By toggling back and forth between several versions, a reader can see how a writer might create subtle variations in expressive quality or mood. Taking this procedure a step further, the computer can produce a version of the passage in which all the instances of hot and cold language are replaced by open spaces. At this point the reader has to take on the quite active role of a writer, creating his or her own network of imagery.

Deep Literacy and Interactive Texts

Clearly, then, to be deeply literate is to interact with the text—to ferret out its different lines of information, to expand it with inferences, to unscramble it. It involves appreciating implicit structures and implied meanings. Moreover, a skilled reader understands that there are many ways to read—for instance, that a literary text (as compared to a biology book), will be "thick" with meaning— that the meaning can be carried in different ways through sound patterns, networks of images, and figures of speech.

In the familiar context of book pages, print lies still. In that static graphic environment, it is difficult to show a young or unskilled reader how to interact with text by sorting, untwisting, and reassembling it, by transforming it, by filling it in. Hence, there is considerable power in computer print displays to make visible what are usually invisible psychological processes of skilled text readers.

SOCIAL INTERACTIONS OVER TEXT: THE POSSIBILITIES OF HYPERTEXT AND COMPUTER NETWORKS

Few activities could be considered more solitary than reading. But on closer examination, even the most apparently isolated reader depends on a community of others. Here the youngest of "readers"—two-year-olds—provide a good model. They learn the most fundamental conventions of reading books in shared *dialogues* over texts (Snow, Nathan, & Perlman, 1985; Wolf & Pusch, 1985). By talking with another person, they learn the boundary between the book world and the reading world, what it is important to attend to in stories and pictures, how stories work. But the social processes behind understanding texts are not limited to the preschool years—they resurface in at least two ways throughout anyone's reading career. First of all, we continue to depend on being able to compare our reaction and understandings with those of other people—10 year-olds discuss whether Judy Blume is babyish, adults debate over whether a news-paper editorial is simply impassioned or twisted. Second, anytime a reader turns to another piece of writing—the dictionary to look up words, more books from the same author, a magazine interview of the writer—he or she makes use of a vital network of information created by other people. In other words, even though we may read to ourselves, the act of making sense of what we read is—or could be—continuously informed by what we have learned about the reading process from other people.

Two relatively recent advents, the design of hypertext programming and com-puter communication networks, provide significant opportunities to *expand,* rather than diminish, social interactions during and about reading. In particular, these two options, if used to advantage, can help students to become aware of fundamental issues in the social construction of knowledge. Chief among these are: (a) the piecemeal nature of individual experience and the consequent need to collaborate; (b) the inevitable role of *stances* (attitudes and values) in shaping knowledge; and (c) the difficulty of translating experience across times, regions, or cultures.

Hypertexts: A System for Collaborative Inquiry

Much human knowledge comes in pieces, with little hope of completing the data not consider the potsherds of an archaeologist, the language samples of the child linguist, the torn or incomplete manuscripts belonging to historians. From another vantage point, consider how much of serious work (whether affective or intellectual) occurs collectively: among parents and children, between siblings, among actors and a director, between a librettist and a composer, between Mo-net and his friends painting together in the fields at Giverney, among scientists working together to find a cure for AIDS (John-Steiner, 1985). Given this, it is surprising how closely most of our learning theories stick to the image of *the* individual up against a problem.

Hypertexts may offer readers what could be called "on-line collaborations" with other minds. A hypertext might best be described as a database that is organized like a cross-indexed encyclopedia and that thus allows a reader to branch out from the text at hand, to follow any number of different lines of inquiry. For example, a reader making his way through *The Adventures of Huck-leberry Finn* could pause to look up a word in a dictionary, to study a map of the Mississippi River, to read about slavery laws, to enjoy letters that Twain wrote about his reason for writing the novel, to scan contemporary and modern reviews of the book. In other words, a hypertext system can model the ways in which an active or sophisticated reader draws on a wide range of human resources available to him or her. In this sense, hypertexts can introduce readers to the way in which their individual understanding of a text depends, in a profoundly social sense, on being able to tap into the work of many other people.

Alternatively, hypertexts can model the kind of interactive conversations that we often have with fellow readers (or ourselves) when we try to make sense of a particularly challenging or problematic work—what current literary theorists call "reader response" (Dias, 1986; Rosenblatt, 1978). Consider what it might be like to read a challenging lyric poem and be able to call up any number of insights from other minds: another reader's diagram of the poem's structure, another reader's paraphrase, or, alternatively, still a third student's appraisal of the poem. In no sense need these entries be preestablished by a programmer or teacher. Some entries might be present to act as models or to spark thinking, but thereafter other readers could enter their own views, revise or amend earlier readings. In this way, readers can become active members of a network of respondents each with a particular point of view to contribute for consideration—they can become part of a conversation in which understanding is no longer piecemeal.

COMPUTER COMMUNICATION NETWORKS: STANCES AND TRANSLATIONS

In recent years, James Levin and his colleagues have developed ways in which computers enlarge not just the size of users' audiences, but their awareness of some profoundly human aspects of data gathering and knowledge use. Notably, they have developed computer news chronicles (Levin, Reil, Rowe, & Boruta, 1985) and collaborative science projects (Levin & Cohen, 1985) where data is gathered at different sites and then collectively analyzed and exchanged through a bulletin board.

Like hypertexts, the projects described by Levin and his colleagues provide interesting examples of the ways in which students could experience reading in ways that highlight the collaborative nature of knowing. (In those projects, students join different texts by taking items off a wire service or by pooling their observations about water conservation and recycling to find out what problems are unique to their region or common around the world.) But the fundamentally interactive nature of the network projects highlights still other potentially social aspects of computer-based learning, notably their awareness of the stances individuals take toward information and the challenges inherent in trying to transport or translate information across situations.

There is no question that computer networks multiply students' sources of information. But one hopes that access can also be made to highlight the different stances that individuals take toward facts. For example, Levin and his colleagues asked students to collect the headlines from newspaper stories about the fortieth anniversary of the bombing of Hiroshima and Nagasaki. Students from San Diego, Tel Aviv, Fairbanks, and Tokyo were involved. Since initially collecting their data, students have been involved in analyzing their data so as to get to the underlying Israeli, American, and Japanese views of the bombings and their consequences. The power, but also the challenge, of this kind of network design is to find situations or problems in which the factual surface of information is unsatisfying and that push students into realizing and discussing the different stances individuals and groups take toward the "same" facts.

Levin and his colleagues have also involved students in Mexico, Alaska, California, and Israel in working on the problem of water conservation. The hope is (the project is still underway) that the problem is vital enough to generate serious research and avid interest in sharing the results. But besides the sheer transmission of information, more is at stake. As Levin describes it, "Once these descriptions have been shared . . . then the focus of the project will be for each site to analyze the techniques used by other sites . . . to understand either why they can't be used in their site or to discover that the technique is in fact useful at their location." (Levin, 1985). Here, then is an opportunity for students to grapple with the difference between *transmission,* or the sheer delivery or information and *translation,* or the understanding that information must be meaningful, useful, and humane, not only at its source, but at its destination. This is no small understanding. Adult exporters of information, goods, and technology do not always grapple well with the issue. Consider the recent consequences of the unthinking export of infant formula to poorer nations: Established patterns of breast-feeding were disrupted, and infant nutrition and health were endangered. If young learners are to grow up attuned to living in a global community, they need to be sensitive to the fit between knowledge or techniques and a particular community of users. Computers and computer networks can be used simply to export and import information. Alternatively, telecommunications capacities *could* be used to focus attention on the issue of translating, that is, selecting and adapting, information.

CONCLUSION

Computers are only as promising as our ability to realize engaging and demanding interactions through them. But powerful interactions have at least two other qualities. One, I would suggest, is *attunement*—a kind of intimacy with both the content and the ways of thinking unique to specific human enterprises. Piaget provided us with a portrait of what it is to educate one kind of thinking—the rigorous problem-solving demanded by hypothetical-deductive thinking. He also illustrated the ways in which particular interactions with hidden objects, stones, or pendulums might promote that rigor. Here I have laid out some of the distinctive skills inherent in being a thoughtful reader. At the same time, I have described possible ways in which computerized texts might provoke, model, and extend those skills. These uses of the computer vary significantly from the strategies and formats used for "geometric supposing" (Schwartz, 1985) or physics problems (diSessa, 1985). And, I would argue, so they should. If, in the course of creating computer instruction, we homogenize what we teach and how we present it, we unnecessarily narrow and diminish what computers can teach. The range of domains for which we create such interactions must, at least eventually, include more than diagnosing diseases, understanding physics principles, or playing chess. It should encompass reading literature, diagnosing clinical syndromes, and writing social history, as well.

A second, equally important quality of worthwhile computer systems is the capacity to provoke complex social interactions, not just chat or data transmission. But such complex interactions are not a necessary by-product of two users confronting a program or the electronic linking of terminals into a network. The art of selecting good problems and science of designing forms of interaction that will draw attention to issues of collaboration and interpretation, to the attitudes beneath data, and to the need to translate information across situations—these skills have to be in the foreground of design.

REFERENCES

diSessa, A. (1985). Learning about knowing. In E. Klein (Ed.), *Computers and children, New Directions for Child Development 28,* 97–124.

Dias, P. (1986). Researching response to poetry. *English Quarterly, 19*(1). 9–21.

Fischer, K., & Silvern, L. (1985). Stages and individual differences in cognitive development. *Annual Review of Psychology,36,* 613–48.

Forman, G. (1985). The value of kinetic print in computer graphics for young children. In E. Klein (Ed.), (Special Issue). *New Directions for Child Development, 28,* 19–36. San Francisco: Jossey-Bass.

John-Steiner, V. (1985). *Notebooks of the mind.* Albuquerque: University of New Mexico Press.

Goodman, N. (1986). *Languages of art.* Indianapolis, IN: Bobbs-Merrill.

Goodman, N. (1983). *Fact, fiction, and forecast.* Cambridge, MA: Harvard University Press.

Greenfield, P. (1984). *Mind and media: The effects of television, video games, and computers.* Cambridge, MA: Harvard University Press.

Levin, J. (1985). Paper presented at Fifteenth Annual Meeting of the Jean Piaget Society, Philadelphia.

Levin, J., & Cohen, M. (1985). The world as an international science laboratory: Electronic networks for science instruction and problem solving. *Journal of Computers in Mathematics and Science Teaching.*

Levin, J., Reil, M. M., Rowe, R. D., & Boruta, M. J. (1985). Muktuk meets jacuzzi: Computer networks and elementary school writers. In S. W. Freedman (Ed.), *The acquisition of written language: Revision and response* (pp. 60–71). Norwood, NJ: Ablex.

Olson, D. (1977). From utterance to text: The bias of language in speech and writing. In M. Wold, M. McQuillan, & E. Radwin (Eds.), *Thought and language/language and reading* (pp. 84–108). Cambridge, MA: Harvard Educational Review.

Papert, S. (1980). *Mindstorms: Children, computers, and powerful ideas.* New York: Basic Books.

Rosenblatt, L. (1978). *The reader, the text, the poem.* Carbondale, IL: Southern Illinois University Press.

Schank, R., & Abelson, H. (1977). *Scripts, plans, goals, and understanding.* Hillsdale, NJ: Lawrence Erlbaum Associates.

Schwartz, J. (1985). Geometric supposer: A program for teaching geometric theorems production and solution. Pleasantville, NY: Sunburst Publishing.

Snow, C., Nathan, D., & Perlman, R. (1985). Assessing children's knowledge about book reading. In L. Galda & A. Pellegrini (Eds.), *The development of children's literate behavior* (pp. 167–182). Norwood, NJ: Ablex.

Weaver, P., & Dickinson, D. (1979). Story comprehension and recall in dyslexic students. *Bulletin of the Orton Society, 29,* 157–171.

Wolf, D. (1985). Flexible texts: Computer editing in the study of writing. In E. Klein (Ed.), Children and computers: (Special Issue). *New Directions for Child Development 28,* San Francisco: Jossey-Bass.

Wolf, D., & Pusch, J. (1985). The origins of autonomous texts in play boundaries. In L. Galda & A. Pellegrini (Eds.), *The development of children's literate behavior* (pp. 63–78). Norwood, NJ: Ablex.

Wolf, D. & Walters, J. (1986). The writer with a word processor: Juggler, sculptor, and director. *Computers in the Schools* (pp. 35–46). New York: Hayworth Press.

Chapter 12

The Child-Computer Dyad and Cognitive Development

Frank B. Murray
University of Delaware

For reasons that are not entirely clear, we know—from several independent lines of research—that when pupils work cooperatively with their peers on an academic task, there is invariably greater academic growth than there would have been had the pupils worked alone on the same task (e.g. Johnson, Muruyama, Johnson, Nelson, & Skon, 1981; Slavin, 1983; and Webb, 1985). Achievement is greatest, in fact, when the only way the individual pupils can meet their own instructional goals is if the members of the group help each other and are thereby successful as a group (Deutsch, 1959; Johnson & Johnson, 1974; Slavin, 1983). When the academic task is a developmental task as well as an academic task, that is, when the task has a strong relationship with age, particularly mental age, we know that the sufficient condition for the young pupil's success may be little more than the opportunity for the child to interact with another child who has an opposing and maturer point of view about the way to solve the task (F. Murray, 1982, 1983).

These developmental tasks, though indicators of important intellectual accomplishments, are only a small portion of the school curriculum (F. Murray, 1979, 1986). The tasks are about the child's understanding of the necessary implications in the concept he or she has mastered, about information that must be true and could not be otherwise. The bulk of the curriculum, on the other hand, is about information that is merely true and could conceivably be otherwise; for that reason there is a potential for conceptual regression and for the acquisition of errors when the pupil argues with, and comes to consensus with, another pupil who is simply wrong about information that is merely contingent and not necessary. Cognitive developmental tasks, tasks about necessity, are by definition not subject to regression in these or any other circumstances. For example, the transitivity relationship (e.g., if $A = B$ and $B = C$, then $A = C$), once constructed by the child, is not forgotten, neither apparently can it be undone by counterargument.

We know also that these developmental tasks are, for the most part, domain specific and that the child's solution of the problem presented in the task does not extend easily to other versions or modifications of the task, let alone to other domains of related tasks. This fact is the so-called horizontal décalage phenomenon in Piagetian theory, or the "p-prim" construct of diSessa (this volume). That the concept of necessity, for example, along with the other Genevan operational concepts, is constructed piece by piece over various materials and contexts has led several researchers (e.g., diSessa 1982; Papert, 1980; Pea, 1985a) to suppose that cognitive development could be facilitated were the child to explore the domain in question in a microworld of a computer—a world in which the regularities of the child's interactions with the environment are simulated with a computer. The notion is that the formalisms and laws that the child eventually comes to construct will develop sooner and more clearly through the child's interaction with a computer. Even if the computer simulation is a poor model of the domain in question, and even if, as a result, there is little positive transfer between the child's proficiency with the computer tasks and their real-world counterparts, the child's proficiency with the computer could entail the very same logical operations that define, for example, the Piagetian operational stages. A similar argument can be advanced about the role of language in the development of logical thought. Even though the Genevans do not give language a central role in the development of intelligence, it is certainly possible that logical operations could be applied reflectively to linguistic stimuli as well as to any other set of stimuli that are ordinarily implicated in cognitive development. Thus it makes as much sense, for example, to speak of the conservation of "letter" under transformations of size, font, case, and so on, as it does to speak of the conservation of number under the transformations of displacement and spatial arrangement (Furth, 1978; F. Murray, 1978).

However, there is another way, often neglected, in which the computer can be supposed to influence cognitive development. Rather than merely simulate the interactions of the children with their environments in certain domains, the machine might simulate their interactions with other children, particularly children who are at a somewhat more advanced cognitive level than they are. These interactions, these cooperative and collaborative events, have been theoretically and empirically established as necessary—and sometimes as sufficient—conditions for intellectual development. What would the computer have to do, what would have to be simulated in the computer's taking on the role of a more cognitively advanced peer?

THE WORKINGS OF CHILD-CHILD DYADS: INTERACTION EFFECTS

There has not been any legitimate doubt that conflict and interaction among peers in small classroomlike settings are effective ways to promote cognitive development and the acquisition of some conceptual information in the curriculum. J. Murray (1972) and Silverman and Stone (1972) reported success with training procedures based on the rather simple micromainstreaming experimental manipulation of having immature pupils argue with their advanced peers until they all came to an agreement or stalemate about the solutions to various problems. When tested alone after the interaction, 80 percent to 94 percent of the lower level pupils made significant gains in performance compared to the very much lower rates of success reported in studies of more traditional training attempts (Beilin, 1977; F. Murray, 1978). These gains fulfilled several demanding criteria for genuine accomplishment. Not only do most immature children make significant gains as a result of social interactions with advanced children, but the gains are of substantial magnitude. For example, in Murray (1972) 8 out of 15 children who scored 0 out of 12 on the pretest had scores of 11 or 12 out of 12 on the various posttests. What has not been clear in this line of research is what in the social-interaction experience produced these gains. A number of factors come to mind, and research since 1973 or so has treated many of them.

We know that the social-interaction effect can be had in different-size interaction groups of one on one (Silverman & Geiringer, 1973; Silverman & Stone, 1972), two on one (F. Murray, 1972), and three on two (Botvin & Murray, 1975) in kindergarten, first, second, third, and fifth grades with normal and learning disabled, although not with those disabled by communication disorders (Knight-Arest & Reid, 1978), with blacks and whites, and with middle and low socioeconomic status (SES) groups. Borys and Spitz (1979), however, did not find social interaction to be especially effective with mentally retarded institutionalized adolescents (IQ = 66, mental age (MA) = 10 years, chronological age (CA) = 20 years).

We know also that no unusual information or instruction is presented in the interaction; that is, no researchers have reported children saying anything or manipulating the stimuli in any way that has not been said or demonstrated in the less effective "nonsocial" training procedures, namely, cognitive conflict, cue reduction, phenomenal-real discrimination, verbal rule instruction, reversibility, and the various learning paradigm procedures (Murray, 1978).

Analyses of the course of the interaction yield no surprises either, except perhaps that agreement is often reached quickly. Miller and Brownell (1975) found that nearly half the agreements were reached in less than 50 seconds and rarely took longer than 4 or 5 minutes. It is also surprising that the advanced children do not prevail because of any greater social influence or higher IQ or because they are particularly better arguers. In arguments about best TV shows and other concepts that have no developmental or necessity attributes, the advanced children won only 41 of 90 arguments, lost 38, and stalemated 11, leading Miller and Brownell (1975) to conclude that relative social influence of the advanced children by itself is not a significant factor in the social interaction effect.

Growth occurs only for the children who yield, which they do 60%–80% of the time (Silverman & Geiringer, 1973). The advanced children seem to initiate discussion slightly more often, state their answer slightly more often, give good reasons, counter the others slightly more often, move stimuli more often, and appear slightly more flexible in their arguments than the immature children, who repetitiously focus on their original opinion and its justifications (Miller & Brownell, 1975; Silverman & Stone, 1972). No differences are found between the pupils in their modes of communication, considered apart from their content, nor between yielders and nonyielders in this regard (Silverman & Geiringer, 1973); thus, the clues to the success of the procedure are not apparent in the analysis of the form or content of interactions between the children.

Despite the magnitude of the success of the social interaction procedures, the authenticity of the children's newly acquired solutions may still be questioned even though, taking the studies as a whole, the principal criteria for genuine solutions are met. It may have been possible for the immature children in these studies to have merely parroted or imitated the correct response because a thoughtless repetition of the right answer could have inflated the posttest performance. Although some researchers controlled for such a response set by including items for which the "right answer" would be inappropriate, a more demanding test of whether the children did more than imitate their tutors would be the degree to which they explained their new judgments by justifications that differed from those given by the advanced pupils during the social interaction sessions. Silverman and Stone (1972) reported only 1 instance out of 14 in which a newly trained child gave an explanation not originally offered by his partner in the interaction. However, Botvin and Murray (1975) reported significant differences in the types of reasons given by advanced children during the interaction and by the immature ones on the posttest. Forty-nine percent of the advanced children gave one kind of reason for their answers during the interaction, and 61% of the immature children tended to give another kind of reason when they solved the problems correctly on the posttest. Similarly, Perret-Clermont (Doise, Mugny, & Perret-Clermont, 1975) found that over half her children introduced one or more arguments or explanations that had not occurred during the social interaction session. There is evidence that the newly acquired solution has a different basis of justification from that which is used by the advanced children (Gelman, 1978; F. Murray, 1981). Although these latter studies bolster considerably the contention that the immature children were not merely imitating others, they do not indicate whether the training procedures merely activated a latent but preexisting competence, or whether the competence was produced by the training procedure.

The group of social interaction training procedures, however, does address the directionality-of-development issue. From a social learning theory perspective, particularly in the dyad interactions, there is no a priori reason to think that the advanced children should not be as affected as the immature ones are by the interaction, especially when the "social influence" of one is no less than the other (Miller & Brownell, 1975; Silverman & Geiringer, 1973). Yet, shifts from correct to incorrect solutions simply are not reported in any significant degree in the literature. Why the correct solution should be a more firmly held position than an incorrect one is not clear from a social learning perspective, because environmental and linguistic support for errors is very great (F. Murray, 1981). For example, because there are so many more large-heavy and small-light objects in the world than large-light and small-heavy objects, it is not unreasonable to expect errors in children's concepts of weight to result, as they commonly do, from transformations of the size and shape of objects. In fact, it is a puzzle in social learning theory as to why children eventually change their minds, because their errors seem to serve them so well for so long. The child, for example, who thinks that heavy objects are larger than lighter objects will usually be correct in his or her judgment about the weight of objects.

Silverman and Geiringer (1973) found 5 cases (of 23) and Miller and Brownell (1975) found only 8 instances (of 69) where the advanced child yielded his or her position during the social interaction session, but in virtually no case did even these correct children regress to an incorrect answer on the posttests. Thus, the directionality requirement of development is sustained in these studies, although it remains to be seen whether more direct or systematic attempts to shift children from the correct to the incorrect answer would succeed. Still, a heavy burden is placed upon social learning theory to explain the single direction of the behavioral change that results from the social interaction procedures that have been applied to various developmental tasks

The Genevan account for the efficacy of the social interaction treatments in facilitating development centers on the claim that logic has its origins in children's need to prove their point of view to others coupled with the shock of their thought coming up against that of others (Furth, Chapter 3, this volume). Logic and necessity, the critical ingredients in persuasive argument, have their origins in the child's cooperation with others, cooperation that necessarily breaks down the equilibrium of egocentrism. The efficacy of the social interaction studies makes sense from the Genevan perspective, although the changes occur over intervals that are too short to be consistent with the general Genevan position that development is a slow process. The question of how much time it takes to advance to a higher, more advanced level, on the other hand, is somewhat meaningless because it involves the quantification of a quality. The Genevan explanation, however, lacks parsimony, and it should come as no surprise that researchers still attempt to explain the workings of social interaction procedures with more parsimonious mechanisms, such as imitation or modeling, even though these mechanisms may require modification to handle the unidirectional character of cognitive growth on tasks that have large components of necessity.

Several researchers (Charbonneau & Robert, 1977; Charbonneau, Robert, Bourassa, & Gladu-Bissonnette, 1975; Rosenthal & Zimmerman, 1972; Sullivan, 1969; Waghorn & Sullivan, 1970; Zimmerman & Lanaro, 1974) have demonstrated that children who were incorrect can acquire the correct answer merely by observing adults model or perform the tasks correctly, and other researchers (Botvin & Murray, 1975; Cook & Murray, 1973; J. Murray, 1974) have confirmed the result with child models, often showing greater gains than with adult models.

In a direct comparison of the power of modeling with social interaction procedures, Botvin and Murray (1975) showed they yield equivalent success. In both cases, the gains met the traditional justification, transfer, and durability criteria. Because F. Murray (1972) in his study of social interaction and Rosenthal and Zimmerman (1972) in their study of modeling both used the Goldschmid and Bentler (1968) Concept Assessment Kit, Forms A and B, as the dependent measure, another comparison of the two procedures is possible, at least indirectly. Both studies yielded equivalent posttest scores (Forms A and B) with children of the same age and background. The posttest scores for children who could solve no problems correctly on the pretests were essentially the same in the two studies and met all the major criteria for being correct. There is some evidence (Charbonneau & Robert, 1977; Charbonneau et al., 1976) that some children exposed to a modeling experience fail in the end to meet the full range of the criteria for genuine achievement (viz., duration and generalization). Also it appears that the cognitive growth that results from modeling is constrained by the intellectual and cognitive level of the observer (J. Murray, 1974) to a greater degree than it is for children in the social interaction experience. It appears that some children rotely memorize the model's response algorithms, but this fact itself does not rule out the possibility that in other circumstances they would respond at a more advanced level. Highly competent persons may still use rotely memorized algorithms as a problem-solving approach in a situation for which they perceive them to be an appropriate, or at least an economical, strategy.

The modeling effects, like the interaction ones, have been shown to hold across various age groups (4 to 8 years), SES levels, language and ethnic groups, and IQ levels. Moreover, they cannot be explained away as merely the assimilation of the information presented by the model, because often the information presented outside a modeling condition fails to produce stable conservation gains (Rosenthal & Zimmerman, 1972), and because the gains are sometimes based upon reasons different from those given by the model (Botvin & Murray, 1975; F. Murray, 1974). To be sure, rules and explanations given by the model often, though not always, enhanced the gain (Rosenthal & Zimmerman, 1972; Sullivan, 1969; Waghorn & Sullivan, 1970), but the effect cannot be attributed solely to their presence. Something more is contributed by the modeling aspect of the information transmission. The social attribute of the message appears to be critical for cognitive growth.

Unlike the children in the social interaction condition who may yield temporarily to the wrong approach but still give the correct response on the posttests, some researchers (Rosenthal & Zimmerman, 1972) report that advanced children who observe children making errors regress and imitate the model somewhat. These reports of regression require close examination because they are a potentially serious threat to the strong directionality claims of developmental theories.

A closer look at Rosenthal and Zimmerman's (1972) 17 children whose mean scores significantly declined after exposure to an adult model who made errors, reveals that the children had a mean score of only 8.59 out of 12 on the Goldschmid-Bentler Assessment Kit and could, on that basis alone, be thought to be not that advanced in the first place. Cook and Murray (1973), on the other hand, had 12 children with perfect scores on the Goldschmid-Bentler Kit observe a child model with a score of 0 and found no regression. The observers maintained perfect scores on the modeled tasks and on the transfer tasks. F. Murray (1974) also found no evidence of regression after his subjects observed a child model make errors.

These regression effects are not found, it seems, when children serve as the model. Robert and Charbonneau (1977, 1978) argue convincingly that cognitive regression from modeling procedures is artifactual and a function of social control and submissiveness to social-influence features of the procedure. They found that extinction or regression occurred only in the presence of adults, and even then it appeared that the children only temporarily adopted the errors simply to conform to perceived social demands (Robert & Charbonneau, 1978). Moreover, Kuhn (1972) found little evidence of regression in the modeling of classification in a study that provided a fine-grained portrayal of regression and progression in terms of the Piagetian substages. In balance, the directionality assumption of the developmental model is not seriously threatened by the results of modeling and imitation attempts to extinguish the correct response in either "natural" or newly trained children. Still, the potential for regression in school tasks that have arbitrary, as opposed to necessary, outcomes is a nagging problem for child-child dyads in school.

Although it is unlikely that the social interaction effects are explainable as essentially modeling effects, other "nondevelopmental" explanations are possible. For example, it is possible that given the very short durations of the interactions, the immature children merely acquiesced to terminate the argument and simply pretended to be advanced. Even though their pretense would not fully explain all the results of the interaction studies, we still might expect that the dissonance between their pretense and true belief, discounting the likelihood of the sufficient justification of the experimental procedure, could motivate cognitive change, as it typically does, in the direction of the subject's public position (viz., the correct response). In this account, the immature would come to believe their public position and genuinely be correct.

Murray, Ames, and Botvin (1977) dramatically confirmed the dissonance or role-playing hypothesis in two experiments. Children with initial scores of 0 scored 14.5 out of 16 in one experiment and 6 out of 8 in the other experiment after they pretended to believe the correct answer publicly. All demanding criteria, including resistance to extinction, were met. In the extinction condition, the newly trained children pretended to be wrong publicly with no ensuing evidence of regression. Thus, they gave all the signs of genuine understanding of the solution—justification, transfer, durability, and countersuggestion resistance. Those who were initially correct and who pretended to be wrong also gave no signs of regression, even after a second dissonance manipulation. They maintained nearly perfect scores on the pretest and throughout the posttests. However, there were signs of regression among those whose understanding was incomplete when they pretended to give a wrong answer that conflicted with their original answer. An interesting case was that of those, also with a shaky grasp of a problem, who pretended to give the right answer. On problems where their pretense conflicted with their initial position, they made the maximum gain, but on problems where there was no conflict (i.e., where there was originally a correct judgment without a correct reason), they made only half the gains that could have been made, despite the fact that all the information needed to solve the problem was presented in the pretense.

The picture that is emerging from these "social" training procedures supports a unidirectional and nonreversible change in children's performance on some tasks, which is supported by something more than the presentation of additional useful information. That is, there is in these studies support for the *development* construct and perhaps for the Genevan *equilibration* construct. There is not support for social learning theories because they are unable to explain the general failure of experimenters to undo correct performance through social interaction, conflict, modeling, or dissonance. In social learning theory, it should be as easy to shift children from correct to incorrect responses as it is to shift them from incorrect to correct answers; that is, change should be symmetrical, but the evidence points more certainly to an asymmetrical change.

If the effects of social conflict, interaction, modeling, and dissonance are greater or more potent than the effects from the presentation of the same informational content in nonsocial formats, the question of the "content-free" motivational aspects of these procedures naturally arises. Inasmuch as uniquely social effects of these procedures are confounded with the information contained in them, before we can attribute a unique motivational feature to modeling, dissonance, and so on, we need to confront the immature children with incorrect information that conflicts with their incorrect judgment but is still equally incorrect. Thus, any gain could not be attributed to the presentation of the correct answer, so to speak. For example, a child who thought that a glass of water poured into a taller, narrower glass held more liquid than when it was poured into a shorter, wider glass could be confronted by a peer who argues it contains less, by a model who states it contains less, or by his or her own public pretense that it contains less.

Both J. Murray (1974) and Cook and Murray (1973) found that children who were wrong and who observed other children who were wrong made slight but significant gains. Doise, Mugny, and Perret-Clermont (1975) found that when children were told by an adult that a displaced stick, which the child thought was longer, was shorter when viewed from its other end, a significant number of them (9/20) came to understand that the length of the stick was constant. Even though they were presented with erroneous information, apparently the fact that it conflicted with their initial position promoted some cognitive growth, although not as much growth as when they received correct information. In that case, nearly all the children were correct on the posttests.

Ames and Murray (1982) also subjected children to conflicting judgments in social interaction dyads, in a model, in a pretense, and in a "nonsocial" information presentation. All social procedures—social interaction, dissonance, modeling—had significant effects on the immature children. Virtually all the children changed their responses to at least one of nine tasks presented, but just a few children (12%) changed only to the correct answer. Most (57%) changed to another incorrect judgment (i.e., the conflicting version), and about 31 percent changed to the correct answer on some tasks and to another error on some others. The changes to the correct answer on the posttests were virtually all from children in the social interaction group. Significant differences in correct performance was found between the social interaction and all other groups in mean posttest scores. Insignificant differences were found among all the other groups and the retesting control. Still, the gains were modest, with final mean posttest scores slightly better than 4 ($sd = 5$) out of 18. These modest gains nevertheless did fulfill the justification, transfer, and durability criteria. Three children with scores of 0 scored between 16 and 18 out of 18, and 11 scored between 5 and 15.

Thus, this approach provides some support for cognitive motivation, but little support for a unique equilibration function in any procedure but the social interaction condition. Here it is shown that conflict *qua* conflict is not only cognitively motivating but that the resolution of the conflict is likely to be in the progressive directions described by the equilibration model. In this limited way, two wrongs come to make a right. The rates that occur from these social procedures when incorrect information content is presented are lower than when correct information content is presented; this indicates that correct and incorrect information are not equivalent. The child more easily changes from incorrect to correct than the other way around.

It is important to bear in mind that the cognitive tasks used to demonstrate the effects that have been cited above are developmental tasks; that is they are tasks, like those on IQ tests, that have strong relationships with the age, particularly the mental age, of the child who attempts to solve them. Thus, the expectation that the result of the social interaction that occurs between at least two children of qualitatively different intellectual levels will be positive, or in the direction of more sophisticated levels of thinking, is only warranted at this time for the kinds of tasks that already have a significant developmental component.

THE CHILD-COMPUTER DYAD

There is no reason to think that the cooperative learning research findings will fail to hold when the instructional task is computer-assisted. In fact, all the cooperative learning effects are found when children work together to solve computer-generated instructional problems (e.g., Johnson, Johnson, & Stanne, 1986). Whether the findings would hold if the other members of the pupil's group were computers is untested. However the success of such a cooperative child-computer group would require, as Slavin (in press) notes, that computers would have to simulate the motivational reward structure of cooperative groups. How successful computers could be in this regard is problematical (Leeper & Chabay, 1985), but failure might not be crippling. For example, the literature on child-child dyads suggests that the computer need only present the opposing and correct point of view to the child, contingently and for relatively brief periods of genuine dialectic. Is there any reason to believe that machines can pass as peers, so to speak, in a situation like the child-child dyad in domains like the Genevan operativity tasks?

In the 1950s, Alan Turing, a British mathematician, proposed a simple test to determine whether a machine is "intelligent," that is whether it could "pass as a person." A machine is intelligent, Turing reasoned, if an intelligent person could interrogate it through a keyboard for half an hour and not know for certain whether he or she was corresponding with another person or with a machine. In limited domains of knowledge, and if the interrogation is gentle, a number of programs appear to meet this test (de Gelder, 1982; Pea, 1985b).

The proposal that a computer simulate a peer in the child-computer dyad calls for the creation of a combination of the expert advisor and surrogate instructor features of artificial intelligence systems (Hayes-Roth & Thorndyke, 1985) that would and could enter into a "dialogue" with the child. When the domains are narrow, as they are for the concrete operational tasks for instance, the development of intelligent computer-assisted instruction (ICAI) is feasible

(Hayes-Roth & Thorndyke, 1985). Such a system, presumably but not necessarily, amounts to the programming of the appropriate operativity structures to create an epistemic subject. Whether the machine would ever pass Turing's test and pass for the epistemic child is an empirical question, but one about which there could be some optimism given the child's anamistic proclivity when interacting with computers (e.g., Turkle, 1984; Dennett, 1978). The lessons from the child-child dyad research are clear in showing that the effectiveness of the message is not easily separated from the medium, in that instance another child. The same information, presented in other formats—especially nonsocial formats—is only marginally effective in promoting genuine cognitive development (F. Murray, 1983).

The Nonsocial Child-Computer Dyad

Apart from the microworld function in the child-computer relationship, in which the child explores and manipulates a rule-governed universe that serves as an analogue for some significant aspects of the "real" world, the computer may provide a more direct tool for the child to use in the discovery and invention of principles in his or her immediate environment. The computer itself can be a tool, like note-taking or measuring, in the service of the child's exploration; in other words, it can be an amplifier of cognition. Pea (1985a) envisions the computer as just such a device for increasing the amount of cognitive workspace the child can bring to bear on a problem by shifting significant portions of the information-processing load from the mind to the machine. One potent consequence of this shift is that aspects of the mind are made available for external examination, inspection, and reflection in much the same fashion as language and logic provide a device for thinking about and enhancing thought itself. There is no question that the child's performance on any number of developmental cognitive tasks can be improved when the task is presented in a format and context that minimize the amount of processing that must take place inside the mind, so to speak (e.g., Case, 1985; Siegler, 1983). It is doubtful that these simplified tasks, despite the child's flawless performance on them, have anything to do with operativity or the child's appreciation of the necessity of his correct response. Nevertheless, the task can be made easier and solvable if the child's expanding, but frail, information processing can be circumvented by a computerized representation of some of the problem's critical variables and their relationships. The issue is whether the child's successful performance on the computerized version of the operativity task is still a theoretically valid indicator of a developmental change. Even though it may be true that children who were not formal-operational thinkers could solve certain formal-operational problems with the aid of a computer program, the question is: How did they do it? Did they just get the right answer or did they employ formal operations in their solution to the problem? If they did employ formal operations, then they were formal-operational in the first place. Or was the child-computer dyad, as a system, formal-operational with each component contributing to a genuine operativity solution by the dyad itself? The former question is the reincarnation of the Genevan issue of pseudo-operativity, that is, the case of the child's correct solution of an operativity problem but by a nonoperativity means.

The latter question has its counterpart in some recent work in the Vygotskian tradition (e.g., Forman & Cazden, 1985). In this research a peer collaborates with or complements the child's point of view instead of challenging or confronting it. It shows that the child-peer dyad performs the task at a higher level than the members can perform it alone, even after their successful collaboration on the problem. In other words, the dyad would be formal-operational, so to speak, but its members would, on their own in the disbanded dyad, remain concrete-operational. Presumably this outcome would be the same for the child-computer dyad and indicates that concrete-operational children would remain concrete-operational despite the fact that with their computer they gave evidence of formal-operational thought. We are left, of course, with the enduring question of what is developing in this dyad situation—the competence of the dyad or of the member, and which competence is of central concern?

With regard to the individual member, the issue is clearest in cases where there is no processing overload, where the child already has accomplished what the computer could provide. This is the case of the last substage in all the Genevan accounts where the child has noted and remembered all the relevant factors and thus has all the information needed for solution, but has no way, apparently, to convert this apprehension of all the relevant information into the required deduction that would be the correct operational answer to the problem. The child, in other words, had no way to convert what was merely true into what must be true. This conversion is the key developmental question.

The Child-Computer Stage

In the end, the question of the centrality of computing in cognitive development will be one of discerning when a technology shifts from being a mere amplifier of the mind to a transformer of the mind. Virtually every new communication medium—the book, telephone, radio, television, and so on—has been introduced with predictions that education and intellectual development would be qualitatively altered as a result of the adoption of these devices. Will the habitual computer users eventually be in a new stage of mental functioning? Will they, with or without their computers, have a way of operating on problems that cannot be explained by the very same cognitive principles that were adequate to explain the workings of the "precomputer mind"? What benefit does or could computing confer on a developing mind—even in the zones of proximal development—that would not be conferred, for example, by collaboration with a peer or by the child's confrontation with some other event?

It is not fully appreciated by many researchers (e.g., Pea 1985b) that the zone of proximal development is a notion that is, of course, completely compatible with Piaget's own view of the necessity of social interaction and collaboration in intellectual development, or his view of the efficacy of the assimilation of information, whether presented by a computer or not, that is a step or substage ahead of the child's current level of development. The Genevan emphasis on cognitive conflict does differ from Vygotsky's emphasis on social collaboration as the critical factor in the zone of proximal development (Forman & Cazden, 1985). Still, the findings from the social interaction studies are clear—children confronted by a cognitively more advanced peer develop in the direction of that peer.

In conclusion, it has been noted, on many occasions, that the epistemic subject or the pure knower, the central phenomenon of the Genevan theory, does without many things—sex, culture, personality, and so forth. It is only somewhat facetious to ask whether the epistemic subject can get along in the future without a computer.

REFERENCES

Ames, G., & Murray, F. (1982). When two wrongs make a right: Promoting cognitive change by social conflict. *Developmental Psychology. 18*(6), 892–895.

Beilin, H. (1977). Inducing conservation through training. In G. Steiner (Ed.), *Psychology of the 20th century, Piaget and beyond* (Vol. 7). Zurich: Kindler.

Borys, S., & Spitz, H. (1979). Effect of peer interaction on the problem-solving behavior of mentally retarded youths. *American Journal of Mental Deficiency. 84*, 273–279.

Botvin, G., & Murray, F. B. (1975). The efficacy of peer modeling and social conflict in the acquisition of conservation. *Child Development, 46*, 796–799

Case, R. (1985). *Intellectual development from birth to adulthood.* New York: Academic Press.

Charbonneau, C., & Robert, M. (1977). Observational learning of quantity conservation in relation to the degree of cognitive conflict. *Psychological Reports, 44*, 975–986.

Charbonneau, C., Robert, M., Bourassa, G., & Gladu-Bissonnette, S. (1976). Observational learning of quantity conservation and Piagetian generalization tasks. *Developmental Psychology, 12*(3), 211–217.

Cook, H., & Murray, F. B. (1973, March). Acquisition of conservation through the observation of conserving models. Paper presented at the meetings of the American Educational Research Association, New Orleans.

de Gelder, B. (Ed.). (1982). *Knowledge and Representation.* London: Routledge & Keegan Paul.

Dennett, D. C. (1978). *Brainstorms.* Montgomery, VT: Bradford Press.

Deutsch, M. (1949). A theory of cooperation and competition. *Human Relations 2*, 129–152.

diSessa, A. A. (1982). Unlearning Aristotleian physics: A study of knowledge-based learning. *Cognitive Science, 6*(1), 37–75.

Doise, W., Mugny, G., & Perret-Clermont, A. N. (1975). Social interaction and the development of cognitive operations. *European Journal of Social Psychology, 5*(3), 367–383.

Doise, W., Mugny, G., & Perret-Clermont, A. N. (1976). Social interaction and the development of cognitive operations. *European Journal of Social Psychology. 5*(3), 367–383.

Forman, G. E., & Cazden, C. (1985). Exploring Vygotskian perspectives in education: The cognitive value of peer interaction. In J. V. Wertsch (Ed.), *Culture, communication and cognition: Vygotskian perspectives* (pp. 323–347). New York: Academic Press.

Furth, H. (1978). Reading as thinking: A developmental perspective. In F. B. Murray, & J. Pikulski (Eds.), *The acquisition of reading* (pp. 43–54). Baltimore, MD: University Park Press.

Gelman, R. (1978). Cognition development. *Annual Review of Psychology, 29,* 297–332.

Goldschmid, M., & Bentler, P. (1968). Concept assessment kit-conservation manual. San Diego, CA: Educational and Industrial Testing Service.

Hayes-Roth, B., & Thorndyke, P. (1985). Paradigms for intelligent systems. *Educational Psychologist, 20,* 231–241.

Johnson, D. W., & Johnson, R. T. (1974). Instructional goal structure: Cooperative, competitive or individualistic. *Review of Educational Research, 44,* 213–240.

Johnson, D. W., Muruyama, G., Johnson, R., Nelson, D., & Skon, L. (1981). Effects of cooperative, competitive, and individualistic goal structures on achievement: A meta-analysis. *Psychological Bulletin, 89,* 47–62.

Johnson, R., Johnson, D., & Stanne, M. B. (1986). Comparison of computer-assisted cooperative, competitive, and individualistic learning. *American Educational Research Journal, 23,* 382–392.

Knight-Arest, I., & Reid, D. (1978, May). Peer interaction as a catalyst for conservation acquisition in normal and learning disabled children. Paper presented at the eighth annual symposium of The Jean Piaget Society, Philadelphia.

Kuhn, D. (1972). Mechanisms of change in the development of cognitive structures. *Child Development. 43,* 833–844.

Leeper, M., & Chabay, R. (1985). Intrinsic motivation and instruction: Conflicting views on the role of motivational processes in computer-based education. *Educational Psychologist, 20*(4), 217–230.

Miller, S., & Brownell, C. (1975). Peers, persuasion, and Piaget: Dyadic interaction between conservers and nonconservers. *Child Development, 46,* 992–997.

Murray, F. B. (1972). The acquisition of conservation through social interaction. *Developmental Psychology, 6*(1), 1–6.

Murray, F. B. (1978). Development of intellect and reading. In F. B. Murray, & J. Pikulski (Eds.), *The acquisition of reading* (pp. 55–60). Baltimore: University Park Press.

Murray, F. B. (1979). The generation of educational practice from developmental theory. *Educational Psychologist, 14,* 30–43.

Murray, F. B. (1981). The conservation paradigm: Conservation of conservation research. In D. Brodzinsky, I. Sigel, & R. Golinkoff (Eds.), *New directions in Piagetian theory and research* (pp. 143–175). Hillsdale, NJ: Lawrence Erlbaum Associates.

Murray, F. B. (1982). Teaching through social conflict. *Contemporary Educational Psychology, 7,* 257–271.

Murray, F. B. (1983). Learning and development through social interaction and conflict: A challenge to social learning theory. In L. Liben (Ed.), *Piaget and the foundations of knowledge* (pp. 231–247). Hillsdale, NJ: Lawrence Erlbaum Associates.

Murray, F. B. (1986). Micro-mainstreaming. In J. Meisel (Ed.), *The consequences of mainstreaming handicapped children* (pp. 43–54). Hillsdale, NJ: Lawrence Erlbaum Associates.

Murray, F., Ames, G., & Botvin, G. (1977). The acquisition of conservation through cognitive dissonance. *Journal of Educational Psychology. 69*(5), 519–527.

Murray, J. (1974). Social learning and cognitive development: Modeling effects on children's understanding of conservation. *British Journal of Psychology, 65,* 151–160.

Papert, S. A. (1980). *Mindstorms: Children, computers, and powerful ideas.* New York: Basic Books.

Pea, R. (1985a). Integrating human and computer intelligence. In E. L. Klein (Ed.), *Children and computers, new directions for child development* (pp. 75–96). San Francisco, CA: Jossey-Bass.

Pea, R. (1985b). Beyond amplification: Using the computer to reorganize mental functioning. *Educational Psychologist, 20,* 167–182.

Robert, M., & Charbonneau, C. (1978). Extinction of liquid conservation by modeling: Three indicators of its artificiality. *Child Development, 49,* 194–200.

Rosenthal, T., & Zimmerman, B. (1972). Modeling by exemplification and instruction in training conservation. *Developmental Psychology, 6,* 392–401.

Siegler, R. (1983). Information processing approaches to development. In W. Kessen (Ed.), *Handbook of child psychology* (Vol. 1, pp. 129–212). New York: Wiley.

Silverman, I., & Geiringer, E. (1973). Dyadic interaction and conservation induction: A test of Piaget's equilibration model. *Child Development, 44,* 815–820.

Silverman, I., & Stone, J. (1972). Modifying cognitive functioning through participation in a problem-solving group. *Journal of Educational Psychology, 63,* 603–608.

Slavin, R. E. (1983). *Cooperative learning.* New York: Longman.

Slavin, R. (in press). Cooperative learning: Developmental vs. motivational perspectives. *Child Development.*

Sullivan, E. (1969). Transition problems in conservation research. *Journal of Genetic Psychology, 115,* 41–45.

Turkle, S. (1984). *The intimate machine.* New York: Simon & Schuster.

Waghorn, L., & Sullivan, E. (1970). The exploration of transition rules in conservation of quantity (substance) using film mediated modeling. *Acta Psychologica, 32,* 65–80.

Webb, N. (1985). Student interaction and learning in small groups: A research summary. In R. E. Slavin, S. Sharan, S. Kagan, R. Hertz-Lazarowitz, C. Webb, & R. Schmuck (Eds.), *Learning to cooperate, cooperating to learn* (pp. 147–172). New York: Plenum.

Zimmerman, B., & Lanaro, P. (1974). Acquiring and retaining conservation of length through modeling and reversibility cues. *Merrill-Palmer Quarterly of Behavior and Development, 20,* 145–161.

Epilogue

Chapter 13

Constructivism in the Computer Age: A Reconstructive Epilogue

George Forman
University of Massachusetts

Peter B. Pufall
Smith College

We asked the authors of this volume to write chapters on "Constructivism in the Computer Age" to share with us their perceptions of educational gains and theoretical insights already realized in the computer age. More important, we asked them, given their sense of what has been accomplished, to speak to the potential of "computers," and the myriad hard and soft technologies implied by that term, for our understanding of the developing mind in formal and informal educational environments. In setting this task, we realized that because we are at the beginning of the "computer age," our authors would have to speculate about the potential of computers. They have speculated about future computer technology and how new technology will transform the way we construct our reality and, particularly, the way we think about ourselves as epistemic beings.

Constructivism is variously defined in contemporary cognitive psychology, giving the authors some latitude in preparing their speculations. The chapters amply attest to these various meanings and to the authors' willingness to speculate. At the same time recurrent themes shared among the authors are critically important to our developing understanding of constructivism.

This epilogue serves several purposes. The first is to succinctly state our understanding of constructivism. We believe the chapters by Furth (chapter 3), Murray (12), and Papert (1), within the present volume, as well as an earlier volume in this series discussing constructivism (Sigel, Brodzinsky, & Golinkoff, 1981), indicate that our understanding is not entirely idiosyncratic. The second

---

[1]References to chapters in the present volume are not listed in the reference section. They are designated in the text by author without an accompanying year of publication. All other references are listed in the reference section and follow the usual citation procedure within the text.

purpose is to specify the recurrent themes. These themes are not exclusively linked to the topic of the computer. Nevertheless, they either have had a formative influence on the educational use of computers or seem to be issues that could be addressed effectively by research involving computers. The third purpose is to relate these themes to constructivism—that purpose is embedded in our discussion of the themes and provides a brief overview in the general conclusions.

PROPERTIES OF CONSTRUCTIVISM

For us, constructivism embodies three properties: epistemic conflict, self-reflection, and self-regulation. *Epistemic conflict* involves two knowing systems. These systems may originate in different individuals, and it may be that in early development we are more dependent on externally induced conflict than we are subsequently (Pufall, chapter 2). Whatever the source of the conflicting epistemic stances, if there is a resolution it is within the individual experiencing the conflict, that is, it is an individual construction. If the resolution is developmental, in the strict sense, it means constructing a new way of thinking about reality and is marked by logical necessity (Murray, chapter 12).

Self-reflection can be construed as a response to conflict. Perhaps paradoxically, it means objectifying our knowledge by specifying our assumptions about reality, about procedures for solving a problem, and so forth. Reflectivity is an opportunity to explicitly construct or transform our way of representing reality. At the same time, and embodied in the same intellectual act, there is the potential for developmental restructuring of thought. Developmental restructuring is *self-regulation*. Through our thinking about our practical and conceptual actions, these actions can be restructured to a "higher" level of knowing. These developmental transformations, though materially linked to empirical transactions, reflect self-organizing properties of the knower that reflectively, but not consciously, abstract structure from action.

In sum, conflict and self-reflection are, of necessity, conscious, whereas the last step, self-regulation, that is to say, developmental restructuring, is in all likelihood unconscious in process and outcome. That is, we do not explicitly construct new logical structures of mind and do not need to be aware of them when they function in our day-to-day problem solving.

RECURRENT THEMES

Knowledge as Skill Versus Understanding

The recurrent themes within this volume echo issues central to contemporary cognitive development. The first is the concern over whether knowledge should be characterized as mastering a hierarchy of skills for doing or as understanding reasons why. This theme emerges when considering the relation between computers and thought for very practical reasons. Can the computer be built to take over mundane and repetitive functions, leaving more time for reflection, questioning, evaluating, and so on, time to perform semantically rich cognitive functions (Ginsburg & Zelman, chapter 9)?

From a practical perspective the skill-understanding contrast may be a remnant of the contrast between performance and competence. By partitioning adaptive behavior into skill versus understanding or performance versus competence, there seems an attractive division between those functions that are computer-appropriate versus those that remain necessarily human in kind. The computer could be responsible for repetitive functions. Computers perform reliably and at high speeds, whereas humans, with paper and pencil, or, worse yet, with only their wits, would be unreliable and slow.

There are several ways in which this distribution of function can be realized. In a very real sense the skillful computer can become a functional prosthesis. Within this volume, Bransford, Sherwood, and Hasselbring (chapter 10), as well as Ginsburg and Zelman (chapter 9) offer an anecdote of the child whose school performance was deteriorating because she was driven to make her letters perfectly when doing a composition. The computer obviated the problem and the child began to perform significantly better in school. In this case the computer provides an option, a prosthetic device, or amplifier (Murray, chapter 12) by which we can circumvent limitations.

The value of word processing programs to circumvent these obsessions as well as the physical demands of using a pen or pencil seems obvious. Every effort should be made to create user-friendly systems designed with specific needs of individual learners in mind. This practical value may be of little theoretical value. As functional prostheses, these computer technologies do not necessarily inform us about the nature of sensorimotor activity or of operational thought (Pufall, chapter 2). As functional substitutes they do not necessarily simulate sensorimotor activity. At best they create conditions within which operational thought may be expressed, but in themselves they do not structure transactions to facilitate development.

How far can we take the distinction between skill and understanding? Could we imagine a cognitive function such as transitive inference as a program or algorithm in a computer of the $5 hand-held type? With such a logic device children would only have to learn to apply the appropriate functions to a data base, a process similar to the way many "learn" statistics. Moreover, in today's calculators the functions are carried out internally, with little information about the structure of the inferential activity, and, therefore, there would be no action on which to reflect.

One could argue that learning to use a data base, say, financial statements from American companies, is a simple process of looking "here and there." The interactive process is one of a person "asking" questions and the computer "giving" answers. Immediately one can see a problem with this characterization. The computer would not give the person an answer, but it would give information. Our interpretation transforms the information into an "answer."

From a developmental perspective, this process bears little resemblance to constructive processes such as self-regulation. There is no implication of building progressively more comprehensive mental structures. In fact, growth appears to be a matter of expanding the data base or the functions for interacting with that data base. This image of development resurrects a familiar concern for distinguishing between operational thought that implies knowing why and pseudo-operational thought that implies knowing how (Murray, chapter 12).

Pufall makes this point nicely by reminding us that performance is not enough. Intelligence is more than symbol manipulation, because knowing is more than symbolical or representational systems. The self-object relation, that is, conceptual object, results only from a conscious reflection on alternative perspectives in the practical domain of self-world relations. The point is that the distinction between skill versus understanding is inadequate, and not merely because it suggests that skills are instrumental and nonreflective whereas intellectual acts are executive and reflective. It is inadequate because skill itself is highly cognitive (Forman, chapter 6, as well as Furth, chapter 3), and elsewhere (Fischer, 1980), a point that has been overlooked by many educators.

The computer's role may be to help us change from doing skills automatically to thinking about their structure. As computer scientists we need to simulate these functions if computers are to act as prostheses. From the standpoint of the child learning to program a computer to carry out ordinary sensorimotor functions such as moving through space (Fein et al., chapter 7), the child has to reflect on the structure of that activity and construct executive functions.

If we can imagine children interacting with logic devices we need to decide whether or not there are developmental goals in this interaction, for example, Furth's (1970) Symbol Picture Logic. If that is our intent, then the psychological problem is not how to distribute intellectual responsibility from mind to computer but to discover ways in which the mind can more efficiently grasp logic through interactions with intelligent, not dumb, computers (McCorduck, 1979).

Wohlwill's (chapter 8) work with children as graphic artists and Wolf's (chapter 11) work on literary composition are examples of employing computer systems to facilitate the development or expression of "cognitive skills." Wohlwill attempts to enhance children's interest in the aesthetic qualities, such as imaginativeness and pleasingness, of their art by matching their presumed desire for "cognitive control" with a "medium" such as BASIC. The assumption is that the latter can be controlled and modified more effectively than direct manipulation of graphic and plastic media. Although his results were, at best, only suggestive, by comparing the developmental effectiveness of two types of computer media, graphic tablets and keyboard languages, he has methodologically structured the questions in the right way (Salomon and Gardner, 1986).

Wolf's (chapter 11) computer software, a type of hypertext, allows children to analyze the literary structure of compositions. Children interact with a layered text that makes the inferences and implied meanings of text visible. This visibility means they can explore the process of composition and not merely compose. They interact with the text's structure, going beyond the simple act of decoding the textual pieces. For example, the figurative mood can be changed instantly by swapping a "warm" for a "cold" metaphor. Wolf's hypertext is not to be confused with a word processing program; it is a microworld within which children can explore textual composition per se.

In a similar way DiSessa's (chapter 4) microworlds of physics provides a convenient means to test ideas about physics. The computer eliminates delay and cumbersome feedback that is inherent in the conventional physics laboratory. Thus students spend more time on the task, but, more important, there is greater opportunity to reflect on the way their "pieces" of knowledge do or do not interrelate. We should not trivialize the role of the computer as a tool to compress the time frame of reflection. By reducing the time between successive tests of an hypothesis about a physical event, their discrepancies are made more accessible for reflection.

The manner in which time can be manipulated differs between the "macro worlds" that Bransford, Sherwood, and Hasselbring (chapter 10) create through videodisc technology and the "microworlds" that Wolf and DiSessa create on microcomputer technology. Macroworlds are worlds of real events that unfold over time. The structure of those events is often too slow, fast, or complex for us to reflect on effectively. Although not all three aspects of time are explored in the work Bransford et al. (chapter 10) have done thus far, all could be or have been explored in other contexts. By accelerating slow events and decelerating fast events, their structure is more clearly perceived, and the kind of questions we ask about them changes. Bransford et al. focus on complex phenomena, events that have multiple subevents, and concentrate on these to teach us to look more carefully for information implied in an event, information that might be useful in letting us answer other questions about the event, and in general to teach children to be better problem solvers.

A way to relate the work of Bransford et al. to the relation between skill and understanding is to draw on Salomon's (1979) idea of "supplantation." The zoom, the freeze frame, and instant replay of the video camera mimic cognitive functions that punctuate our instructional parlance as we implore students to "concentrate," "stop and think," or "think about what you just said." Becoming skillful with these technologies may lead the viewer, the thinker, to simulate these functions even when the video event or the real-world observation is playing straight through.

Salomon's conceptualization of technical literacy, and the literacy in any programming or word processing language is a critical area of educational research. Although the computer is fascinating to many, it is not to all (Ginsburg and Zelman, chapter 9), and therefore, if there is some specific advantage in working in micro- and macroworlds, we may have to design alternative methods for engaging children with different learning strategies. Fein, Scholnick, Campbell, Schwartz, and Frank (chapter 7) understand that fluency in a computer language, LOGO in their case, demands preliminary skills. These "primitives" must be invented and, in some cases, reinvented by the child as he or she masters the computer language. They point out that these inventions have a developmental course. In fact, their research suggests that skill with a technical system may have an interesting developmental path. As we move to fluency (Fein et al, chapter 7), that fluency may transform the quality of expression, making it more or less imaginative (Wohlwill, chapter 8), and work with hypertexts may make fluency itself the object of thought through a new generation of word processors (Wolf, chapter 11).

Intuitive Versus Formal Thought

Central to constructivism is the assumption that to know is to continually reconstruct, to move from a more to a less intuitive state, or from intuitive nonanalytical understanding to explicit formal understanding. In short, knowing is always intuitive to some extent or in some way. From a developmental perspective, a corollary is that coming to know is always reconstructing what we already know. To fail to appreciate the centrality of the knower's intuitions runs the risk of pseudo-constructions that are restricted in their contextual application (Murray, chapter 12; Bransford et al. chapter 10) and probably short lived. Bransford et al. effectively teach junior high school children using *Raiders of the Lost Ark* as a unit by which to measure distances. This may work with children prepared to consider distances as objective voids. However, younger children's conceptualizations of distances may be intimately related to the energy needed to jump, climb, or carry. As a consequence Indiana Jones' height may be less relevant to their intuitions than his heroic proportions.

There are several interrelated issues in this "natural" epistemology. One is a familiar Genevan lament, that constructing an explicit understanding of logic (Furth, chapter 3) or composition (Wolf, chapter 11) has a developmental pattern and perhaps a maturation time course to it, and hence cannot be hurried. Two is that, as a natural epistemology, changing the environment may change the path of development. Neither Furth nor Wolf adopt this second and more radical stance, but rather they have constructed hierarchically organized microworlds through which children can move effectively at their own pace. Both of their microworlds capitalize on intuitive knowledge structuring interactions of knower and object.

Yet another understanding of the relation between intuitive and formal is contained within Papert's (1981) concept of *powerful ideas* first articulated in *Mindstorms*. Powerful ideas are metaphors that have a developmental history. Papert recalls playing with gears as a child. His intuitive structuring of gears was gradually transformed into explicit mathematical principles. However, these principles were always best understood by using the metaphor of gears. In a similar manner Frank Lloyd Wright's play with block structures was gradually transformed into basic design principles. For both their rich intuitions about the gears and blocks was the developmental springboard to their understanding of mathematics and design, respectively. More important, that play created a "powerful idea" within which their thinking about issues of mathematics and design could be analyzed. That is, it is not completely accurate to categorize their thought as formal-operational. It is accurate to say that they can think about formal relations in rich contexts of gears and blocks.

Whether all minds can create metaphors as powerful as "great minds" or whether great minds are distinct because they create powerful metaphors is an open question. Papert's view would seem to be that the former is true, and his development of Turtle Graphics is an effort to provide a metaphor commodious to all. It is designed in particular to allow us to think about aspects of mathematics not so easily understood through current educational curricula. He explains its novelty in terms of mother structures. One property of a *mother structure* is that it combines two important themes or ideas. Turtles can be anthropomorphized and therefore invite assimilation to our knowledge of human movement. On the other hand, the fact that the symbolized turtle embodies both location and heading means that turtle geometry is based not on idealized points, as Euclidean geometry is, but on vectors of movement.

In this volume, Papert (chapter 1) points out that turtle geometry may not be a general metaphor, and therefore, as do Ginsburg and Zelman (chapter 9) he wonders whether interacting with the same microworld leads different children to construct different ideas and even different powerful ideas. It seems likely that there may be distinctively different powerful ideas, but it is not likely that formal thought would differ from individual to individual. The general research challenge is obvious: one must do longitudinal studies of children who have engaged these microworlds to determine in what ways these worlds seem to continue to serve as powerful ideas.

Personal intellectual histories reveal only a small part of the developmental story. They do not contain details about the development from intuitive to formal thought, neither do they indicate how the computer may play a special role in that intellectual transition. Other aspects of Papert's writing and other contributors to this volume take seriously the potential that computers have for transforming intuitive to formal thought.

Fein et al. (chapter 7) distinguish between intuitive spatial knowing and an egocentric performance. Egocentric performing is rooted in sensorimotor knowing. Adaptive moment through space is sensorimotor knowing that involves representation. Initially these intuitive representations are organized in large measure with reference to self. The developmental course from self-referential systems to explicit descriptions of a space and finally to formal geometric systems is marked by a continued decentering of intuitive knowing.

Decentering begins with children giving another person (or turtle) objectively specific directions. Paradoxically, the turtle was chosen as an anthropometric metaphor. Hence, Papert invites children to be egocentric and use their knowledge of personal movement through space when organizing their thinking about moving the turtle. Papert emphasizes the fact that the turtle embodies the properties of location and direction, allowing children to think about movement as vectors. Children "communicate" their knowledge through LOGO, the command language. There are several interesting psychological characteristics to this microworld. First, because they have to communicate their knowledge of movement by a set of command functions, children have to specify properties of that action, for example, heading, how to achieve that heading, and distance to be traveled. Second, they have to transform continuous, or analogic, action, into a set of discrete commands that procedurally specify the act. Third, they know whether their procedures are an adequate description of intended action as soon as they "run" the program. Finally, and perhaps most important, to successfully communicate they have to move from an egocentric assimilative mode to an accommodative turtle-centered mode, that is, they cannot specify the turtle's action as if they were performing the act.

But what kind of transformation of intuitive knowing is involved in this communicative system? Pufall (chapter 2) points out that the children have to abandon their intuitions of personal locomotion to write efficient commands; for example, they should use the "Backwards" command to move toward something behind them rather than turning and moving forward as *they* would in *their* world. In short, if children take an anthropomorphic stance too seriously they may never learn to move the turtle efficiently through its space. It may be that progress is made by abandoning one's intuitions rather than transforming them into a formally more explicit system of LOGO command procedures.

This suggests that not all aspects of one's intuition are transformed into a higher level of knowing. In this case, the microworld of the turtle reveals self as the point of reference, forcing children to deal with the relation between the command language and the movement of the turtle. Although this is a big step, it is not evidence that the microworld of the turtle spawns powerful ideas.

In a similar manner, diSessa (chapter 4) outlines the value of microworlds to challenge college students' thinking about physics, to move the student from intuitive assumptions to a formal "theory." It would appear from his analyses that our intuitive accounts of reality are necessary outcomes of trying to understand. From a developmental perspective they provide the foundation for epistemic conflicts. For diSessa, as for Papert and Fein et al. (chapter 7), microworlds of computers made that conflict immediate and ongoing. Moreover, because we are communicating with a dependent but obedient system we must make each aspect of our knowledge explicit and correct if the system is to behave adequately.

If computer worlds are to generate development, then they must not only be expert systems but they must also be sensitive to the intuitive pieces of thought that constitute bad theories. They may have to be designed to move us from intuitive pieces to "bad" intuitive theories and only later to comprehensive formal theory. Karmilof-Smith and Inhelder (1975) would argue for the necessity of the intermediate step of a bad intuitive theory, a sentiment echoed by Lochhead (chapter 5), whose criticism of current education is that its dedication to instrumentality and immediate indoctrination into formal statements may well preclude developing more comprehensible and real-world-related bad theories.

Bransford et al. (chapter 10), and Forman (chapter 6), in this volume, and Levin, Reil, Rowe, and Boruta (1985) elsewhere assume that intuitive knowledge is a worthy place to start instruction. Each portrays the function of computer or video systems in different ways. We have already discussed Bransford's et al. utilization of macroworlds as a rich resource of information, but they also point out the potential of video disc productions in which students view the structure of their thoughts as they themselves as produce effective videodiscs.

Forman (chapter 6) goes beyond the advantage of reflectively examining self in video playback by speculating that it forces students to take responsibility for their lack of expertise, to "own" the cognitive base of performance rather than to dismiss it as a random error. This process may be enhanced, Forman argues, by representing knowledge in various digital and analog symbol systems. Although this is intriguing, Wohlwill's work (chapter 8) on aesthetic development contrasting analog and digital programming did not yield dramatic differences. This may only indicate the obvious, that we have a long way to go before we understand how to construct each of these systems to serve simultaneously as a means for representing intuitive knowledge and as the basis for constructing new knowledge.

Domain Specific Versus Universal Knowing

What is the best way to characterize human intelligence? Does our intellectual power come more from a vast store of real-world knowledge, or should we give more weight to general procedures of deduction and induction? In the first case, intelligence is primarily a search through domain-specific knowledge. In the second, intelligence is primarily a constructive synthesis of principles and rules. Both views of intelligence have advocates among cognitive scientists. Can we say that one view is more consistent with constructivism than the other? Probably not!

Those identified with a Piagetian persuasion, correctly or not, are accused of focusing on the general structures in rational thought, for example, transitivity, *modus ponens,* class inclusion. Murray (chapter 12), for one, defends logical necessity as the transcendent feature of human intelligence, reminding us not to mistake inductive for deductive thinking. To be sure, he does not suggest that logical structures are to be interpreted as general stages of knowing. Logical necessity may be acquired domain by domain. But in noting that fact he and others vividly remind us that the question of "how" necessity "occurs" to us may not be answerable. What may be able to be answered is: What conditions increase the likelihood of it occurring? And, having done that across various domains, we may be able to induce reasons why some domains are mastered earlier than others.

These conditions will probably not be the same for all domains of knowing or for all individuals in the same domain (Ginsburg and Zelman, chapter 9). As a consequence, in principle we may be faced with the challenge of matching children and educational media, as well as matching teachers with children in their preferred media. This goal, though laudable, is obviously unattainable at this time. Currently, computers are designed as universal expert systems that function as tutors of the universal, not the individual, learner. Until computers are constructed to be sensitive to individual styles, the question of whether teacher, student, and educational media need to be matched to attain the most significant developmental gains remains open.

We suggest that there are two procedures that could be adopted in response to this situation. One is to develop computer software to help teachers identify their own styles as well as those of their students, so that both can be effectively matched to the microworlds designed to teach content areas. Alternatively, we may opt for rich problem-solving microworlds that give the student multiple means of entry. Papert's Turtle Graphics provides one example. Turtle Graphics is an environment in which children do geometry with "turtles" that have location and orientation and "sprites," which add velocity. Some children adopt the turtle, whereas others adopt the sprite. The former is the "planner," seemingly dedicated to precise figurative statements, whereas the latter is the "negotiator," interested in representing the dynamics of a system. Providing a microworld that capitalizes on individual styles is only part of the story; of course, the students still have the responsibility for exploring that environment to discover the compatibility between their cognitive styles to instructional alternatives.

DiSessa (chapter 4) responds to this challenge of creating microworlds for teaching physics by staying close to specific content that challenges students to reflect on their primitives of thought, that is, "p-prims." P-prims are not general theories. They are intuitive and domain specific. For example, diSessa offers evidence that students do not use *impetus* as an organizing principle across contexts. Lochhead (chapter 5) agrees with diSessa's general characterization of thought, and both diSessa and Lochhead undoubtedly accept Murray's criterion of necessity in logical thought. Nevertheless, neither would assume that necessity is generally achieved but might be achieved in only a few sub-areas of physics. In sum, that aspect of knowing with which diSessa and Lochhead are principally concerned predates necessity. Their practical goal is to create conditions that challenge us to reflect on the inadequacies of our primitives so that we might reconstruct our thinking about physics.

Murray, diSessa, and Lochhead analyze the foundations of the antecedent conditions differently. Murray notes that debates between peers about commonly held primitives yields progressive and stable change. DiSessa constructs computer enhancements. Lochhead suggests we reintroduce sense-based experience in the form of Newton's brass equipment. If we are trying to capture the entire process of intellectual development, even within a specific domain, both diSessa and Lochhead leave us to struggle with the self-regulated reconstructions that bridge the steps between antecedent conditions and subsequent structures of mind.

The clearest advocate of the potential of computers and technology in general for contextualizing (concretizing) learning is Forman (chapter 6). It is obvious that he believes that development from intuitive to explicit or formal knowledge takes place best in the context of practice, a position echoed in Pufall's review of functionalism in Piaget's theory (chapter 2).

More to the point are Forman's several suggestions for specific types of contexts that force children into a procedural mode (Papert, chapter 1) and into a cognitive state appropriate to reflective abstraction. For Forman there is no practical separation between the transition between intuitive and explicit thought and context of practice. Hence, new microworlds must be developed with the understanding that intuitive reasoning occurs in highly textured contexts. Intuitive rules are not decontextualized; they become explicit within contexts—in fact, consciousness of our intuitive rules may mean raising consciousness task by task. The new symbol systems of computer and video graphics present opportunities for learners to become fluent in self-analysis.

Bransford's et al. (chapter 10) use of videodisc in consort with computer graphics is another example of contextualized learning and development. In contrast to Forman's, their macroworlds are not structured explicitly to teach a single concept. Rather, various concepts can be reflectively abstracted from their rich video environments. They use context-specific knowledge as scaffolding for the development of context-free concepts and problem-solving functions.

More subtly, though no less important, Bransford et al. force us to think about the value of rich contexts as motivational tools and the place of domain-specific knowledge as an educational objective. Their educational objective is to develop individuals who understand the relation between knowledge and problem solving in everyday and academic life. Their epistemology bridges the extreme positions of contextual and universal knowing by assuming that adaptive knowing is necessarily knowing within a context. The central educational challenge is to bring children to understand that they are seeking to know what knowledge is relevant to what problem-solving situations.

Let us return to the questions that framed this section, but do so by looking at the computer as a simulator of intelligence, not as an environment for intellectual development. Computer scientists have discovered the power of computers with a substantial store, a data base, of simple facts. For example, Mycin, used to diagnose viral infections, can relate over 400 diagnostic facts as accurately as can the average physician. Teiresias is a program that helps Mycin learn from its mistakes. In contrast with Mycin, Teiresias is not filled with real-world facts, but rather uses a small set of heuristics and backtracking strategies. Are we willing to say that properties of construction are embodied in Teiresias and but not in Mycin systems?

This may be a simplistic hypothesis. It may be mistaken to simulate constructive processes only within Teiresias-like systems. Among other semantic functions, such a program would neglect the practical constructions of selecting facts as relevant to a domain. Context-free functions cannot make those decisions. To simulate the acquisition process we have to connect a question-asking computer to the real world. Parents, teachers, and peers (Murray, chapter 12) can serve and have served in that capacity. Indeed, the new trend in programming computers consists of computers asking many questions once the general goal has been defined. In this fashion, we can model how real-world facts are organized into semantic networks and how the well-formed networks require constructive processes.

Solitary Versus Social Constructions of Mind

A frequent criticism of computer micro- and macroworlds is that if they become the worlds of cognitive development, then we truncate social construction of knowledge. Paradoxically, another criticism might be that the computer may become the "expert" so that self-regulated construction is truncated. Each concern is predicated on an expectation of what the computer must be and, moreover, what the relationship between self and computer can be. The authors of the present volume all seem convinced that we do not know the limitations of the computer and therefore do not know what it can be and how we will be able to interact with it.

Our authors see advantages for both the solitary and social aspect of computers. To the timid child, interacting with an intelligent machine provides a nonevaluative method of learning (principally see Ginsburg & Zelman, chapter 9; Furth, chapter 3). On the other hand, computers can be a context for collective problem solving (Murray, chapter 12, Papert, chapter 1; and Wolf, chapter 11) as well as perspective taking (Levin, Reil, Rose, & Borvta, 1985). Perhaps when computers are perceived to be nonevaluative, students working alone may be more playful, more exploratory, and more divergent in their thinking. Students working in groups may be more concerned with validation of agreed-on propositions, cross-referencing competing positions, and sensitivity to consistency in an argument, because the proponents of various perspectives will not tolerate the intuitive, less explicitly stated approaches of solitary thought.

We are aware of the problems of capitulating to authorities by accommodating or withdrawing in order that evaluation will be positive or avoided. The literature on the dynamics of group decision making is also substantial. The issue is whether the computer adds a new twist to these dynamics, particularly with reference to the constructive process. Does the student, as Ginsburg and Zelman (chapter 9) suggest, actually take feedback more easily from a computer than from a person? By contrast, might the nonjudgmental status of the computer deteriorate as students become more familiar with being tested by a computer? There is no doubt that children attribute intentionality to computers (recall Papert's citation of Turkle, chapter 1). Computers are thought to be alive because they cheat. It would appear then that children's perception of computers as nonevaluative benign entities in other circumstances is due to the way the child and the computer can interact.

As the computer becomes more and more frequently a teacher surrogate, its human attributions could increase. Anyone who has failed on repeated attempts to beat Sargon, a computerized chess player, soon develops emotions of resentment, anger, and embarrassment that are appropriate, objectively speaking, only as a response toward a being who knows you as a person. It might be that as the next generation of computers mimic ordinary properties of mind, the next generation of computer users will attribute many more human qualities to the computer than did their older cohorts.

Certainly assigning attributes to the computer will vary according to developmental level. This anthropomorphizing may also vary according to cognitive style. As Papert mentions (chapter 1), some students prefer to develop elaborate plans before writing "programs," and others dive in immediately to negotiate program structure as they go. There are several questions we need to address carefully here. One is whether or not these styles of interacting with computers affect our perceptions of the computer as evaluative? That is, our personal style of interacting with computers and the ways computer software are constructed may not be psychologically independent dimensions.

Another question is whether cognitive styles are specific to working with a computer or are they more indicative of individual styles independent of contexts? The likelihood that these are context free seems doubtful, given the inconsistency of personality traits (Mischel, 1981). We need to study the possibility that cognitive style might be transformed through careful selection of the types of computer worlds with which one interacts.

Murray's (chapter 12) review of the literature on what makes peers effective agents for cognitive change reveals that we are more certain about what does not account for their effectiveness than what does. In general, when children are grappling with structured systems, that is, systems that have the property of logical necessity, peer interactions appear to be more effective than interactions with adults, even though the type and amount of information may be similar. Computers can simulate styles of interaction, store, retrieve, and present types of information, and adopt evaluative and nonevaluative stances. If we can systematically control these dimensions, then we can explore questions concerning social constructions such as the relative value of social conflict (Piaget) versus social collaboration (Vygotsky) to cognitive development.

The value of peer interaction in the construction of knowledge may be related to children's perception of the relation between child and parent in the discussion of ideas (Pufall, chapter 2). Parents may be perceived as autocratic and as creating an asymmetric relation in the developing perspective. Conformity rather than mutual trust marks the parent (adult)-child interaction. A parent may be perceived as asking the child to "think about the way I think" and not to "think about the way you are thinking." On the other hand, peers cause the child to the latter, more self-reflective mode of thinking.

If this analysis is valid, the role of the computer is unclear, or at least uncertain. Computers are not self-reflective. They are not aware of their own metaphors or even that they are operating metaphorically. If they are restricted in this way, then can they be co-constructors, as peers are? Put more basically, is self-reflection, or awareness that knowing is metaphorical, incidental or central to successful co-construction? One test is to look at cognitive development with computer systems that are expert or replete with information but by any acceptable criterion are not self-reflective.

The final challenge is to continue to develop computer programs that mimic the conscious self-awareness of peers. Setting this as our goal means that we are involved simultaneously in testing our theories of conscious self-reflection and, at the same time, testing whether interacting with a computer system can yield knowledge that is "new" to both parties (i.e. co-construction of knowledge).

Whereas coconstruction with a computer may seem future oriented and other-worldly enough, we end with an idea discussed by Murray (chapter 12) but first introduced by Pea (1985). Is it possible that the human and the computer interacting together construct a "mind" altogether more developed than either functioning independently? This is different from the human functioning only as the eyes and ears of the computer and, as such, being the prosthesis of the computer, picking up information and transducing it into the symbol system of the computer. Coconstruction is also more than the human telling the computer what programs to use. In these types of person-computer interactions the discourse itself is not self-evaluating nor does the computer have a theory or a perspective. As a consequence it is difficult to believe that together the person and computer are functioning at a higher level than when functioning alone. Nevertheless, if this is possible, then we have created a new species of being, one in which self-reflection and construction are not self-regulated within the skin of the person, but within the relationship of self and computer.

GENERAL CONCLUSIONS

Constructivism in the computer age has been examined with respect to four issues: skill versus thinking, intuition versus formal thought, concrete versus universal ideas, and social versus solitary intellectual constructing. Our goal has been to reconstruct the manner in which microworlds of computers and macroworlds of video technology may facilitate constructive processes that we believe to be inherent in the developing child. There is always a risk in reducing complex, and yet rather diverse, work to a singular conclusion; nevertheless, it is our belief that computer worlds are and will be developmental forces when they promote constructive processes. Their successes though limited at this point, in our minds, have not challenged but validated principles of constructivism. If there is a challenge, it is practical in nature. The challenge of the Computer Age is to create new worlds that provide more degrees of freedom to construct knowledge.

Specifically, micro- and macroworlds are constructive when they provide new representational systems (e.g., Forman, chapter 6) within which we can more effectively "think about" what we know and what we have yet to know (Pufall, chapter 2). These representational systems are constructive in that they provide practical and explicit procedures for solving problems with the microworlds (e.g., Papert, chapter 1).

Equally important, constructive microworlds are manifestations of conceptual realities and not simulations of specific realities (Pufall). As a consequence, general intellectual adaptations are achieved when children understand that microworlds are not to be treated as practical realities. It may be that microworlds are most effective when children are not bound to the practicalities of direct sensorimotor transactions but nevertheless build on that intuitive knowledge, for example, Papert's Turtle Graphics, or when these computer worlds extract the conceptual structure from the complexities of natural language, for example, Furth's Symbolic Picture Logic to teach logic.

Ultimately the effectiveness of these worlds to intellectual development will be measured in terms of transfer. To be sure, many have ignored that issue, and wisely, as they develop their first microworlds. Nevertheless, transfer will be critical, and it will raise old questions in a new format. The years of a separate literature and conceptual systems to explain structural knowledge, such as class logic or spatial concepts, and functional knowledge, such as reasoning and problem solving, must come to an end. The transfer of types of knowing will be explored in the same study. Fein et al. (chapter 7) have demonstrated this possibility. One of the beauties of operating in computer microworlds is the possibility of studying both the structural, for example, Papert's powerful ideas, and the functional, for example, intellectual styles and aspects of thought, and, we would add, to do so within as well as between domains.

REFERENCES

Fischer, K. W. (1980), A theory of cognitive development: The control and construction of hierarchies of skills. *Psychological Review, 87,* 477–531.

Furth, H. (1970), *Piaget for teachers.* Englewood Cliffs, NJ: Prentice-Hall.

Karmiloff-Smith, A., & Inhelder, B. (1975). If you want to get ahead, get a theory. *Cognition, 3,* 195–212.

Levin, J., Reil, M. M., Rowe, R. D., & Boruta, M. J. (1985). Muktuk meets jacuzzi: Computer networks and elementary school writers. In S. W. Freeman (Ed.), *The acquisition of written language: Revision and response* (pp. 103–135). Hillsdale, NJ: Ablex.

McCorduck, P. (1979). *Machines who think.* New York: W. H. Freeman.

Mischel, W. (1981). Personality and cognition: Something borrowed, something new? In N. Cantor & J. Kihlstrom (Eds.), *Personality, cognition, and social interaction* (pp. 75–96). Hillsdale, NJ: Lawrence Erlbaum Associates.

Papert, S. (1981), *Mindstorms.* New York: Basic Books.

Pea, R. (1985). Integrating human and computer intelligence. In E. Klein (Ed.), *Children and computers. New directions for child development* (No. 28, pp. 75–96). W. Damon (Editor in Chief). San Francisco: Jossey-Bass.

Salomon, G. (1979). *Interaction of media, cognition, and Learning.* San Francisco: Jossey-Bass.

Salomon, G., & Gardner, H. (1986). The computer as educator: Lessons from television research. *Education and research, 15*(1), 13–19.

Sigel, I. E., Brodzinsky, D. M., & Golinkoff, R. M. (1981). *New directions in Piagetian theory and practice.* Hillsdale, NJ: Lawrence Erlbaum Associates.

Author Index

Subject Index